▬▬▬▬▬ Did You Know You Can: ▬▬▬▬▬

Minimize your fear of heights with backrubs?

Relieve your claustrophobia with sore muscles, walking sticks and sex?

Make yourself less anxious about animals by reading and fantasizing?

It's all here in this extraordinary book with all the new techniques for breaking the Fear Habit; including unique "workbook" sections with mental puzzles and exercises to help you overcome specific phobias.

Kicking the fear habit

"[Dr. Smith's] characteristically catchy prose explains how phobias operate and how to unlearn the Fear Habit by systematic exercises to relieve anxieties. Will be one of the most requested books of the season."

—*Library Journal*

Bantam Books by Manuel J. Smith, Ph.D.

KICKING THE FEAR HABIT
WHEN I SAY NO, I FEEL GUILTY

Kicking the fear habit

Using your automatic orienting reflex
to unlearn your anxieties,
fears and phobias

Manuel J. Smith, Ph.D.

*This low-priced Bantam Book
has been completely reset in a type face
designed for easy reading, and was printed
from new plates. It contains the complete
text of the original hard-cover edition.*
NOT ONE WORD HAS BEEN OMITTED.

KICKING THE FEAR HABIT

*A Bantam Book / published by arrangement with
The Dial Press*

*PRINTING HISTORY
The Dial Press edition published September 1977.
Bantam edition / May 1978*

ISBN 0-553-11656-8

Published simultaneously in the United States and Canada

Bantam Books are published by Bantam Books, Inc. Its trade-
mark, consisting of the words "Bantam Books" and the por-
trayal of a bantam, is registered in the United States Patent
Office and in other countries. Marca Registrada. Bantam
Books, Inc., 666 Fifth Avenue, New York, New York 10019.

PRINTED IN THE UNITED STATES OF AMERICA

To those whose ideas, work, writings and
teachings I have learned from—as
well as from themselves:

Petr Anokhin
Sigmund Freud
Harry Harlow
Donald Lindsley
Irving Maltzman
Ivan Pavlov
Joseph Sidowski
Burrhus Frederic Skinner
Zev Wanderer
Joseph Wolpe

And two special people whose insights
continually amaze me:
Jennifer Patten Smith and Joyce Engelson Keifetz.

acknowledgments

I wish to thank sincerely my colleagues, associates, and friends who over the years have helped me formulate and develop the orienting reflex training methods for the treatment of fears and phobias by their hard work and sweat in the laboratory or clinic; their expert tutorials; their ideas, feedback and critiques; their suggestions for improving my manuscript; and their support and encouragement.

In particular: Harold Sanford Kant, Esq., Beverly Hills, California; William Kantor, Nelles School for Boys, California Youth Authority, Whittier, California; Susan F. Levine, Los Angeles County Mental Health Clinic, Long Beach, California; Irving Maltzman, Professor and former Chairman of the Psychology Department, University of California at Los Angeles; Fred Fromme Sherman, Training Consultants, Escondido, California; Joseph Sidowski, Professor and former Chairman of the Psychology Department, University of South Florida, Tampa, Florida; Zev Wanderer, Director, The Center for Behavior Therapy, Beverly Hills, California; and Joyce Johnson, Executive Editor, The Dial Press, New York.

contents

1

Fears and Phobias:
how we get them

one
Flight into fear

How I Became Phobic

About twenty-two years ago, I was in the U.S. Army. I mostly remember the funny things about the army that happen when warm civilian bodies are crammed into khaki. But I also remember one thing that scared the hell out of me—so much that it gave me a phobia which lasted close to five years. It was an airplane flight from a U.S. Air Force base in Japan to one on the island of Okinawa.

I was being reassigned to a new duty station along with some thirty other soldiers, most of us privates. I remember sitting on my duffel bag at the edge of the airstrip where the truck from the Tokyo Arsenal had dropped us off at five in the morning. I was bundled up to keep from freezing in the predawn winter cold. Even after watching the slow beauty of the clear Japanese sunrise, I was still cold. We couldn't leave the asphalt strip to go into the flight lounge, directly behind us, for hot coffee or to get warm. The flight lounge was taken over by officers. A general was sleeping there on a couch surrounded by his staff of lieutenants. They thought we might wake him up. We sat there bitching and griping for several hours until a strange-looking aircraft making a hellish racket pulled up in front of us and woke the general. This airplane was the most feared thing in the sky, not for its combat abilities but for the number of people who had died flying in it. The plane was called the Flying Coffin.

The Coffin was a strange aircraft, both inside and out. It had two skinny boom sections that ran back from the engines across the wings into a single tail structure. This puny-looking arrangement held up and surrounded a huge sausage-shaped main body that resembled a stretched football.

Needless to say, I wasn't too happy with the travel plans the army had made to get me to Okinawa. I had never flown in the Coffin before, but I knew its reputation. As I sat there staring, two giant doors swung open at the end of the sausage, and ramps were pushed out by the plane's crew. The general suddenly emerged from the lounge and went on board followed by his flock of door openers, who were followed by us. We walked in and tossed our duffel bags up on a row of freight lashed down along the center of the deck. We sat down facing one another on metal bucket seats lining each side of the cabin. Everything was painted a depressing military olive drab. The bucket seats were painted too, but they all had a bright, shining spot in the center where squirming rumps had worn off the paint. Above us, behind the pilot's cockpit, was officers' country. They sat in cushioned seats on a second deck level that was open at the back. The general settled into a passenger seat with arm rests and a tilting back. After he had adjusted himself he sent a lieutenant to tell the pilot to proceed. The crew pulled in the ramps and closed the doors. We taxied out onto the runway and sat there waiting.

By now the winter sun had superheated the inside of the aircraft. Even the general had sweat running down his face. At last, with a great revving of the engines, the pilot jerked us forward and we lumbered down the runway gathering speed for take-off. This act was merciful in that it caused a cooling onrush of wind to flow through the cabin ventilators, but at the same time, it also set up a tremendous vibration throughout the plane that made me think it was going to fall apart. For an eternity I thought my spine was going to dislocate and my teeth rattle loose. Then suddenly the pilot jammed on the brakes and cut the engines' power thrust. We screeched to a halt near the end of the runway.

The airplane hadn't been able to get up enough ground speed to allow it to become airborne. Or at least I hoped the pilot thought we were going too slow to become airborne safely. Back we came to the start of the runway where we sweltered again in the heat. After a few minutes of revving the big engines, as if we were in the start of a drag race, down the runway we went for another try, propellers screaming, rivets and teeth rattling, seats jerking and vibrating. As we closed on the point of no return, the pilot hit the brakes again, but much harder this time, jerking us against the seatbelts with our forward momentum. We came to a stop faster than before and much nearer to the end of the asphalt. On this return trip, the pilot took much longer in getting us back to the starting place for a third try at takeoff.

About this time, I began to know fear. I was hoping the pilot would give up, tell us to get off and fly his load of freight down to Okinawa without us. No such luck. Pilots don't do sensible things like that in front of a general. Instead, he aimed us at the distant end of the runway, set his brakes and slowly turned the engines up to full power—and held them there. As the vibrations from the straining engines grew more violent, the whole airplane began to shake and lurch from side to side. It was clear that the pilot was going to get us off the ground on this try, even if he had to perform the equivalent of shooting us out of a cannon. When he released the brakes, he did just that. On this third try, we shot down the runway going much faster than before. I looked at the reaction of the other passengers to this new tactic. Maybe I was the only one who was afraid, but all their faces were serious and drawn. Gone was the wisecracking GI humor and griping of an hour ago.

As the point of no return rushed past the window, we lifted off the ground for a moment, hit the runway and bounced back into the air again. The pilot kept the throttles on full power—we were committed this time. We would either lift off or spin out and crash when we ran out of airstrip. We kept bouncing into the air and falling back to the runway.

My arms went rigid. I looked at my hands. They were locked onto the edge of my seat. There was nothing else to hold onto. I looked up at the officer deck. Did they know something I didn't? I can still see the general digging his hands into the ends of his cushioned armrests. He had white knuckles too. That was when I really knew fear. The only thought that came into my head was idiotic. The general was in front and, if we crashed, he would do his nose dive at the end of the runway before me. I could see that lack of rank sometimes had its privileges. This train of thought was broken off when the feel of the vibrations under my rump changed. I felt another bump as we hit the runway once more, but it was a gentle one. We were in the air. I started to breathe again. The pilot announced that the smoking lamp was lit but instructed us to stay in our seats. He wanted to gain some altitude before everyone rushed to the rear latrine and tipped the airplane backward into a stall.

The rest of the trip was also colorful. We were treated to a roller-coaster ride in the turbulent air pockets along the thousand-mile East China Sea route between Japan and Okinawa. Going up and down like that, I found it easier not to look out the porthole windows to see how high we were. Shortly after leaving the seacoast of Japan, the navigational system went berserk and we followed an erratic zigzag course southward to Okinawa, delaying our estimated time of arrival by an hour and a half. We touched down at Kadena with a mighty thump.

After landing most of the men just sat there out of military courtesy waiting for the general to exit first. Not me. With a few others, I was out the door as soon as the ramp hit the ground. No one stopped us or even seemed to care about military protocol.

For the rest of my time in the army and for three years afterward, I didn't go near a plane. I had flown in airplanes since I was twelve years old. It used to be fun. But not anymore. I had acquired an irrational fear of airplanes—a phobia. Thank God the army sent me home by troopship. After I was back in school, my aerophobia had subtle side effects. Perhaps because I felt the fool with my irrational fear, I shied away from the topic of flying entirely. My major professor then, Joe Sidowski, was continually frustrated in trying to get feedback from me on his ideas for improving aircraft safety with better design of the pilot's working space. All I would ever reply was "Uhuh . . . uhuh . . . uhuh," to anything he shared with me on the subject. He was always muttering that there was no accounting for personal taste. He finally wrote my behavior off with, "Some people have to be dragged kicking and screaming into the twentieth century!"

What a Phobia Is and What It Can Do to Your Life

How can you tell if you or someone close to you has a phobia? The meaning of *phobia*, in my experience, is about as loose in professional usage as it is in lay language. It has been used to mean anything from mild nervousness about taking an examination or a job interview to the paranoid thoughts of a psychotic patient desperate with worry over the Communist plot to poison his food. A more limited and useful way of thinking about phobias is to characterize them as having at least two elements: irrational anxiety, sometimes bordering on outright panic, and a fairly specific situation or thing that triggers off the irrational fear, such as airplanes, animals, high places, and elevators. Most patients who come to the psychological clinic for treatment of their irrational fears can be quite specific about what frightens them. Some, however, cannot. Their type of anxious reaction may be more general and include, for instance, any social situation where they must interact with other people. Often these patients realize that people upset them, but they explain their nervousness to others by telling a little white lie and arbitrarily picking out something in a social situation as the reason for their anxiety. "Dogs," they might say, "always make me uptight and I have a phobia about them." And then to demonstrate that they are working on their problem, they sit with the host's dog during an entire evening and very effectively avoid what they really fear: social contact with other people. Or they might say that subway trains make them nervous as they are traveling on one to the cocktail party—which is what they really dread.

Although such *social fears* are not uncommon, there is not much point in treating them as if they are specific phobic reactions. Instead, a program of social assertiveness training is typically used to teach this type of patient how to cope with the things that cause his or her anxiety: social embarrassments, lack of confidence, social mistakes and fear of criticism. Such social fears are also not in the same league with the specific phobias when it comes to the devastating effect of the phobic anxiety. One of my patients had a fear of blood tests and things medical. But he was unaware, as I was also, of how sensitized he had become even to the medical paraphernalia by itself. Wondering what I could use to begin his behavioral anxiety reduction, I thought we would try just a hypodermic syringe, without needle. That wouldn't be too extreme, I thought. So I put one in my pocket before our second meeting. With his permission, I pulled the syringe out and showed it to him from across the room, hoping it would evoke at least some anxiety with which we could then begin to work. He promptly fainted dead away from the psychological shock of being that close to part of the feared thing. This extreme reaction of the phobic patient is not uncommon.

Even though the anxiety responses may range from mild to panicky fear, most phobic patients avoid like the plague the thing that frightens them. Consequently, their daily living patterns may be grossly distorted, even to the point of not taking a good-paying job on the fifteenth floor because they have a fear of heights or elevators. Or they may only work within walking distance from their homes because of an irrational fear of driving a car or riding in public transport. Their marriages may become hellish because of phobic impotence of the husband, or, in the case of many women, the phobic frustration of being orgasmic through self-masturbation but never in the psychologically more exposed situation with their husbands or lovers.

These are just some examples of what a phobia is and the effect it can have in crippling a whole area of a person's life. Considering this description of the problem, and perhaps your own experience of irrational fears, you might suppose that a phobia is a difficult condition to eliminate. That depends greatly upon how you go about it. Let's look at what happened to my own aerophobia that I acquired thanks to the U.S. Army Transportation Corps.

According to one particularly moldy and archaic but still popular theory of clinical psychology, my phobia was a symptom of an underlying hidden psychic conflict in my makeup, probably due to a frustration that I could not deal with during my period of psychosexual development between birth and six years of age. Well, at the time of my flight in the Flying Coffin, I had a conflict—but it was with the U.S. Army and it wasn't psychosexual. The army thought I was a soldier, but I knew better. My soldiering impulses pooped out in the second week of basic training.

According to a more modern theory of clinical psychology, developed in this century and called behavior therapy, my phobia was learned; it was a conditioned emotional response. This theory shows us, at least in my clear-cut case, that my feelings of uncomfortableness during my five flightless years were triggered by things peculiar to airplanes and were conditioned by my last fearful flight in the same way that Pavlov's dogs were conditioned to automatically salivate to the sound of their keeper's footsteps at meal time. Like Pavlov's dogs, I had been conditioned to produce a similar automatic, involuntary emotional response, only mine happened to be negative and about airplanes instead of hamburger. This behavioral notion of how we acquire phobic responses has several advantages over the analytical theory developed in the nineteenth century by Freud and his followers. First, the evidence of research clinicians shows a clear-cut superiority in treating phobias using behavioral methods. Second, the behavioral methods don't require us to examine our pasts for the original trauma that caused the phobic reaction—it is only necessary to know what triggers off the anxiety now. Third, it isn't necessary to resolve any hidden psychic conflict to make the phobia go away.

How I Lost My Phobia

What ended my five-year battle with modern transportation? Did I see a behavior therapist? No, at that time they were quite rare and usually associated with the big universities and research hospitals. What happened was a lucky set of circumstances that resulted in my phobia being eliminated in about thirty minutes of "reconditioning" by one of my old undergraduate friends who had become a naval aviator during my last year in the army. Now back in graduate school with me, Fred was still full of enthusiasm for flying and kept pestering me to learn to fly and join the local flying club. What he wanted, I suspect, was a partner to share flying expenses. I resisted until he suggested that we fly up to Palm Springs in a club plane to see the Grand Prix auto races being held there the following month.

To understand why this trip was of particular interest to me, I have to tell you something else about Fred. As an undergraduate, he was one of the slickest charmers on campus. Every girl I had seen him date was just beautiful. The clincher Fred put on my flying to Palm Springs with him was his assurance that he had already made arrangements for two girls to meet us at the races. Afterward they were going to drive us into Palm Springs to be their houseguests for a weekend, and we would fly back on Sunday. I was not going to miss that weekend if I had to fly to Palm Springs in a strait-jacket with my eyes blindfolded. With obvious mixed feelings I agreed to Fred's offer, but he laid on one more condition. Before we flew to Palm Springs I was to go up on one local flight with him so he could teach me some of the basics. With reluctance I agreed. He pulled a small booklet on single-engine flying out of his pocket and told me to study it before Saturday. He had already reserved a plane for us.

Saturday morning came and we met at the airfield. He had me climb in and around the airplane to confirm what I had learned, pointing out things, asking their names and what they did. A few minutes after this check-out, I was heaving on the propeller calling out, "Brakes? Ignition off? Contact?" and then running around to climb in the cockpit and take off. Within a half an hour I was piloting the plane, running through turns, spins, climbs, stalls, dives and trims under Fred's direction. I didn't do them very well, but that didn't matter. At first I was very ner-

vous. Then I found myself too busy to be afraid.
Then I began to even have fun. My fear of flying
was gone.

Some few minutes later my "cure" was put to an
acid test. I was taking the airplane along a straight
course toward a mountain peak Fred wanted to show
me when a loud thump hit the top of the cabin. Instead of panicking, I turned to look at Fred anxiously
and asked him, "What was that?" Chewing on his
cigar, he looked at me and said with a grin, "I don't
know, but we're still flying." Taking over the controls, Fred asked me to keep a sharp lookout for flat
land in case we had to make a forced landing. As it
happened, we touched down with no difficulties at
the nearest landing field a few miles away. Our problem was caused by a thin aluminum weather strip on
the top of the Plexiglas windscreen used to keep out
rain seepage. It had worked loose in flight and bent
over from the wind pressure, making the loud
thump as it doubled back on itself. After scrounging
some screws and a screwdriver, I refastened the weather strip. We were back in the air and on our way in
less than fifteen minutes.

Since that Saturday morning with Fred, I have
logged over 100,000 miles in the air as a passenger
on commercial airlines, and seventeen years have
passed without my fear of flying coming back to
haunt me.

If your experiences are like mine and those of millions of other people and you find yourself subject
to irrational fears or phobias, then you probably ask
yourself the same kinds of questions that concern
most of us: Why can't I control my feelings of anxiety
in this situation? How did I wind up with these unpleasant feelings in the first place? Does my phobia
mean that there is something profoundly wrong with
my personality? Should I try to get rid of the phobia
or just avoid the situation that makes me uncomfortable? Can I get rid of it? What's the best way to

do it? How long will it take? Do I need to see a therapist to eliminate my phobia?

All of these questions, of course, are important if you have a phobic condition—especially the last three: What to do? How long will it take? With whom do I need to work? There are, of course, no simple one-line answers—none that would fit all of our individual situations. Answers with the most hopeful outlook, however, are already suggested by the story about my own experience in conquering a fear of flying.

What did I do about my phobia? I reentered the phobic situation, even though reluctantly, under a set of lucky circumstances, and my feelings of fear were replaced with positive feelings. Fred didn't know of my irrational fear of airplanes. I'd previously avoided flying with him by telling him that I wasn't interested in flying, which was true, and that I was too busy, which was not true. As things turned out, it wasn't even necessary for Fred to know about my phobia. All that was necessary to eliminate it was for him to set up conditions in advance that would motivate me strongly to step into an airplane and force me to pay attention to other things besides my fear.

In the light of later research on phobic treatment, Fred's counter-phobic procedure was ideal. If, for example, he had just let me sit passively as a passenger during the flight, my phobic condition would likely have remained the same or perhaps gotten worse. That is the typical result for people with aerophobia who force themselves onto passenger liners and then just sit and suffer for several hours between Los Angeles and Chicago worrying about every squeak and strange noise they hear.

There is a wide variety of things Fred could have made me do in the airplane that would have worked just as well as making me learn to fly it. Learning hand and eye coordination tasks in the feared situation is among the best of antiphobic procedures. And the learning task doesn't have to be related to the phobic situation! Fred could have, for example, made me learn to juggle three oranges simultaneously in flight with similar good results. Or he could have had me practice being a bombardier by dropping oranges from the open window to learn how to hit a target on the ground as the plane passed over it—or any number of other things limited only by our imagination.

Clearly I didn't require the services of a psychotherapist of any stripe—analytical or behavioral. What I did need was the help of someone I trusted in the phobic situation, and, for my particular problem, it was ideal that Fred was a pilot. Since then, however, my colleague Zev Wanderer and I have helped a number of fearful passengers seated next to us on commercial flights by suggesting some of the methods and tasks described in later chapters. These "cures" were effected without advance preparation and without telling our chance seating partners that we were shrinks.

two

Our negative survival emotions and behaviors: freezing, fainting, fleeing, fighting and feeling rotten

All of us have three basic negative emotions: fear, anger and depression, and they are not independent of one another. If we become fearful, for example, and then become angry or depressed, our fear may be either reduced or intensified by these later emotions. So let's take a look at all three to see how they interact and how they can help or hinder us in reducing our learned anxieties.

Each of these emotions is innate and involuntary, genetically built into us for the survival of the species. Our original animal brain that has come down to us from our successful prehuman ancestors is often called the "emotional" brain in laboratory slang by neuroanatomists and physiologists. It automatically controls not only our negative emotions, but also all the bodily functions and involuntary reactions that keep us alive—temperature level, digestion, gland squirts and muscle contractions, blood flow and circulation, heart rate during stressful exercise or rest, sleep and wakefulness, and so forth.

Layered over our primitive animal brain structure is our great human brain, the cortex. This is the part of our brain responsible for what we think of as mankind's achievements: from 2 + 2 to theoretical calculus; from the wheel to the spaceship; from cave draw-ings to the Picasso print; from primitive drum rhythms to Bach, Beethoven, Mozart, and then back to acid rock. We use the cortex whenever we perform some voluntary action like talking, listening, reading, solving a problem, learning something new or even actively doing nothing. Because of the physiological process of learning and the way the cortex is organized, we don't have to think through every step of these activities. The cortex, like our primitive brain, does much of its neurological business without our having to command it, without our even knowing how it does it.

Put your hand behind your back where you can't see it. Move one of your fingers up and down. How do you know your finger moved when you commanded it to? You felt the movement because your cortex automatically, without "you" requesting it to do so, picked up nerve impulses coming back from your finger and organized them so "you" could tell if the finger moved a little, a lot, all the way, or not at all.

Although the cortex is the seat of our voluntary actions, it cannot *directly* control the basic operations of our emotional brain, even with all our commands. If, for example, we have to move our bowels and there is no john handy, we can usually exercise voluntary control over the sphincter muscle so we do not commit a social no-no, but we can't tell the emotional brain to stop letting us know about our discomfort or, at times, our outright pain. In the same way, we can't control our survival emotions of fear, anger and depression.

What Fear Does to Us and for Us

We can't voluntarily rid ourselves of fear, as you may have observed from your own experience. Even though all of the U.S. Marine Corps claim that ability, many of them have been known to faint at the sight of a hypodermic needle. Conversely, we can't voluntarily become fearful. How many times have you told yourself, "I think I'll make myself afraid?" We can sit around worrying about things and making ourselves mildly anxious and nervous, but it takes a specific threat in our surroundings to trigger off real fear or panic: a burglar in the middle of the night, a mugger on a deserted street, a near miss on the expressway, etc.

We are built to become afraid when the situation demands it. This capacity has evolved over eons of trial and error, because the human species had a greater chance for survival during hard times if the reaction to something dangerous was automatic. When we become frightened, research psychologists tell us, we "freeze" momentarily or run without having to think about it. When our ancestors were startled by something huge and hairy that came too close to them without warning, it was often best for them to remain motionless. The easiest thing for the nervous system of animals (including ourselves) to perceive is a change in sound, and next, movement in the visual field. So there was a good chance that our ancestors would not come to the attention of a predator if they remained quiet and still, instead of thrashing about in attempting to escape.

If you are like myself and many others, you may experience a similar freeze paralysis yourself upon suddenly being awakened in the middle of the night by unusual noises. If you are terrified because you can't move a muscle for several minutes, relax. You are not undergoing anything neurotic, psychotic, or even cowardly. You are "wired" to behave that way under those conditions. During parts of our sleep cycle, we dream. To keep us from physically acting out in the dream sequence, the primitive emotional brain cuts off nerve transmission from our cortex to our skeletal muscles, effectively paralyzing our whole body. Obviously, this neurological paralysis keeps us from flailing around in bed at night and collecting a lot of scrapes and bruises. In a harsh primitive environment, where we would be at the mercy of predators when sleeping, it would keep us from attracting large things that walked in the night. So if you find yourself awakened out of a dream stiff as a board, relax and take joy in the fact that you are built to survive under almost any condition.

The second major way our primitive emotional brain protects us from dangerous events is to make us run without having to think about it. When our successful ancestors saw something hairy with big teeth coming at them, they didn't call a committee meeting to analyze the problem; they got frightened and ran like hell. I have a poster on my wall that reminds me of this part of our emotional heritage: "If you remain cool, calm and collected while everyone else is running around losing their head, perhaps you don't understand the seriousness of the situation."

When you sense that churning, weak, panicky feeling of fear throughout your body, you are really sensing the result of messages sent by your primitive emotional brain to the rest of your body, preparing it to make a maximum physical effort in avoiding danger. These messages are both phasic and tonic in nature (fancy words for short and long term). The tonic commands are chemical. While we know relatively little about the chemical changes that produce fear in us, it appears that adrenalin (an organic enzyme) does most of the work in priming the pump. Adrenalin is a general biochemical arouser that prepares our skeletal muscles to consume large amounts of energy. In simple words, it sets you up to run like hell. Once you stop running, you often aren't afraid any more. By then you have metabolized (burnt up) all the adrenalin your primitive emotional brain had ordered released to enable you to run fast and far. On the other hand, if you are prevented from running when you are afraid, the adrenalin stays in your system unmetabolized and raises hell with your disposition. You feel weak all over. Your hands, legs and arms may start to shake and tremble. This happened to me once when I stupidly jaywalked in front of a truck without looking. At the same instant the front fender swerved past, me, a blaring air horn shocked me into a startle response. The side of the truck literally brushed my nose. When I unfroze, the truck having gone down the block, I told myself to be calm, to walk, not run, across the street. "Be cool at all costs," I said to myself. That was a big mistake. If I had taken off full speed down the street away from the truck, I wouldn't have spent the next fifteen minutes walking around in a daze, shaking and wondering what I was doing and where I was going.

Part of the sensation of fear is due to great changes in blood flow through your body. The lower, emotional brain diverts large amounts of blood away from your interior digestive organs where it would not be needed during running. The emotional brain also diverts large amounts away from the areas of your head, neck, face and brain itself, where blood would not be needed. This large blood reserve is sent instead to the skeletal muscles of your arms, legs, back, chest and belly, which need most of your energy in dangerous situations.

If this diversion of blood to the skeletal muscles is carried to the extreme, we then see the pale chalk face of fear that precedes fainting. This faint from fear is not that which is caused by illness, physical problems, or chemical toxification from inhalation of smoke or ingestion of spirits. Its cause is purely mechanical—a severe drop in blood-pressure level in the area of the brain, depriving it of oxygen. With this fear-induced reaction, the emotional brain will shut off consciousness. In other words, it will totally inhibit the action of your voluntary cortex on the rest of your body in as few as five seconds, allowing only the minimal involuntary life support functions to persevere: continued slow heart beat, slow breathing rate, and so forth. This wonderful, automatic action of our primitive brain insures that, while unconscious, we will remain as independent of conditions in our physical environment as possible. We are temporarily "shut down on idle," requiring only the minimal amount of energy exchange in heat and oxygen between us and our physical world.

Stretched out flat in a horizontal position, we are speeded toward recovery of consciousness by our evolutional design. Our blood pressure is equalized between our toes and our nose, insuring that our brain gets an equal chance at the blood nutrients and oxygen with the rest of the body. Also, if we faint because of a toxic atmosphere, the greatest concentration of oxygen is found at ground level, since oxygen is heavier than most other gases. If conditions on the ground where you have fainted are not too pleasant, you will automatically recover within seconds. For example, if anything painful happens, the primitive brain will bring you out of the faint. If you fall on a sharp rock, you will recover immediately from the faint. Pain stimuli are routinely used to revive someone from a faint or anesthesia—smelling salts or spirits of ammonia, a slap on the face, a heavy blow to the chest.

While it is popular to think that more women faint than men, there is no clear data to validate this belief. I have seen many full-grown men pass out at the sight of a hypodermic needle taking a blood sample from them. I have done it once myself. Why any of us faint when fear strikes is a mystery.

We could write off fainting as a malfunction of the body and the nervous system—an overreaction that lowers the blood pressure near the brain too rapidly to be mechanically compensated for. We could also argue that fainting is the result of a deliberate command by the emotional brain when it is impossible to either bluff or run away. This decision of the emotional brain may be based upon a realistic appreciation of general animal behavior that our ancestors faced and we would today in primitive surroundings. Most predators display aggressive behavior for two reasons. One is to obtain food. And they do this, not with aggressive rage but with the stalking skill and coolness of a Beverly Hills lawyer. The second reason is to protect themselves and their territory. If we wander into some animal's private domain and it charges us, screaming or snorting, it is not necessarily interested in us as food. It may even be a vegetarian. It may only see us as a possible threat and want to frighten us off. Watch dogs, for example, growl and rush at us because they are protecting their territory. Lie flat on the ground, looking helpless and harmless, and they are not likely to attack. So fainting may not be such a bad ploy. We can bet with some assurance that if fainting is in our portfolio of fear responses, it serves some survival purpose.

Another part of the sensation of fear is its automatic inhibition or blocking of our thinking process. The primitive part of our brain automatically shuts down the action of the thinking cortex at the same time it physically prepares the body for flight. This slowdown of voluntary actions is again a built-in part of our evolutionary heritage that insures we will not indulge in idle speculation when there is danger to life and limb. If we think about it, this involuntary control of our behavior makes a lot of sense. It wasn't very important for our ancestors to do much complicated problem solving when running full out with some hairy beast in pursuit. Tree height analysis wasn't needed. The closest tree was the right tree. Not much thinking prior to climbing was required.

What Anger Does to Us and for Us

Before we go on to look at how our survival emotion of fear can become a learned phobic response, let's briefly examine our other negative emotions—anger and depression—and their effect on our anxiety level at any time. Anger competes with fear in our nervous system. We are not physiologically built to be fearful and angry at the same time. Like fear, anger is also a survival emotion. When you feel real anger or rage, you are really sensing the results of the biochemical messages sent by your primitive emotional brain to physically prepare your body to exert a maximum aggressive effort against another person or animal.

Part of the sensation of anger is the massive transfer of blood supply to different parts of the body. Just as when we are afraid, the same external skeletal muscles have to do most of the work. In anger, blood also rushes to our face, neck and head in large amounts, causing that flushed, burning sensation. Consequently, unless some rare physical condition exists, we never faint when we are angry as we sometimes do when we are afraid. The human head is a potent offensive weapon. It can be, and is, used for fighting and is guaranteed its full measure during anger by our primitive emotional brain.

The emotion of anger has played an important part in the survival of our species. There is absolutely no doubt in my own mind of the effect of the physiological state of anger in multiplying the physical intensity of aggressive behavior and the fear-inducing effect of this truly enraged aggression upon opponents within our own and other species.

There was only one time in my life when I personally experienced the sensation and effects of this total anger. I was fourteen and a newcomer at my high school when I was challenged to the inevitable bare-knuckle fist fight that preceded social acceptance. Looking back now, it seems a very silly thing, but then it was more important than most things in life. After school my opponent and I, and all my opponent's friends, trooped around to the back of the gym building. Surrounded by about thirty spectators, we squared off with each other, neither of us wanting to throw the first punch. A jab here, a feint there, just as we were taught in physical education class. If it were up to me, we could have just sparred a few rounds and let it go at that. I knew I was going through a social puberty rite, even though I didn't know what it was called by cultural anthropologists. It was a kids' game you went through at every new school. Evidently my opponent didn't feel the same way, or perhaps the taunts and jeers of his circle of friends made him need to prove something, for he threw a solid punch that caught me on the ear. Boy did that smart! Out of reflex, chance—who knows what—I let him have one right on the jaw. He went down on his back stunned. He was out of the fight. For a moment all of us were silent. We stood there looking at him. Then about a dozen of his friends jumped at me. All of them tried to hit me at once. Most of their blows struck me on the shoulders and the back. I threw my arms over my head and tried to see an opening to run through. There were so many of them trying to get at me that the ones in close were thrown off balance by the ones in back shoving and pushing. I was in the middle of a mugging, a riot. This was no longer kids' stuff. Most of their punches were wild but a few struck home.

Then something strange and totally new happened to me. To this day, nearly thirty years later, I am still amazed at my involuntary reaction and its results. From somewhere within me a scream of pure primeval rage came rushing out. (Thank God it did or I would have been beaten into a pulp!) Everything after that scream happened so fast my memory of it is blurred. My arms, which were covering my head, swung out with tremendous ease and force, catching two of the boys alongside the head. They were pole-axed and dropped to the ground. They just lay there, not moving. Still screaming, I spun around at the other boys in the mob striking out with one arm that covered my head, then the other. Without thinking, perhaps instinctively, I charged the boys who were between me and the gymnasium wall. They struck at me but got out of my way. Free of the mob, I turned my back to the wall. Shouting all the obscenities in existence, I charged back at them. This was no longer a social puberty rite; I was trying to kill them. Then another strange thing happened. All of my attackers retreated. None came within reach. In a half-crouch, I stopped and stood there, still screaming at them, taunting them, daring all of them to attack me. They surrounded me in a wide circle: some of them in a half-crouch like I was, some just standing there, two of them still on the ground. But none of them said anything or made any move to come near me. A few turned and walked away. My rage was gone. I didn't want to kill them anymore, but I still wanted to fight and scream at them. This standoff went on for another minute. Then all of us were saved from ourselves when the vice principal arrived. When he walked up it was all over. Civilization had returned.

Anger dominates fear. It makes us disregard most everything, especially things that usually make us anxious. Part of the voluntary action of our cortex is overridden by our primitive emotional brain. However, we seem quite able to predict the consequences of our behavior. We know what is going to happen, but at the time we just don't seem to give a damn. I have another poster on my wall that reminds me of this part of our evolutional heritage. It reads: "Yea, though I walk through the valley of the shadow of death, I shall fear no evil, for I am the meanest son of a bitch in the whole valley!"

Both anger and fear energize our body and simplify our thought processes and actions down to the bare essentials for physical survival. If we can run to avoid danger, our inherited neurophysiology insures that we will run well and fast. If we can aggressively defend ourselves, it insures that we will fight hard and without reservation. It's as simple as that.

What Depression Does to Us and for Us

Depression is our third negative survival emotion. Depression in psychological terms is an involuntary survival reaction of our nervous system when rewards or positive experiences become infrequent in our everyday experience. We become mildly depressed or sad when someone or something we are used to is missing from our daily lives. We become deeply depressed when someone or something very important to us is removed. When we are depressed we withdraw from the everyday things we normally do. We accomplish very little beyond eating and sleeping. We are not productive at home or at work. We have little interest in positive things like sex, going to the movies, having fun with friends and family. Most importantly, from the point of view of reducing fears, we show little motivation to explore novel or otherwise interesting happenings in our lives. A new book, a puzzle, a game, a TV special—all these things that would regularly capture our interest seem a dreadful bore.

The common depression we find ourselves in may last from several hours to several days. Although my fellow therapists and myself see patients who may complain of depression lasting several months or longer, we have no valid clinical evidence that long-term depression is any different, except in degree, from the depressive states we all find ourselves in from time to time. As a matter of fact, the clinical effect of chemical mood-elevating drugs on the behavior of depressed patients is still quite controversial. Some claim they help. Others say they do nothing but make them edgy and irritable. The standard clinical treatment for depression—long term or short—is to help the patient get reconnected with positive experiences, no matter how difficult this may seem at first to the depressed individual. The results of such behaviorally oriented treatment methods are remarkable, often clearing up months of chronic depression within a few short weeks of the patient making deliberate attempts at trying to live normally, even if he or she has to fake it initially.

When you feel depressed, you are sensing the result of messages, sent to your whole body by your emotional brain, slowing down the physiological processes necessary to maintain your normal level of activity. For our ancestors, this involuntary reduction in bodily activity may actually have been beneficial during hard times. When game was scarce, or the winter harsh, people who got depressed and just sat around in their caves, grumping and complaining about the good old days, conserved what energy they could get from their meager food supply until better times came along.

When we are not engaged in something—anything —that gives us even minimal rewards during most of our waking hours, our primitive nervous system puts us on hold, shuts us down, turns us off. In other words, it makes us depressed because this depressive state worked for our primitive ancestors. When they didn't get involved in many activities it meant that times were excessively harsh, risky, demanding and unrewarding. It was much better for their own and the species' survival that they get depressed and not squander their energies when the odds were stacked against them. If you find this very speculative, you might ask what your own outlook on life is when you get depressed. Most people say things like: "What's the use. I can't do anything right. I haven't got a chance, so why should I try anything?" We see this reaction very often today with patients who have suffered a physical trauma like major surgery or a broken leg. Technically it's called the postsurgical depressive syndrome. But again, we are very likely seeing in these patients the results of genetic traces laid down in our nervous system eons ago.

If an early ancestor got injured, it was in his best

interest to become depressed. Any of our ancestral cousins who kept enthusiastically hopping around on one healthy, and one broken, leg instead of holing up and feeling rotten until it healed, was out of touch with reality. In the same way, any of our ancestors who remained optimistic and perky in spite of their long and fruitless explorations in search of more food were less likely to survive. So this psychological "hibernation" mechanism of depression, which naturally evolved in our ancestors to increase their chances of survival during hard times, is still with us.

Fear, anger and depression are all naturally occurring human emotions. They do not, by themselves, indicate some deep-rooted psychological fault or hidden conflict stemming from a twisted personality, even though in therapeutic jargon these emotions are known as the neurotic triad. Most people who go to psychotherapists cope poorly with life's problems. They also complain of these normal negative feelings. It is their difficulties in coping that are the real problems, not the negative emotions of anger, fear and depression. Coping with life's difficulties is the only key to feeling good about ourselves.

What Is an Abnormal Fear?

We could call our survival emotions neurotic or abnormal or any of the other frightening clinical labels, such as "unsocialized aggressive reaction" or "endogenous depressive state." We also could run rampant in making up pseudoclinical names for the many possible fears we could have, and even some improbable ones. All it takes is a Greco-Roman dictionary and a vivid imagination. You could even be "scientifically" afraid of being attacked by a swordfish while strolling along in the middle of the Sahara Desert. If so, you would be suffering from xiphodesererephobia. Unfortunately, all we do in using such fancy names is relegate the solution for our problems into some limbo thought to be controlled only by God, the Devil, or by some sophisticated but otherwise just as superstitious minds, by the medical profession.

You may be surprised to find that there are at least three models or descriptions of what is abnormal: the Medical Model, the Statistical Model and the Coping Model. Abnormality means different things according to the model used to describe it. The models don't always agree.

The Medical Model of Abnormality

The most widely known and used of the three is the Medical Model. This description of abnormality, used mainly by physicians, is set up for two purposes: first, to give physicians some common language for communication and, second, as a convenient category for legal and medical insurance forms. Its major practical use is to give some sanction and authenticity for making expert decisions on matters such as permanent and temporary disability, sick benefits and leave, and compensatory injury awards. The Medical Model is based on the assumption that there is an ideal state for the human condition—within very narrow and known limits, and that any deviation outside these limits is, by definition, abnormal. It's very simplistic and therefore gets its users into trouble whenever they try to describe anything beyond specific physical problems like having the Bubonic Plague, advanced arteriosclerosis or a broken leg. According to the Medical Model, anything outside the limits of normality must be fixed. It has problems, however, with any suspected deviation that can't be measured with a rectal thermometer, a stethoscope, a tongue depressor, an X ray, or with a biochemical analysis of what's in the specimen jar. Medical Model enthusiasts have been known to substitute their own narrow, personal value systems for clinical standards on how things "should" operate when they get into behavioral and social areas *that the medical model has no valid information on*, such as sexual preferences, philosophical and moral judgments or social problems. Medical Model enthusiasts have even claimed such things as racial discrimination, antisocial behavior and the rises in the crime rate as "social diseases," implying with this territorial labeling that there is a reason for such things that will be "cured" as soon as one of the major drug companies finds the correct pill to administer. One recent example was the long, bitter fight within the American Psychiatric Association over the issue of homosexuality. Traditionalists claimed that homosexuality was a sickness, a psychiatric disorder, while practitioners trained more recently felt that there was insufficient validation for this claim, while there was much data to the contrary. As far as phobias are concerned, the Medical Model way of thinking assumes that a phobia is *wrong*, a disease in the broadest sense of that term—in short, an *abnormal* condition, with all the frightening implications of that word.

The Statistical Model of Abnormality

The Statistical Model, on the other hand, sets up no a priori limits or standards on what is normal or abnormal. It looks only at the frequency of a specific condition, happening or behavior for the whole population. If we can believe some of the figures that various statistical studies give us on the number of practicing homosexuals, for example, they range from 10 to 25 percent of the total adult population, not counting childhood experimentation. The Statistical Model looks at a subject only as frequencies charted on a particular curve, used mainly for prediction. The statistical curve charted on the graph may be the one used to grade us in school: the "normal" bell-shaped curve which predicts 10 percent A's, 15 percent B's, 50 percent C's, and so on. Or it could be the

Poisson Distribution, made famous because it accurately predicted the number of Prussian Army sergeants who were kicked in the head by a mule in the year 1881. The curve didn't predict how many mules hurt themselves doing this. In the case of homosexuality, anything that happens to as many as one quarter of the total population doesn't seem that far out statistically. In other words, being homosexual, in a statistical sense is something like getting a test grade between A and B or between D and F. Which end of the statistical distribution you choose is determined by your personal value judgment.

The Coping Model of Abnormality

The most useful of the definitions of normality and abnormality is the Coping Model. This is the model used by experienced clinicians and therapists. The Coping Model makes no reference to arbitrary or statistical norms but looks at how a person is coping with problems on an everyday basis. For example, the Medical Model says it is normal to have 20–20 vision, two arms, two legs and a lot of other good things that make life a lot easier. If you have only one leg, you are, by definition, abnormal and something should be done about it. The Statistical Model agrees with the Medical Model on one-leggedness. Not very many of us have only one leg, so one-legged people are statistically abnormal. The Coping Model, however, sees one-leggedness *only as a possible problem* and asks; "How are you making out getting around with one leg?" If the patient says it's no problem, then there is no abnormality present, according to this model. If, on the other hand, the patient complains of depression and difficulties because of one-leggedness, then the condition is diagnosed as an abnormal one requiring some treatment.

The Coping Model takes a similar view of homosexuality. If the homosexual patient says that his or her sexual preference presents no problems, or only problems that can be dealt with effectively, then the Coping Model does not see homosexuality as abnormal. Or, if the homosexual complains of the difficulties of being gay, the option for treatment change is open between improved coping or working on the homosexuality. And this is the working model of therapy used daily by psychologists, psychiatrists and clinical social workers in helping people with their difficulties. The long and bitter fight over the classification of homosexuality within the American Psychiatric Association was really a conflict between the misuse of the Medical Model to impose narrow, arbitrary philosophical values and the use of the Coping Model, which is more in touch with the realities of everyday life.

Having a phobia is not unlike having only one leg or having any other problem. If you ask yourself, according to the Coping Model, "Self, how are you getting along in spite of being phobic?" and your fear presents no great difficulties, then your phobia or irrational fear is really not worth your time and effort to eliminate it. If, for example, you have a morbid fear of snakes and there have been no reported sightings of snakes in your area for the past seventy-five years, it makes little sense to worry about your snake phobia, let alone be treated for it. If, on the other hand, you plan a vacation trip to the highlands of Arizona and New Mexico, your snake phobia then becomes important—just like my aerophobia was no great problem until I was offered a free weekend with a real dish of a girl, but I had to fly to Palm Springs to make the date. When the prospect of that fun weekend came up, I had a real coping problem. My aerophobia became abnormal immediately!

three

Psychoanalytic symptoms
or learned fears: phobias, freud,
dr. watson and other fellows

There are two popular theories on how we become phobic about certain things and situations. One is the theory held by many analytical therapists, which derives from the original work of Sigmund Freud. Most behavior therapists, however, derive their theory from a different body of data collected primarily in the twentieth century.

The Old-time Analyst's Viewpoint: Anxiety that Covers Uncivilized Impulses

In brief, the analytical theory of phobia assumed that the phobia, like other irrational or strange behaviors is nothing more or less than a symptom of an underlying personality conflict. The more rigid analytic types would not directly attempt to treat the phobia. Instead, they urged us to work, preferably in a prone or seated position, on gradually achieving insight into the cause of our hidden conflict or personality fault. When this insight occurred, our symptom would disappear—hopefully. The old-time analytical therapist assumed that a fear of flying in airplanes, riding in elevators or driving on the freeway was a product of a hidden psychic conflict between an individual's animal nature and civilized upbringing.

The analytical viewpoint also assumed that the conflict was usually sexual in nature and was initiated in your childhood sometime before the age of six. It was useless, therefore, to deal with your phobia without first resolving childhood sexual wishes to make it with your mother, father or both. Since the phobia was assumed to be an outlet for the "psychic energy" produced by a hidden conflict over the desire to do something naughty, some other outlet or symptom would rapidly appear if the phobia were taken away without resolving the conflict.

This theory borrowed its ideas from eighteenth-century physics. Our conflicts were viewed as comparable to two sticks rubbed together to produce friction, heat and fire. These two sticks, smoldering with conflict, kept the psychological teakettle simmering away with bits of libidinal steam puffing out around the rim of our civilized cover. If we pressed down on one edge of the cover, the steam would only escape from some other place on the rim. If we pushed down on both places, the steam would seep out somewhere else. The analyst sincerely feared that a new symptom, caused by removing a phobia, would probably be more destructive to the patient's well-being than the phobia was.

This analytical "teakettle" theory about the treatment of phobia is truly dated. It is not supported by the results of controlled clinical and laboratory research done over the past twenty-five years by psychologists, psychiatrists, physiologists and other scientists. If you have a phobia, and it is eliminated by dealing with the phobia directly, instead of looking for hidden "psychic conflicts," your chance of getting something worse in exchange is about as likely as getting a shark bite at high noon in the middle of an Iowa cornfield. Nevertheless, some of the more traditional practitioners still fervently believe that, consciously or unconsciously, your phobia serves some psychic purpose, even if you come in complaining bitterly about how it is screwing up your business or social life. If, however, you want to keep your phobia, whatever the frightening Greco-Roman label is that describes it, then I agree with them that you should not part with it. If there is some payoff to you personally, if it gets you out of work or out of social complications, or if your spouse and family place fewer demands upon you because of it, then who could blame you for quitting halfway through the treatment? But that's the only justification I know of for just sitting and talking about causes and coping, instead of getting out and doing something about the problem.

There is an alternative to turning belly up on the traditional analytical couch for months or even years. The alternative is behavior therapy, with its various treatment methods.

The Behaviorist's Choice: Bad Luck in Learning

Behavior therapists assume that irrational fears are learned fears and that what can once be learned can also be "unlearned." The behavioral types draw this conclusion from three sources of evidence: general learning studies carried out over the past seventy-five years, reports of phobic patients who claim that they suffered a specific trauma—a fall before becoming acrophobic, a frightening air trip before becoming aerophobic, a putdown during sex before becoming erotophobic—and experimental laboratory studies which show the acquisition of irrational fears through the simple learning process of pairing two things together the way Pavlov's dogs learned to pair the appearance of food in their cages with the footsteps of the animal keeper.

Let me use an example I have given to my students at UCLA to explain how we can become phobic through this involuntary learning process. Suppose you are driving your custom sports car, the Marinara Longostino. This car is a striking red color with a long and slender nose that gradually widens into a rounded shape around the driver's cockpit and abruptly squares off just over the rear wheels. It would be unkind to say it resembles a ketchup bottle on wheels, but in fact, your friends who drive the more conventional Chevys and Fords call it exactly that: "the ketchup bottle." On this particular day, you are driving your Marinara over a winding mountainous road. Just as you make a turn, a semi-tractor-trailer runs you off the road down into a sheer 300-foot drop. As you fall straight down to oblivion, you try to scramble out of the car, helplessly attempting to survive while your whole life flashes before your eyes. Refusing to admit that the end has come, you wonder whatever happened to Virginia Lapmarsh, that cute co-ed with a gap between her teeth whom you dated as a freshman in college. Still wondering, you close your eyes as the ketchup bottle plunges the last fifty feet to the rocks below. You feel your body snapped up and down violently as your beloved sports car smashes into the rocks with a horrendous bang. You still keep snapping up and down and wonder if this is the way everyone feels when they go down in flames in a ketchup bottle. Eventually the up-and-down movements stop and you decide to open your eyes. There lie the smoking remains of your Marinara Longostino fifty feet below you. There you are dangling by the back of your belt on a spruce branch fifty feet above it. You are not a highway statistic but a person who has had the hell scared out of him. The rescue team of the paramedics lowers you down with only a few bruises and sore muscles. Nothing has happened. You're the same as you always were. Right? *Wrong!* Conditions have been set up that may produce in you a severe phobic reaction about cars and driving.

Two weeks later, your insurance agent calls to say that a replacement Marinara Longostino has arrived at Ostentatious Motors. You rush down to see it. On the way in the taxi you can't help but think about the old ketchup bottle and what happened. As you walk into the auto showroom, you see its identical twin, Marinara II. You notice your hands are trembling but not with the anticipation of feeling that genuine Rhino-tail gearshift lever. Also, your stomach is a bit uneasy and quivering. As you finally run your hand over the red-lacquered side wheel cover, you notice that your palms are positively clammy and leave a trail of sweat on its elegant surface. Suddenly remembering an important appointment you just happened to forget, you apologize to the salesman, decline to stretch out on the Wombat-skin seats and leave promising to give him a call. As the weeks go by, you find one excuse after another not to go back to Ostentatious Motors. You have acquired an irrational fear of automobiles and driving.

Also, you notice something else is bothering you. The rented Ford you picked up as temporary substitute is a tomato red color. Each morning when you leave the house and approach the car, you get that same clammy, queasy feeling you had with Marinara II. You exchange it for a yellow Chevy. Still, even in the Chevy, you feel uncomfortable if the road curves ahead and you cannot see what is coming. Steep grades bother you and you get nervous driving in the foothills. The mountains you avoid like the plague. The more you drive, the worse the feeling gets. Finally, you turn in the rented Chevy and travel only by bus and taxi. If you have been waiting fifteen minutes in the rain and a red cab stops, you get in only reluctantly. Yellow cabs are all right, but red means dead! Six weeks later, you meet Virginia Lapmarsh at a party. It's obvious she still has the hots for you. But just seeing her again makes you a bit nervous and you wonder what you ever saw in such an oversexed amazon. Especially one with a gap between her teeth. You resolve never to go near women with such gaps again; there must be a genetic connection between teeth and sexual drive!

Of course this is an overstatement of the phobic

learning process. But it shows how things we see, hear or touch in one situation will trigger off our fear response in another, similar situation. It also is indicative of how a learned fear can complicate our behavior, our emotions and our thinking.

One of the classic cases reported in the professional literature points this out dramatically. A young girl, about seven years old, ran away from her aunt on a picnic, after she promised her mother that she would be good and not get lost. The aunt found her sometime later wedged in between two rocks in a small creek with a waterfall cascading over her head. The young girl was terrified both of the situation and what her mother would do to her when she found out. The aunt took her to a nearby farmhouse to dry her out and promised not to tell mom about her naughty behavior. The next day, aunty left for the city and the child had no one she could talk to about her frightening experience; she had no way of "reliving" her experience with a friend under more normal and relaxed conditions. Shortly after this traumatic incident, any sound of running or falling water produced a panic in the child. Her parents sometimes had to carry her screaming to the tub to bathe her. When other students at school splashed the water from a drinking fountain outside the classroom she panicked; once she fainted from this sound. This case is not unlike my hypothetical example of phobic conditioning, only less exaggerated.

During the 1920s, two very famous psychologists, John Watson and Rosalie Rayner proposed to induce a phobia in the laboratory and then "cure" it with counterconditioning. To test this procedure they selected a very young boy, Albert. First, they showed Albert a white rat and allowed him to pet it. Albert showed no fear at all of this white rat. Then Watson and Rayner pulled a sneaky trick on him. They sat him down with his back to a four-foot-long, three-quarter-inch-thick steel bar hung from the ceiling. Whenever the white rat was brought into Albert's view, they struck the steel bar, suspended in back of Albert, a mighty blow with a hammer. Needless to say, Albert got quite upset whenever they did this to him. After a very short time, just the sight of the white rat caused a negative emotional response. Like people with phobias acquired outside a laboratory, Albert showed a typical fear pattern. Just as with non-laboratory trained phobias, his fear generalized to other things similar, but not identical, to the white rat. If you showed Albert a white fur muff he would get upset. Even a man with a white beard triggered off the learned fear response. Although Watson and Rayner intended to decondition Albert to his fear of white furry things, they never did—for some reason. One story has it they ran out of research funds before the second part of the experiment was completed. Another has it that Albert's mom took him away before Albert could relearn his joy in petting the white rat. Somewhere out there today is a sixty-year-old Albert with his conditioned fear of white furry things intact.

What a Phobia Is and What It Isn't

Some therapists are of the opinion that phobias are learned indirectly through mental association of ideas. Another classic case illustrates their viewpoint. A young girl had made a mental association between two physically unrelated objects: a minister's collar and fresh falling snow. As it happened, this teenager had become sexually active and then felt very guilty about it because of her strict religious and puritanical upbringing. The *pure* white snow reminded her of her uncle's *pure* white collar, which brought to mind what uncle would say about her sexual escapades as well as her guilt feelings. Her uncomfortableness was reported to be so severe that she would go to bed and cover herself up whenever it started to snow.

In this unfortunate girl's case, she was not fearful

of snow itself. The snow only made her think of what her supermoralistic uncle would say about her sexual experimentation. I would have difficulty in calling her condition phobic. Frankly, from my experience of dealing with thousands of persons with psychological problems, a case like this one showing such bizarre thought patterns and coping behavior would suggest, at worst, a prepsychotic condition and, at best, a very passive, nonassertive personality style. Here I am not engaging in professional nit picking. The appropriate characterization of her problem would have told us how to remedy it. If she were phobic about snow, we could have made her feel better about snow. But her real problem was feeling terrible about not knowing how to cope if and when her puritanical uncle criticized her sexual desires. If anything, she was realistically afraid of the effect her uncle would have on her. One effective answer to the young girl's problem might not have been too different from that worked out for a young woman I mistakenly treated for autophobia, the fear of driving a car. This patient became quite upset when driving —but only when there was traffic on the street.

For a few fruitless sessions, I went on the assumption that the thing she said she was afraid of produced a phobic condition, i.e. driving a car and perhaps getting into an accident in heavy traffic. After trying all sorts of behavior therapy techniques and failing to relieve her discomfort in driving, I came to the obvious conclusion that what I was treating was not her problem. To see what made her anxious on the streets, I suggested we take a short drive for a few blocks around the clinic. As we pulled out of the parking lot onto Wilshire Boulevard, I had to push my old beat-up VW microbus into heavy traffic. Right away, my patient became nervous. She got quite upset when I signaled to a big Cadillac that I was going to cut in. When I was in the traffic flow, I asked her what had troubled her. Did she think that we might have an accident? "No," she replied, "I was thinking what that man in the Cadillac must have thought of us for cutting in front of him." This answer puzzled me because the guy in the Caddy smiled and waved me on as I signaled him. Right then it hit me. I knew what her problem was. It wasn't a fear of driving. She was afraid of what people might think of her if she drove in the aggressive manner needed in many situations. Still pursuing the source of her discomfort, I asked what the Cadillac driver must have been thinking and she said: "He must have been grumpy and didn't like it." "But," I countered, "he smiled at us and waved us on." "Yes," she said seriously, "most people put on a front and don't say what they are really thinking about you." With that I gave up trying to work within her slightly paranoid system of classifying people's behavior and tried a different tack. "You know me quite well now. Guess what I would say back to him if he acted grumpy with me?" She grinned: "You would say, 'Fuck'um!'"

For the next half hour we kept cutting in and out of the heavy traffic on Wilshire with her looking at the person who had to stop for us and saying aggressive things like: "Screw you. . . . Up yours too, buddy. . . . Your horn works fine. Now try your lights!" That half-hour session on Wilshire Boulevard eliminated her feelings of discomfort entirely. At her next appointment, she reported that she was driving all over town with no upsets and only an occasional expletive. Like the snowflake girl, she did not have an actual phobia but only an anxious sense of inadequacy when she imagined that other people were thinking bad things about her. Perhaps some of her expletives were truly angry ones that wiped out her anxiety over what people thought of her. My bet, however, is that most of the anxiety elimination work was accomplished by her learning a method—any method—that allowed her to do something *active* in the face of her anxieties instead of just passively accepting them. She discharged herself from further treatment after that one session with my approval.

These cases point out why it makes sense to look at phobias as fairly specific learned fears. This viewpoint gives you the great advantage of being able to detail the situation or thing that causes you anxiety and, by so doing, determine if you have a specific fear caused by the situation itself—a phobia—or an abstract, yet realistic, fear caused by something else that is only incidentally related to the situation— generally a lack of a specific coping skill. For instance, the majority of people with a fear of public speaking do not have a fear of crowds, auditoriums, standing up on a stage in full view, or even a fear of speaking to crowds. The fear that paralyzes their minds is the fear of making a mistake, or of appearing less sophisticated than other speakers, or even of having no answer to some heckler in the audience who questions them. And these concerns are not irrational. For most people, the answer to fear of public speaking is to work on the fear of looking foolish before crowds and learn effective ways of coping with it gracefully.*

Some of the Behavioral Ways to Lose your Phobias

Keeping in mind this distinction between a true phobia and a more general anxiety over "What would happen if . . . ," let's look at some of the many different behavioral methods that can be used to eliminate a phobia, and then, in later chapters, tie them together by seeing that they all do one important thing—replace bad feelings about a situation with good feelings.

Mary Cover Jones, a contemporary of John Watson, developed the first laboratory treatment procedure for phobia back in the middle 1920s. She worked with

---

*See Manuel J. Smith, *When I say no, I feel guilty* (New York: The Dial Press, 1975).

a young boy named Peter, who had an unnatural fear of rabbits. If a white rabbit was brought into the same room with Peter, he would get nervous; if it was brought close up to him, he would panic. After observing Peter in her laboratory, Cover Jones formulated the most important question in treating a phobic state. *If a phobia is a learned fear, what do you "teach" the patient to replace the fear response to the phobic stimulus with?*

I've asked myself the same question. What is the opposite of fear? Is it relaxation? Or something else? What about excitement? People are always saying that they could use some excitement in their boring, day-to-day existence. How do you teach people to become excited? How about enjoyment? People don't appear to be frightened when they enjoy something. How could Cover Jones teach Peter to enjoy his rabbit instead of fearing it?* The simplest procedure was to get Peter in a jolly mood, or at least feeling good, and then to use that psychological state to replace his fear of the rabbit. Since Peter, despite his fear of rabbits, was like most children, Cover Jones could feed him something he liked, put him in a jolly mood with the food, and then sneak the rabbit up on him, first from afar and gradually bringing it closer with each enjoyable meal. With this simple procedure, tested nearly fifty years ago, Mary Cover Jones both "cured" Peter's rabbit phobia and started the whole movement we know of today as behavior therapy.

Jones published her results in an obscure profes-

---

*As you may recall from the previous "autophobe" case, I taught the patient to make an aggressive response whenever she was anxious about what people thought of her driving. Her anxious response was partly extinguished, because anger and anxiety are incompatible within us. We cannot be angry and anxious at the same time. But would this work for little Peter? I doubt it. I can just hear what Peter's parents would have said to Cover Jones about her treatment method if she used aggression as the counterconditioning response to replace fear: "What did you do to our little boy? All week he's been going around saying 'Up yours Mr. Rabbit!' and then kicking his stuffed toys all over the house."

sional journal, and for nearly thirty years this type of behavioral treatment for phobia was ignored. No one picked up on it and used it for general clinical treatment. Perhaps because Freudian psychotherapy was becoming very popular then, no one believed that this exotic clinical malady called the phobia could be dealt with so simply and quickly. Then late in the 1940s Dr. Leo Reyna, a student of Clark L. Hull, the great American learning theorist, took a job overseas in a South African university. It just so happened that Leo Reyna became friends with another faculty member there, Joseph Wolpe, a physician. Dr. Reyna talked to his friend about his research in learning, and Wolpe listened. In fact, Dr. Wolpe began to apply learning theory in the laboratory with animals and then started using it with his phobic patients. He found himself confronted with the same problem Mary Cover Jones had solved in 1925. If irrational fears are learned fears, what can you have the phobic patient learn in place of his fear response?

Dr. Wolpe picked relaxation. It seemed to make sense that you could not be afraid of something and be physically relaxed at the same time. Here he became quite ingenious. He borrowed the techniques of deep muscle relaxation developed by Edmond Jacobson in 1938 and taught them to his patients. Then he had his patients make up lists of situations about their phobia and rank them from least to most fear provoking. (For example, "I'm three miles away from my office building, and I'm only thinking about that damned elevator," versus, "I'm in the elevator and the door is just closing on me.") With this rank order set up, Wolpe had his patients relax and then reminded them of the scenes they had made up about the phobic situation. He started with the least uncomfortable ones and worked up the list, laboriously —sometimes two steps forward, one step back—toward the most fearful scene.

Wolpe called this method of treating phobia "systematic desensitization." This term was borrowed from dermatology wherein allergy sufferers were gradually desensitized to larger and larger amounts of an irritating substance like pollen. This method is, of course, the same one used by Mary Cover Jones when she gradually introduced the feared rabbit into Peter's lunch hour. With systematic desensitization, the patient eventually would be able to imagine himself in the elevator and feel no twinges of anxiety. He or she would be "cured."

This method has one major disadvantage—it often takes up to six months of weekly or biweekly sessions to extinguish the patient's fear. In light of the newer and much shorter ways of eliminating phobias, it seems that the choice of relaxation to replace anxiety was impractical. It makes sense to me that if there is a common element in making anxieties go away and if many other treatments make it go away quickly, the slower methods must have less of whatever it is that makes anxiety go away.

Albert Bandura of Stanford, for instance, helped people with snake phobia simply by letting them observe another person without a phobia pick up and handle snakes, first from the vantage point of an adjoining room and then up close. This method, called "modeling," seems to have little to do with the food and relaxation methods of relearning used by Mary Cover Jones and Wolpe—or does it?

Victor Meyers of London's Maudsley Hospital was also innovative. He found he could reduce the fears of people who avoided city streets and stores by having them play a game of "hide-and-go-seek" with him on the garden rooftop of the hospital. Dr. Meyers would hide in the bushes and the patient would have to explore the garden to find him. Later they would do the same thing out in the city streets. Again, game playing seems to have nothing in common with food and relaxation, yet it works just as well in overcoming phobias.

Still another ingenious treatment method called "paradoxical intention" was developed by Victor

Frankl. Dr. Frankl "cured" a patient of his pathological fear of having a heart attack by persuading him
to try to induce one. The patient, who was quite
healthy, huffed and puffed for some time. He could
not bring on a coronary, but, in trying, he eliminated
his irrational fear of having one. While this method
can be used in some restricted situations for reducing anxiety, I wouldn't want to recommend it to
people who are afraid they will act compulsively or
who are afraid someone might do something to them
—people afraid of jumping or falling off a tall building, for example, or who fear their work is going
downhill so fast that their boss will fire them. In
cases like these, the use of paradoxical intention
might not be an antiphobic treatment but a self-fulfilling prophecy.

The most radical and surprising of the new phobic
treatment methods is "contact desensitization" developed by Brunhilda Ritter of Stanford. With this
intuitively brilliant method, Dr. Ritter was able to
eliminate a fear of heights *within thirty minutes* simply by keeping physical contact with the patient during the phobic deconditioning period. Dr. Ritter
found that she needed only the stimulus of touch,
keeping her hand lightly on the arm of the patient
as they gradually went step by step above ground
level. Of all the dozen or so different methods tested
for reducing phobic anxieties in the last twenty
years, Brunhilda Ritter's technique is the one least
predictable by common sense. Food, relaxation, games
and perhaps even demonstration can be viewed as
fun and therefore counterphobic. But the elimination of a phobia simply by maintaining a light physical touch with another person is amazing. But then
the applied uses of our innate, constitutional sensory
processing system—the "orienting reflex,"—called by
one researcher, "the observable unconscious" are more
amazing still as we will see in the next chapter.

2

The good feelings
we can use to overcome
our fears and phobias:
how we get them

four

The triggers of our good feelings

How We Learn to Like Something

I became interested in treating phobias because of my interest in psychophysiology—a fancy name for the simultaneous study of the basic positive and negative responses of our nervous system to all sorts of stimuli and how these responses limit or enhance our everyday behavior. To be quite honest, I'm not a scholarly type. So I didn't get interested in the field of psychophysiology because of all the publishable gold nuggets lying therein just waiting to be picked up. I got into psychophysiology because of some subtle—and not so subtle—arm twisting by my major professor at UCLA, Irving Maltzman. While Irv was, and still is, one of the world's leading psychophysiologists, I was the only graduate student in the department who could fix all the complicated electronic recording apparatus in his laboratory. But this mixing of differing talents didn't produce friction as you might guess. It produced a lasting friendship and true affection between student and teacher. For in addition to his formidable intellect and scholarly knowledge, Irv also has a down-to-earth, common-sense way of reasoning things out that made the translating of nervous impulses and gland squirts into our everyday behavior much more sensible and realistic.

For example, a short time after I received my doctorate under Irv, something happened that started

me on figuring how we could make our physiology
work for us in changing a phobic response in the
same way many of us acquire a genuine liking for
questionable things like Scotch whisky. Now, I am
one of those people who can't stand the taste of
whisky. I never told that to Irv, though. At parties
and scientific meetings with him, I was one of the
boys. I tossed it down straight with the rest of them,
smiling without showing my teeth, because they
were clenched holding back the shudders.

Irv and I were sitting down over coffee theorizing
on alcoholism and toying with ideas for pilot research to investigate its basis. I argued that clinical
work showed that many drinkers (like myself) dislike the taste of booze. Many alcoholics prefer vodka
because it has very little taste. They swallow the
stuff like medication to get the afterglow and the
blurring of painful reality. "Psychophysiologically,"
I said to Irv, "we ought to test out in the laboratory
this clinical hypothesis that alcoholics really don't
like the taste of booze." Or, stated more precisely, the
alcoholic's primitive nervous system—*wherein lie all
the positive and negative feelings*—doesn't respond
positively to booze. I argued that the alcoholic voluntarily overrides the natural, negative response of
his nervous system to liquor in much the same way
we all put up with the dreadful taste of aspirin, because it will make us feel better later.

Now this hypothesis, coming right out of my personal dislike for whisky and my middle-class background, was a pure misapplication of the Medical
Model. In this case, I reasoned that the noble human
body and the constitution of our primitive nervous
system could never be perverted. It could only be
attacked by external disease processes or warped personality quirks against which it would fight valiantly
but with which it would never, never collaborate. I
argued with Irv, therefore—a bit arrogantly and with
right and common decency on my side—that we
ought to be able to measure a negative reaction of the

nervous system to the unpleasant, burning whisky as it hits the sensory receptors of the tongue, mouth and throat. "Whisky is a medication," I said, "taken solely for its afterglow. No one likes unpleasant-tasting things. Have you ever heard of an aspirin user who sucks on the tablet?" I asked.

Irv, a Scotch lover, pointed out with his pipe stem jabbing at my nose that we ought to be able to measure a positive reaction of the nervous system to whisky, a reaction of interest, of heightened perceptual awareness. We ought to, Irv added, if he were allowed to pick the brand—J & B, eight years old, aged in Scotland in casks. "If you're so sure of it," said I, "let's test it out in the lab and loser pays for the fifth." "Pays for the quart," said Irv, sucking on his pipe with a solemn poker face.

Some days later, with the bottle of Scotch tucked under his arm, Irv, followed by Dr. Bill Kantor and me, went down to the laboratory to run a classical one-subject study in the tradition of Pavlov. Who won the bet? Who do you think? Irv showed a strong positive nervous system response the first time we placed a few milliliters of J & B on his tongue. He did the same the second time and the third and the fourth. And so it went for ninety minutes. To distilled water randomly given there was no response, but to Scotch whisky a positive response every time. To rub it in, when Irv swallowed the J & B after each measurement he would smack his lips with gusto and chortle things like, "Ambrosia, a work of the gods!"

The Orienting Reflex: Our Automatic Decision Maker

In this mini-experiment, we were measuring Irv's orienting reflex—the "What is it?" response of the nervous system—each time we gave him a taste of Scotch. Called the OR for short, it is our fundamental perceptual–arousal system that neurologically sorts out what we see, hear, smell, touch and feel. It is our automatic attention response. When we are hungry, for instance, our orienting reflex makes the smell of a steak cooking (unless we are vegetarians) much more interesting than the sound of a bee buzzing nearby. The OR does this sorting out automatically and quickly. We don't have to say to ourselves, "Gee, that steak on the barbeque is more interesting than the bee buzzing in the back yard. I think I will concentrate on the steak and ignore the bee."

On the other hand, if the bee takes a keen interest in exploring your ear closely, your OR will automatically make you pay attention to the bee while it blocks out the sizzling and the smell of the steak. This choice is made without our having to think of it. And it's done on a level about as basic and innate as each beat of our heart.

You can actually see the OR at work if you snap your fingers at your pet dog. The dog will automatically perk up its ears while turning its head to orient its sense organs toward the source of this unexpected sound. Were you to keep snapping your fingers, however, this sound would be evaluated as nothing of significance by the dog. It would lose its unexpected or novel quality and the dog would stop orienting to it. When I do this to my dog Wimpy, he always perks up for at least three or four times. Then he just stares at me, his head lying between his paws with the most disgusted look. Although it's not a "scientific" observation, I can swear he's thinking to himself: "What's that turkey want from me now? He just keeps snapping his finger as if it's some big deal. So what? I heard it. He'll have to do more than that to get some action." Also compare your dog's short-lived orientation to a finger snap with its persistent OR to the food bowl at dinner time or to that bitch in heat that somehow always seems to get loose during the mating season and parade up and down in front of your house. So, for animals as well as for humans, the OR is the fundamental, first-line mechanism by which all incoming stimuli are sorted out according to their importance, their threatening nature, or their plus value concerning our well-being and survival.

Needless to say, without the orienting reflex our existence would be quickly reduced to a schizophrenic jumble of impressions. Or, at least, we would have a hell of a job trying to decide: "What should I look at now—the moving leaf on that tree that looks like a visual Japanese haiku or the cute girl in the tight skirt walking down the street in front of me?" Without the OR, we would be continuously making choices about every little thing that happens. We would be buried deep in thought and do nothing in life but sort out stimuli. The way nature evolved a means of having us involuntarily orient to things according to certain priorities is a lot more practical, and, as it turns out, these priorities are the keys to reducing our fears and phobias.

In our mini-experiment, Irv's nervous system produced an OR to Scotch whisky that was identical to the OR that your dog's nervous system would produce if you snapped your finger at it, showed it a bowl of hamburger, or said, "Get the ball. We'll play." Irv's ears didn't perk up each time we gave him a sip of Scotch, but we measured the internal changes in his brain and nervous system produced by his orienting reflex to whisky on a polygraph recorder much like a lie detector. But most importantly, Irv's nervous system failed to produce a negative response to Scotch. And this was the same liquor that often triggered off a gag reflex in me.

This simple fact shocked me. How could a reflex so basic and important for our survival be suborned into responding so positively to an acquired taste, especially a vile one for Scotch? Being able to mess around with your OR and have it listen to a different neurological drummer than the one Mother Nature intended was perverse, I concluded. Therefore, in my eyes, Irv's positive response to Scotch had to be unnatural. "No one goes around giving positive nervous responses to negative things," I reasoned, "unless they are sick." For example, I could make my dog Wimpy perceive my finger snap as a threat if, each time I snapped my finger, I then proceeded to beat the hell out of him. His nervous system would then also produce a learned "defensive reflex"—a name for all the nerve impulses, gland squirts and enzyme drips within us that *are* what we call fear, anxiety and unpleasant feelings. This defensive reflex, called the DR for short, is a normal reaction under those circumstances and would get Wimpy's body activated and ready to expend a lot of energy in running away from the expected beating that would follow my finger snap. In fact, we would judge Wimpy abnormal if he gave only a positive reaction to my finger snap—a large orienting reflex—and no defensive reflex.

This positive reaction of Irv's nervous system to Scotch made me face a simple but inescapable fact about the orienting reflex and my own shabby, limited view of it. Up to then, I'd thought that much of how we automatically oriented to stimuli in our environment was according to some grand scheme of what was good for our species and its survival. I had naively assumed that our basic, innate nervous system schematic, evolved over eons of time through countless billions of trials and errors, was set up by Mother Nature only for survival through what we might call middle-class means.

Irv and the mini-experiment made me realize how much I had bought the Medical Model way of thinking—lock, stock and scalpel. My naive perception of our fundamental nervous constitution—how our wiring worked—was the opposite of Freud's. Freud assumed that we all have an underlying bestial neurological foundation intent upon pleasure gratification—*I wanna eat, I wanna fuck, an' if I can't I wanna kill*—tempered only by civilization's overlay of humanity and false caring. I, on the other hand, nobly assumed that our fundamental wiring system was benignly motivated and above vice. It tolerated only our superficial personality corruptions. The involuntary operation of our innate nervous system, I reasoned, kept each of us, as much as possible, from committing genetic suicide by not allowing us to like things that were bad for us. It certainly wouldn't gleefully join in such a venture, I told myself. So, I figured that, if like Irv, you responded positively to Scotch whisky, it must be due to some weird thing your mother did to you before the age of six and not the result of a choice made by your nervous system.

But Irv, Bill and I had collected some simple data in the laboratory that shot these naive ideas to hell. The squiggles on the polygraph sheet in front of me spelled out Irv's changes in electrochemistry and in the supply of blood to his brain when he tasted Scotch. They were all positive. I didn't have to see my own squiggles. I knew in advance what they would say. My involuntary gag reflex to Scotch already indicated that I would respond with a consistent defensive reflex that would be a testimonial for Carrie Nation and the Women's Temperance League. But still, there it was in front of me. Irv's squiggles agreed with what he had said beforehand: *He and his whole body* really liked J & B Scotch whisky!

To keep my intellectual vanity from being bent out of shape, I still could not accept the evidence of my eyes. I came up with a lot of totally useless Medical Model diagnoses to explain away what I saw: "Irv must be a degenerate. What do they really do in the faculty club after the academic senate meetings?" Or, "He has a masochistic personality problem. That must be why the psychology department asked him to take over as chairman." Then, after this foolish moment of refusing to face the obvious, the data in front of me began to make sense. Irv was not perverse because his nervous system had learned to respond automatically and positively to Scotch. He was, in fact, a connoisseur of whiskies and other liquors. He didn't just drink liquor. He studied it. For Irv, good Scotch whisky was an occasion. For me, it was just a jigger of whisky. *He paid careful attention to the quality of the experience when drinking it. I ignored it and just swallowed.*

My God, did I feel dumb! I had learned a simple, inescapable fact: Not only can the decisions and preferences of our nervous system be "perverted" according to any value system man has yet devised, but this is also the innate way it is designed to function. Our nervous system is fundamentally optimistic. It is designed to look at everything that happens as a potentially positive event. Our nervous system is built so that it can learn to respond positively (or negatively) to *anything*. Any other design of Mother Nature's would drastically narrow the range of conditions under which we could survive. Without this flexibility, it would only take one big ecological dust-up to finish us as a species.

An old joke about the Great Apocalypse makes this point. After God's messenger angel tells the world that all will perish within forty-eight hours of the Second Flood, there is a general call for forty-eight hours of prayer, fasting and repentance to prepare us to meet our Maker. All the religious leaders join in, except for the chief rabbi of Jerusalem. He summons all the members of his congregation so that they can sit down together and figure out the best way to learn how to breathe under water—and like it!

Even though certain things may displease or frighten us, our nervous system is built in such a way that *we have to experience something as unpleasant before we can learn to fear it* (unless it comes up behind us suddenly and makes a hell of a racket!).

By any age after birth, we have learned that some things are to be avoided. Nevertheless, we are still built to respond positively to anything and everything as if it will be rewarding to us. And the physiological mechanism built into us that makes us respond this way is the orienting reflex. When the OR is triggered off for any reason, our body and nervous system experience a positive reward. A lot of things in our everyday lives can be rewarding. It may be a smile from a sexy-looking man or woman, some simple praise, a taco when we are hungry or just a wag of a dog's tail when we come home at night. These external things we take for granted as rewards, but within our nervous system, before we can get that good feeling that goes with a reward, an orienting reflex must be triggered off. On the neurological level, *the orienting reflex is the reward and the only reward.*

Now, there are rewards and there are rewards. What pleases you may leave me cold. Also, most rewards that we experience within our nervous system are nickel and dime stuff. Some occasional rewards make us feel like a million dollars. But the important point for our nervous system, and how we feel over the long run, is that nickels and dimes add up to dollars. Especially since the big rewards are few and far between, the nickel and dime stuff we get on the neurological level is very important to keep us operating from day to day without plunging into a depressive state. *Unless you are orienting to something—anything—during most of the day, you are going to feel anxious and depressed.* This statement is not derived from some mountain top, touchie-feelie, avant-garde psychophilosophy game but from clinical histories and hard psychophysiological laboratory data.

Now let's see how the orienting reflex affects our basic emotions by making us feel rotten when it is absent and optimistically good when it is active.

The Plus and Minus Emotional Sides of Our Primitive Nervous System

Our primitive emotional brain, you may recall, controls our emotions and the other bodily functions that nature has given us little say over. This whole involuntary part of our nervous system—the primitive brain structure, the nerve tracts, the nerve endings, feedback loops, etc.—is called the autonomic (involuntary) nervous system (or the ANS, for short) by anatomists. The ANS is looked at by neuroanatomists and physiologists as if it has two different parts that take care of different functions in our body. One half, when active, makes us feel good. The other half, when active, makes us feel uncomfortable. For our present purposes, let's use psychological lab slang for these parts of the ANS. The part that is active when we feel good, we call the "fun" system. The part that is active when we feel uncomfortable, we call the "fear" or "flight-fight" system. Technically, they are called the parasympathetic and sympathetic systems respectively. The sympathetic half was called that because early researchers noted that its response was in "sympathy" to extreme mood swings like fear and anger. The other, fun, half they couldn't figure out too well so they just called it parasympathetic—meaning around the sympathetic—because at least they knew its nerve tracts came out of the top and bottom of the spinal column while those of the sympathetic system came out the middle.

As you have already guessed, the flight-fight half gets our bodies ready to run or fight like hell when it is strongly activated. When it is mildly activated we just feel nervous and uncomfortable. We still don't know much about the other half of the ANS, the fun part. It controls digestion and parts of our sexual response, like foreplay and intercourse, but not orgasm. It is active when we are feeling good but not when we are bored. Most of what it does, let alone the details of how it does it, is still uncharted territory. Part of the problem is our lack of understanding what fun and good feelings are. How do you describe fun? One person gets off a roller coaster and says, "That was fun. Let's do it again," while two others in the background are about to throw up. What is feeling good? We can play and feel good. We can work and feel good. We can even do nothing, apparently, and still feel good. We can just look at something we like and feel good. There are so many activities that can inspire what we call feeling good that figuring out what is common to all of them is the major problem in understanding how to use them constructively and systematically for our benefit.

Fortunately, one thing is quite clear about how each half of the involuntary system operates. Both halves, fun and fear, are in competition with each other. They operate something like two children on a seesaw. If one child goes up, the other comes down. If the fear half is active, the fun half is inhibited. If the fun half becomes stimulated, the fear half's activity is reduced accordingly. If the fear half is active and the fun half is active also, the half with the greatest activity will be dominant and rule the other. This, incidentally, is the purpose of general psychotherapy: to set up conditions where we can stimulate the fun half, allowing us to think about what is going on when we deal with uncomfortable material about ourselves.

After all this chitchat about what we know and don't know about our involuntary nervous system, you just might be asking yourself, "Can we get control over our involuntary feelings of discomfort and fear?" The answer is yes—but only by indirect means. Willpower doesn't work but something else does. The orienting reflex is the "backdoor" to the involuntary nervous system. It is an indirect way of getting some control over how we feel that we can't directly achieve by telling ourselves not to feel a certain way. The "keys" for this backdoor to our uncontrollable feelings are the different ways the orienting reflex can be triggered off. When you know what these keys are *for you*, then you will have found a variety of ways to swing the activation of your nervous system out of the flight-fight half and into the fun half. Now let's look at these ways to orient and, by doing so, learn a variety of things, some of which will work for most everybody and some of which will be personal to you—but all of which can be used in eliminating irrational fears and phobias.

five

The five keys to the backdoor of our
involuntary emotional system:
food and sex, body sensations, orders,
something old and anything new

Over the past seventy-five years we have learned a
number of things about the functioning of the OR
as well as how each of us uses it, and how it can be
misused. Research into the orienting and defensive
reflexes began in the laboratory of Ivan Pavlov, the
great Russian psychologist and psychophysiologist. It
was continued in Russia by colleagues and students of
Professor Pavlov, then in other countries as well. In
the United States, most of the work has been concentrated at UCLA by Don Lindsley, Horace Ma-
goun, Irv Maltzman and their students.

Unfortunately, the significance of what these researchers in many countries studied has not been
widely understood, perhaps because of the "publish
or perish" edicts of academic institutions that prompt
isolationist empire building of many scientists. Consequently, the application of our knowledge of the
orienting reflex to real life difficulties, such as learned
fears and chronic depression, or even to things like
overweight and dieting problems, has proceeded at a
snail's pace.

We know now both specifically and in broad terms
what categories of things will make us orient at the
fundamental, bedrock level of our primitive nervous
system:

Stimuli with *novelty:* Anything that is unexpected or new.

Stimuli with *biological significance:* Anything that satisfies our biological hungers.

Stimuli with *innate signal value:* Anything that we instinctually orient to such as bodily sensations.

Stimuli with *learned or acquired signal value:* Anything that we have learned to pay attention to by any means.

Stimuli with *instructed signal value:* Anything that we have been told or instructed to pay attention to, either by others or ourselves.

Novel Things that Quickly Trigger Off the Plus Side

Let's look at these OR triggers and see what each of them means in your personal life.

First, the novel or unexpected happening. If all the birds sitting in the trees in your neighborhood are quiet, you will not orient to them consciously without telling yourself to do so. Your nervous system will automatically decide that these quiet birds are insignificant. It will do this while it still scans your surround for anything else going on. If all the birds start making noise, you will orient to them without having to think about it. For our ancestors out in the bush, this kind of response to sudden changes was very important. When the birds started making noise and flapping around, it usually meant something big was coming toward them. It could be an animal that our ancestors could eat, but it could also be an animal that could eat them. Nowadays, it's only the scruffy neighborhood tomcat trying to keep his ancestral heritage alive. He, incidentally, is the one that makes you orient out of a deep sleep at 2 A.M. during mating season with his unexpected howl.

You orient to unusual stimuli from other people just as to what's going on around you in your physical surroundings. For example, if you are deeply engrossed in an interesting book or TV show and your wife wants to make small talk—"Was work pleasant today?"—her statements don't seem to penetrate your consciousness after the first or second try. You literally pay attention only until your brain determines that she is not talking about something of greater significance (signal value) than your book or TV show. She may go on talking, but a continual "uh-huh" on your part may keep her satisfied and your attention elsewhere. Then she says casually in the same low monotone, "The monkey went into the refrigerator and took out a banana." Suddenly, you find yourself automatically, without having to think about it, *orienting* to what she just said with a "What was that?" and, at the same time, feeling slightly sheepish trying to figure out what was so strange about her last comment. It also doesn't help a bit to have her looking at you with that suspicious little smile. Now as this example points out, just something new or novel happening doesn't make us go into an orgasm of pleasure from anticipation, but even this "finger snap" reflex causes our fun system to swing momentarily into action.

Anytime we process new information, solve a puzzle or figure out a problem, even to copy a grocery list, we orient. And in doing this our nervous system makes us feel more positive and alive and less uncomfortable and bored.

Now although novelty is good for reducing our level of anxiety, unfortunately it poops out—quickly. All novel stimuli lose their newness as they are repeated. As soon as our cortex "records," in short-term memory, what is different about this new thing, we are done with it. And, in truth, why should we pay attention any longer?

In using our orienting reflex to reduce our fears and anxieties or to recondition our phobic situation, the trick is to keep orienting as long as possible in the unpleasant situation. Since novelty produces only a phasic OR (one that phases in and out), what we need is a tonic (longer term) OR to combat our fears. The other classes of things we orient to, stimuli with *biological significance* or *innate* or *acquired signal value* affect our nervous system for a much longer time than something that is merely novel. These are the things that really do the work in reducing our anxieties.

Biological Things that Trigger Off the Plus Side in Cycles

Biologically significant stimuli are all those things in life that satisfy our bodily needs. These things are easily recognizable as stimuli that make us feel good or hold our interest. They are also a class of things that we orient to consistently and tonically. For example, when we are thirsty we will orient consistently to something cool to drink: a frosty beer, a soft drink, maybe even water. On a hot day we will orient each time a cool breeze fans our sweaty body. Food is an obvious example of what our nervous system considers biologically significant. Common sense tells us that if we didn't orient to food—even minimally— we would soon waste away and die. Sex is another of these stimuli, but perhaps one a bit less obvious to some of us. Without sexual orienting our species would soon be extinct. If you find yourself with sexual inhibitions or embarrassments, these are learned nervous system negatives that tend to override your orienting reflex to sexual matters and can be relearned—often in a matter of weeks.

Even pictures of food or a sex partner are enough to make most of us orient. If we are hungry enough (about eight hours) or sexually deprived enough (about two hours), a written description of food or a sexual act will hold our attention for a considerable amount of time. Now you know why cookbooks and sex novels are bestsellers.

Hunger is a simple name for a complex sensation

produced by your nervous system's *learning to antic-ipate* your regular meal times. Like other biological orienting reflexes, it waxes and wanes depending upon conditions in our bodies. About a half-hour before breakfast, lunch and dinner, if you eat these meals regularly, your nervous system causes a batch of insulin to be dumped into your blood stream. The insulin quickly metabolizes, or burns off, the sugar in your blood to get things ready for the fresh nutrients coming in with the next meal. Your low blood sugar level, caused by your conditioned insulin release cycle, is what we call hunger As long as your blood sugar is low, you will continue (for about forty-eight hours) to orient to food: the sight of it, the smell of it, the taste of it, even the thought of it. It is not unusual to find people who go most of their adult lives without breakfast and feel no discomfort, no matter what the breakfast cereal manufacturers claim on the side of their boxes. The nervous systems of these people have learned that insulin is not to be released into the blood stream shortly after waking up, simply because there will be no food to digest at that time. And these people report that food in the morning does not particularly interest them.

About thirty minutes after you eat, the first part of your meal is partially digested and your blood sugar level begins to rise. When this change occurs, you do not automatically orient to food as food any longer. For instance, remember the last time you cooked steak and onions? At the time you prepared this marvelous dinner, your mouth keep watering and the smell of the onions sizzling was delicious. Then after dinner you took a walk around the block in the fresh night air. As you walked back in the front door, your nose was assaulted by the overpowering smell of cooked onions and you wondered why in the world that dreadful smell was so appealing sixty short minutes ago.

Often, our bodily states, like hunger, will trigger off an orienting reflex to such a degree that it inter-

feres with our thinking brain. We make stupid decisions. For example, it's not too smart to do your
week's grocery shopping just before dinner. When
you are hungry, you will orient more than you normally do to a lot of junk displayed in the supermarket
and buy it. Later, fully fed, you will wonder, "Why
did I buy that jar of pickled elephant rump?"

Since some of the things that cause us to orient
are biologically tied to the bodily states we experience
at a particular time, what value does this have for us
if we are concerned with getting rid of phobias? *Take
your phobia out to lunch!* Which is exactly what
Mary Cover Jones found out from Peter and his white
rabbit phobia nearly fifty years ago.

You're phobic about airplanes? You can shave the
odds in your favor way before you get on a flight. Go
to dinner at the airport restaurant in your city. While
you are enjoying your favorite meal watch the planes
take off and land. Do this a number of times with no
intention of ever flying on a plane. Then, when and if
you do decide to board a plane, starve yourself for
about eight hours first. Aboard the jetliner, break out
one of those fabulous cookbooks to read before takeoff—the ones with those scrumptious pictures of wonderful food that make you drool just to look at them.
Also try bringing along a few of your favorite snacks
to enjoy during takeoff and later. Indulge yourself,
bring real goodies! Don't wait for the stews to feed
you. The food on most airplanes is dreadful (unless
you fly in first class).

"But no one else will be eating!" you complain,
afraid that you will look odd. Let me reassure you
that with the number of people around who feel uncomfortable flying—the airlines themselves estimate
about twenty-five million—you will receive only en-
vious stares clearly saying, "Why didn't I think of
that?" Also, if your fellow passengers have read this
book, they will be too busy to pay attention to you.
They will be orienting to their own bootlegged gusta-

tory delights, ranging from Hershey bars to cold aspic of duck cordon bleu en dixie cup.

But food is only one way to OR your phobia away. Don't drop this book right now and rush to the phone to make a reservation with United Airlines. Read on until you have a few more tricks in your bag!

There is no doubt that sexual matters have an innate interest for us. Sexual stimuli will cause you to orient greatly and consistently with only minimal "down time" after orgasm.

In his fascinating book, *The Tell-Tale Eye*,* Dr. Eckhard Hess tells us of his research on involuntary changes in the size of the pupil of the eye in response to sexual stimuli. The pupil is that part of your eye that gets larger in the dark and smaller in the light. This response of the pupil to changes in light is called the "adaptation reflex" by psychophysiologists. If the light is too bright, your pupil will automatically constrict to protect the cells of your eye. If the light is too dim to see well, your pupils will dilate so more light will reach the inner eye cells. This adaptation reflex is also used by the physician to see if an unconscious person with no heart-beat or breathing can be helped. He shines a small light into the eye, and if the pupil does not constrict, the person has suffered brain damage to the extent that recovery is unlikely. In medical parlance, the adaptation reflex is one of the *vital signs* that the body and nervous system are still functioning. With the adaptation reflex, our involuntary nervous system automatically controls other things like body temperature, blood pressure, breathing and heart rate.

Given a constant light in Dr. Hess's experiments, if someone's pupils got larger, it was not a result of the adaptation reflex—that person was orienting to some-

---

*Dr. Eckhard Hess, *The Tell-Tale Eye* (New York: VanNostrand Reinhold Co., 1975).

thing that had just happened. If the pupils got smaller, the person was responding with a defensive reflex. Although Dr. Hess only casually connected his research on pupillary responses to the orienting and defensive reflexes, it does a disservice to him and his brilliant work not to place it in its proper context, so we can recognize what it tells us about ourselves.

For example, Dr. Hess reasoned that if the pupils of the eye respond so consistently to sexual stimuli, it was likely that these enlarged pupils, indicating an OR taking place, would have a definite effect on a possible sexual partner observing them. Very ingeniously, Dr. Hess made two identical color slides of a young, pretty girl, retouching them so one had large pupils and the other had small ones. Then he asked a group of men to look at both slides and tell what they thought about the two pictures. Not one of the men was able to point out that the only difference between the two was in the size of the pupils. Yet most of them described the small pupil face as "cold, selfish or hard" while the face with large pupils and the whopping big orienting reflex was described as "soft, loving and warm." What does this consistent interpretation indicate? Simply that in sexual matters, we instinctually orient to each other without realizing it. We tell each other in effect, without saying so, "If you play your cards right, I can be had."

You may recall this innate sexual orienting message from your own experience. Think back to a party where, as you walked in, there across the room was a woman with the most interesting, sexy look on her face looking back at you. For that moment, the "vibes," the "chemistry," is all there at a peak. You are both communicating without knowing how you do it. You both turn each other on because of a perceived, but not understood, mutual orienting reflex. She is biologically significant to you. You are biologically significant to her. Next time you walk into a cocktail party and this mutual turn on happens, at least you will know what is going on. You will, that is, unless she is orienting over your shoulder to the guy who came in right behind you.

This phenomenon of "big eyes" being part of a sexy-looking face has been known by women for thousands of years. The drug belladonna, meaning beautiful woman, dilates the pupils when applied with eyedrops. It was used in earlier centuries by women to make their eyes appear larger and sexier.

You may find it difficult to believe what some eye shadow and mascara can do to the orienting reflex. I was amazed at my own reaction to the Plain Jane at the supermarket check-out counter. This gal had served me for years and we always had a few words of greeting for each other over the groceries. One time she put on a "face" just before quitting time so she could make an early date. I couldn't believe it was the same woman. My God, what a difference! If I weren't with my wife, I would have asked her out myself. The change in her sexual appearance was dramatic. The makeup forced attention to her eyes, and she didn't have to dilate her pupils to get this effect.

The billion-dollar cosmetic industry is based entirely upon this OR dilation substitute. Without some way of calling attention to the eyes, all the pancakes, creams, lipsticks and rouges wouldn't be worth a plugged nickel.

Aside from how we turn each other on sexually with overt signs of our orienting reflex, or its substitutes, you may have puzzled over the question of why you have your own sexual preferences. How come you chose *your particular* mate? We have no authoritative answer to this question, but the choice depends upon your innate or learned persuasion. One behavioral view held by many psychologists, for example, is that homosexuality, like Irv's preference for Scotch whisky, is learned. Homosexuals, somewhere along the way, have learned to orient to those of their own sex, probably because they have previously been conditioned to exhibit a defensive reflex

to members of the opposite sex. Bisexuals, according
to this point of view, would have been conditioned to
orient to their own sex, as well as having an innate
sexual orientation to members of the opposite sex.
This notion that heterosexuals involuntarily orient to
the opposite sex while homosexuals involuntarily
orient to the same sex is backed up by hard experimental data from Dr. Hess's laboratory. He found that
heterosexual males and females oriented to pictures of
nude females and males respectively. Homosexuals,
on the other hand, oriented to pictures of the same
sex.

So your personal preferences in sexual partners are
most likely learned preferences. It is not inconceiv-
able that we could become conditioned when we are
young children, and at our most pliable age, to orient
to physical characteristics of mom or dad, favorite
uncles or aunts, older cousins, etc. And these early
learned characteristics may well play a part in mate
selection in later years as many clinical psychologists
argue. Perhaps Sigmund Freud wasn't too far off the
mark with his Oedipal ideas but just stretched them
one complex too far.

Stimuli with either innate or acquired *signal value*
are even more useful for triggering off your orienting reflex than sexual or other biological stimuli. Our
innate OR stimuli are those things to which we all
orient from birth, even before we are psychologically
or physiologically mature. Infants orient to sounds,
lights, smells, tastes, touch and temperature without
prior experience outside the womb. We respond automatically to changes in all our classic senses at all
ages. For example, when it gets light in the morning
and the daily noises begin, we wake up because we
orient to these happenings.* It is difficult to go to
sleep when any of our senses are being stimulated.
You don't bed down at night in a quiet, comfortable,
dark place because of social custom or learned habits.

---

*One accompaniment of chronic oversleeping is chronic depression,
a state in which we do very little orienting to anything.

You seek out your little nook when tired because your orienting reflex demands the absence of relatively strong sound, light, smell, taste, touch and temperature stimuli. You may even find it difficult to fall asleep the first night or two in a new home or apartment, because the novelty of it keeps your orienting reflex active, and the OR keeps you awake! Only strong bodily deficits like sleep deprivation, sickness or physical exhaustion will override an active OR and allow you to fall asleep.

Bodily Sensations that Reliably Trigger off the Plus Side

The fact that we instinctively orient to stimuli in all our physical senses may sound so obvious that it hardly seems worth pointing out. But there is one striking bit of data that is not so obvious and ties into phobic treatments. If someone touches you, you will orient. In fact, you will orient longer to bodily sensations than to any input from your other senses. This is so reliable a way of triggering off the orienting reflex that it can be used to check the proper dosage of anesthetics for surgical patients. To see if a patient is "under" with no sense of touch or pain, the physician can repeatedly touch the surgical area until the pupillary dilation OR ceases. When the pupil no longer responds, the area is properly anesthetized.

The orienting reflex will be consistently triggered off by other bodily sensations as well. Why do you think you don't habituate to the itch of a flea bite that keeps bothering you? Or to a tight collar? Or to a new pair of tight shoes? Bodily sensations are quite important to our basic functioning. This particular way of involuntarily triggering off the OR has some important implications for treating phobias and for psychotherapy in general. The whole point of psychotherapy, for example, is to help us gain "insight" into our anxieties and other negative emotions. To get the brain functioning intellectually we need to orient, because in that process our anxieties come under control of the thinking part of our brain and don't interfere with our thought processes. One way to make us orient is to make our bodies protest. So what do therapists do in general psychotherapy? We get the patient to sit or lie on comfortable furniture for about fifty minutes, telling him or her to relax while talking about the problem. I think we may have it all ass-backwards! In many therapists' experience, including my own, the most productive psychotherapy seems to happen when the patient is obviously uncomfortable. We, rather grandly, assume that our gentle probes and directives have uncovered one source or another of the psychological discomfort and that the patient is now dealing with it. But how much of this discomfort, showed by the patient's wriggles, squirms and shifting from one buttock to another, is caused by our good psychotherapy and how much because the patient is getting over a case of the flu, stayed up late last night, or had to run all over town this afternoon getting things done to be on time for the therapy appointment? With the prices paid for private psychotherapy in New York, Chicago and Los Angeles, I suppose the patient expects comfort and room service. But if the way we organize our therapy sessions minimizes the patient's orienting reflex, it's no wonder that general psychotherapy can take so long.

Several years ago a friend of mine, an aerophobic, was told by her husband that if she didn't want to fly on trips with him, he was going to start taking vacations on his own. This ultimatum put her into a crisis. Her husband suggested that she fly with him on his next trip to Buffalo. It would be only a short trip of forty-five minutes and she might get acclimatized to flying. She agreed with apprehension. On the day of the trip, she boarded the plane irrationally terrified.

As the minutes passed by in the air, she gradually noticed only one thing that penetrated through her fear. The bra she had on was killing her. It was one of the waist-to-armpit types that was in fashion then. She worked for a bra manufacturer, and each of the women in the office was given a sample of every new experimental model. The women were asked to wear it for a few days and let the designers know how it felt. Fortunately for her, it wasn't one of their better efforts. In fact, it was more like a medieval torture device with bony stays and wires, which kept jabbing her as she breathed. It was so tight she felt that her stomach was pushed up just below her tongue. When the plane landed in Buffalo, she was not thinking, "Let me off this plane. I'm terrified." Instead, all she could think was: "I can't wait to get into the women's john at the airport with my suitcase so I can change my bra." That was the first thing she did upon landing—and with a big sigh of relief. The same evening, she flew back to New York City with her spouse and a comfortable bra. She said she really enjoyed that flight. Her fear of flying was gone, and it has not returned on any of her frequent flights taken over the years. *Now that's self-help!*

This story doesn't prove anything, but the laboratory and clinical data collected on the orienting reflex provide the only explanation I can find for this particular woman losing her phobia. As long as it took for her aerophobia to be counterconditioned, her bra kept triggering off her OR with all sorts of uncomfortable little pokes, jabs, pinches, squeezes and general pressure.

Now you may be saying to yourself: "But that's masochistic. Are you advocating that people punish themselves to lower their anxieties?"

Think of it this way. If you are out of shape and you undergo some uncomfortable physical exercise that makes you feel in the pink afterward, is that masochistic behavior? The most important question to

ask yourself is: Which is the more uncomfortable—
the retraining you must undergo or the phobic anxiety you already suffer?

Upon further analysis of this anecdote, I even have
some understanding and empathy for the early monks
who chose to wear hair shirts under their robes—as if
they enjoyed the incessant crawling, itching sensation
that this torture device gave their bodies. Now I
understand that they were just like us, only they suffered a greater sense of guilt and anxiety. They wore
their hair shirts because this device consistently triggered off an orienting reflex that lowered their anxieties and guilt when the early church demanded
more of them than they could give.

Perhaps this notion sounds farfetched to you. But
then how are we to explain the consistent observation by thousands of psychotherapists and physicians of psychosomatic reactions—physical ailments
that are only uncomfortable like rashes, aches, pains,
numbness, etc., in patients with chronic anxieties. If
you are scratching at a rash that drives you nuts,
you haven't much time to worry about other things.
Itchy rashes are guaranteed to make you orient.

At this point you might ask, "You said that the OR
is a positive response that makes us feel good. How
can we orient to things like pain and feel good at the
same time?" An excellent question. Our response to
pain is not as simple as we may think. A mildly painful stimulus can actually be pleasurable, like the
burning sensation of paper on the tongue. We know
very little about pain even though we experience it
every day of our lives.

It's not even clear that physical pain and the defensive reflex—fear or anxiety—are the same thing in
our nervous system. Some behaviorists argue that fear
and anxiety are the anticipation of pain. But we can
also be fearful and anxious about things that have
nothing to do with pain—criticism for one, fear of
failure is another. The list of things we can get
anxious about is endless. As a matter of fact, there is

a wealth of clinical evidence that not only are pain
and fear neurologically different but also that *pain
will reduce anxiety*. For example, people who slit
their wrists—an ineffective way to attempt suicide—
often report afterward that their anxiety leaves them
and that the reasons for killing themselves don't seem
so pressing. Patients who practice self-mutilation are
generally thought to be severe anxiety neurotics and
not psychotics. I treated one such case several years
ago. Because of his severe social anxieties, over the
years he had burnt a continuous V along the inside of
his left thumb and index finger. When his negative
feelings got too intense, he lit a cigarette and burnt his
hand through the skin to the flesh underneath. After
that, his anxieties were quieted for a while. With some
assertive therapy for his social fears, his self-mutilation stopped. At last report—some five years later—he
has not thought it necessary to injure himself again.

Pain transmission within our nervous system also
seems contradictory. Specific nerve fibers that trans-
mit the sensation of pain have priority over every
other happening within our nerve tracts. (Perhaps
this is the reason why pain blocks our feelings of
fear and anxiety.) Yet, as every student of clinical
hypnosis learns, the easiest thing to do with hypnotic
techniques is to block the sensation of pain. It's so
simple to do that it's invariably part of the demonstration of hypnosis to clinical learners and theater
audiences as well. But hypnosis doesn't work well at
all in eliminating fears and anxieties, as we shall see in
Chapter 6. Now that's a paradox. The highest priority
incoming signal in our nervous system is the easiest
one to block! And to complete the paradox, the standard advice of current researchers on pain is to get
your attention focused on something else happening
around you. These therapists are telling their patients,
and with success, to orient outside themselves, not
just to sit or lie there experiencing pain. And their
advice makes sense. How many times have you been
interrupted from moaning over your headache by

someone at work who needs your help in solving a problem immediately? Ten minutes later you come back to your desk and you remember you have a headache! Even more fascinating, when we orient to the location and feeling of our physical pain—instead of to what or who caused it—the intensity of the pain diminishes. How many times have you gone to the doctor and complained about a twinge and when he asks you, "Is it sharp, dull, throbbing?" or, "Exactly where is it, here, here or here?" you feel like a fool, a hypochondriac, a malingerer? When you look inside yourself and try to analyze your pain, it often disappears. We even do some automatic things to reduce our pain, without being told how to do them. Hit your finger with a hammer and you will automatically grab the throbbing thumb with your other hand, tuck it between your thighs, under your arm or stick it in your mouth. Why? Because if you touch or put pressure on the painful area, the pain seems to lessen a bit. What do you automatically do when you get a cramp, a sore muscle or a bellyache? Nobody taught you to rub the painful area with your hand. But you invariably do it. And somehow—who knows how— the deep pain eases. What clinical data do we have that shows positive touch sensation ORs are helpful in eliminating phobias? Brunhilda Ritter and Joseph Wolpe give us the only reported examples, although it's not uncommon to come across patients with experience of faith healing where the laying on of hands seems to have helped them. Dr. Ritter has used the touch OR—which she appropriately calls contact desensitization—with good results for anxiety about snakes and with dramatic results for fear of heights. Dr. Wolpe has successfully used Pavlov's idea of "external inhibition"—stimulating the surface of the skin with a mild electric shock—to eliminate phobic anxieties in some patients.

If some young clinician in the future shows us that a back rub in the phobic situation is the only thing required to get rid of irrational fears, I wouldn't blink an eye.

Instructions that "Tell" the Plus Side to Be Active

One of the best ways to get you to orient in any situation is to tell you to pay attention to something that is happening or may happen. "What's that?" someone asks you when the usual California tremor zips along one of the thousand geological faults under Los Angeles—and you orient automatically to what's going on. At work, or in a therapy session, however, the instructions telling you to orient may be deliberate and planned: "Every time the second hand on the clock reaches thirty, let me know." We can give this kind of stimulus *acquired signal value* for your nervous system instantly and with very little effort for as many times as we need to.

If someone were to say to you, "Stop thinking of the word hippopotamus for thirty seconds and I'll give you a thousand dollars," you would never collect your money. You would know, if you had ever played this mind game, that it's impossible not to think of the word hippopotamus when told not to, because you really have been instructed to orient to it in a devious way. We can use this irresistible OR in phobic situations as well and produce an involuntary, neurological reaction that reduces your fears automatically.

Using instructions to give something in your environment the ability to reduce your fears has some distinct advantages over other ways of getting you to orient. You can use instructions anywhere and the OR to instructions poops out slower.

And when it does, we can always add on other instructions to trigger off the OR again. *Playboy* and *Playgirl* magazines are not always available. Neither is an attractive lunch. But instructions . . . they are always available and cost nothing. Ask anybody a question and they will be delighted to tell you what to do.

Mothers with small children seem intuitively ac-

quainted with this OR technique. Go to the municipal park in your area on Sunday. Look for a two-
year-old child crying, and what is mommy saying?
"Look at the white birds on the lake. Aren't they
pretty. See them all swimming together. See the little
baby ducks following their mommy? And look at the
pretty trees over there with the clouds on top of
them. You see the big cloud in the middle? What
does it look like? Do you see the horsey in the cloud?
You don't? Look closer. See his feet at the bottom.
His nose is that little bit of cloud sticking out at the
side. And his ears are those two tiny little puffs on
top." Mom is getting her child to orient to the many
things in his environment and she does it simply, successfully and with minimum effort. So successfully do
most mothers accomplish this natural fear-reduction
process of instructed orienting that they pay a price
for it. The children soon keep bugging their mothers
to take them out of their boring old house to a place
where things are really happening.

Now one of the things that mom was doing in my
example was to get her anxious child to orient and
then perform a mental task—to look at the details of
the cloud and mentally join up the different pieces
into a total picture of a horse. The orienting reflex to
instructions can be kept active—and consequently
keep you feeling less nervous—for a much longer period of time if you are required to perform some
meaningful mental or physical job while you orient.
It can be as simple as yelling out when the second
hand on the clock reaches thirty. It can be as complex
as piecing abstract cloud parts together to form an
image. Or it can be as earthy as rating each of the
three or four male or female flight attendants on an
airliner with respect to sexual appeal. It can even be
as mundane as studying an illustrated textbook in the
municipal library on reptiles before your tour of the
snake house at the zoo. Or, as Dr. Bandura showed at
Stanford University, *it can be as basic as* to telling
the patient to pay attention to what he was doing

(modeling) as he handled a live, harmless snake. If you get nervous riding in automobiles, your OR can be kept active for hours at a time playing license plate poker. As the game starts to lose interest for you, your OR to the license plates can be reinstated full force when you start to play for money.

You can be instructed to orient—and consequently lower your fears—to anything happening in a phobic situation. You can also be instructed to pay attention to the phobic stimulus itself.

Let's suppose you have a morbid fear of snakes. Let's also suppose you have some skill in drawing—a skill that triggers off one of your learned orienting reflexes. With this natural OR going for you, after explaining what we were going to do and why, I would trot you and your sketch pad down to the Los Angeles Zoo and take you directly to the door of the snake house. First I would have you orient to things in the situation having nothing to do with snakes. Later, I would instruct you to orient to things about the snakes themselves. In each case, I would give you a long list of questions and instructions. We would spend hours at the snake house making you orient to different things about snakes, but long before we ran out of things to which you could orient, your fears would have been reduced to zero.

Learned Things that Trigger Off the Plus Side

There are, as we have seen, other ways besides the use of instructions to make you orient in the presence of snakes, sharks, airplanes, elevators, etc. To defeat your fears, you can use as many ways as possible— and in all different kinds of combinations. Use your own personal interests as OR stimuli—those things with *learned signal value* that have been continuously associated with your orienting reflex. For you it may be baseball, tennis or football—or perhaps knitting, crocheting or needlepoint. (Don't laugh! Remember, this was Rosie Grier's way of relaxing in between bone-crunching tackles for the Los Angeles Rams!) It may be your stamp collection. Or perhaps you have a "nose" for good French and California wines. You may be a nut about archaeology or movie stars, or you may collect ostrich feathers. It doesn't matter what the rest of us think; it's your personal thing. It's what turns you on, interests you, attracts your attention consistently—makes you orient—that counts. The most important characteristic about things with learned signal value is that they are not boring to you or so routine that you can do them without having to think about what you are doing. Learned signal values, then, make you think and orient to process information in the phobic situation even though your primitive emotional brain wants you to drop everything and get the hell out of there.

We could use the rest of the space in this book just to list the thousands of things that we all have learned to orient to during our lives. Instead, use the OR Checklist on pages 301–303 to get material on about a half-dozen topics that interest you before you tackle your fears and phobias *in vivo*. Right now, in the following chapters, let's put all these ways of evoking your orienting reflex together and see how we can use them in a practical way to eliminate your fears.

3

Some simple ways to eliminate your fears and phobias

six

Fear of flying conquered by female forms, luggage carts, fence poles and twenty-one chimpanzees

Fear of flying is one of the most common fears of the general population. About twenty-five million Americans have this unpleasant emotion about airplanes, or so the commercial passenger carriers estimate. Now this fear of flying that the airlines are talking about may not exactly fit the definition of phobia used in this book. Some of these twenty-five million Americans (nearly one quarter of the adult population) undoubtedly have had scary or unpleasant experiences in the air, which could condition a defensive reflex to airplanes. Others undoubtedly have had vicarious defensive reflex conditioning by reading or hearing about air disasters with all the gory details. Some have seen movies where the passengers go down in flames with the aircraft or into some primal hell of a jungle or into the cruel sea, and some have seen news footage of actual air disasters on television. All these things are quite enough to set up, if not a conditioned phobia about planes and flying, then at least very cautious thoughts about this way of traveling.

Another way to become uncomfortable about flying in airplanes is to take a trip to an unpleasant place or happening. For instance, you might have to fly to a business conference where you expect to be confronted with our poor—or even imagined poor—performance during the last fiscal quarter. You are likely to spend several hours in the air mulling over all the terrible things and unpleasant confrontations you will find waiting for you when you step off the plane. Or what if you take an air flight immediately after you and your spouse seriously decide to divorce each other. You will be worrying: "Who gets the kids? How am I going to get a job after all these years of being a homemaker? How am I ever going to socialize again?" And so on and so forth. Again, the list of things we can get upset over and worry about is endless. Worrying about them during an air flight is a nifty way to condition unpleasant feelings to flying. Your involuntary autonomic nervous system doesn't care what causes you to be anxious. Your emotional brain isn't too smart or sophisticated. As a matter of fact, it's quite dumb. Dumb enough, as best we can tell, to connect an inordinate amount of anxiety felt during an airplane ride with airplanes themselves: "Let's see now. Four hundred and fifty-five standard units of anxiety and it happened in this funny-looking thing with wings that keep humming and blowing cold air at me out of that nozzle. Okay. . . . Check! I've got that recorded. What's next?"

We know from clinical experience that phobic-like reactions, if not phobias themselves, can be set up by dwelling on all the disastrous and horrible things that could happen to us in certain situations.* In clini-

---

*Phobias can be learned by just becoming anxious in a situation, and the anxiety doesn't have to be related to the situation. For example, phobias can be set up by hypnosis in a very clever way. This was done by J. T. Barendregt and F. S. van Dam at the University of Amsterdam in the late 1960s. They demonstrated that volunteer experimental subjects could be induced to fear innocuous, simple things like tones sounding and lights going on by means of hypnotic suggestion. They then implanted the posthypnotic suggestion that later, out of the hypnotic trance, the lights and tones would still be fearful things. But these two researchers went a step further and came up with an interesting new twist. *Without the subjects being in a hypnotic trance,* they simply kept presenting the light over and over again. But before each time they turned on the

cal slang, this is called mental *incubation* of fears. The more we indulge in morbid thoughts, the more, it seems from case histories, that we can develop aversions to situations with which we have had little actual experience. Perhaps this tendency toward morbid thinking is the reason why two people, who otherwise experience the same upset in a car, a plane, while swimming, during sex, etc., react so differently. One person develops a phobic reaction while the other does not. My best bet is that the person who becomes phobic dwells on the experience and mentally relives it over and over again *without talking it over with someone else who can interject something else besides more fearful thoughts*. Who knows why one person keeps anxiety to himself or herself? But to stop this fear incubation, the anxious person may need no more than the ear of a sympathetic friend, who can, in the most homey, cornball manner,

---

light, they always showed the subject another stimulus, a star-shaped object, for instance. After a number of paired presentations, with the star always announcing the oncoming of the fearful light, the star began to make the subjects nervous and finally fearful all by itself. Phobic learning had taken place. This phobic conditioning was so effective and strong for one subject that she had great difficulty in holding the star in her hands for any significant period of time. Even when she was offered relatively large amounts of money, she refused to do so.

Now a critical point for psychotherapy was investigated by these two workers. In a second hypnotic trance, they removed the posthypnotic suggestion that the original light or tone was fearful. Then the light and tone no longer induced fear—but the star still did. It was a learned phobic stimulus and not one subject to hypnosis. Then the experimenters tried to overcome a learned phobia with hypnosis. Back into the trance the subjects went with a new posthypnotic suggestion that said essentially: "You will not fear the star stimulus." This posthypnotic suggestion worked for about three days—the typical time-span of an effective posthypnotic suggestion—and during the fourth day, the star again produced fear. Hypnosis did not seem to work on a learned phobia—a result which matches clinical experience of failure with hypnotic techniques to effectively rid patients of phobias. It was necessary to retrain the subjects, without these methods, to remove their phobias. The experimenters used behavioral methods with success. The use of hypnosis may have great promise for working with phobic states but not in the manner typically used by therapists.

say something like: "I know exactly how you feel. That was scary. Would you like a cup of tea? Let me tell you about the time I almost fell off the cliff when Albert and I were on our honeymoon."

I have no clinical evidence, but my hunch is that this homegrown therapeutic procedure is quite common and that an OR which eliminates fears is prompted by such kitchen table talk. We happen to be very versatile beings. We know our human cortex is able to reproduce scary scenes—either real or imagined—that trigger off our defensive reflex. With our ability to construct the same scenes, detail by detail—orienting all the while to each one—we can also make our fears and phobias wither and fade away. And I for one, bet this is done daily over mid-morning coffee without professional help of any sort!

We can also convince ourselves that we don't want to have anything to do with some activity, because it has no payoff for us.

Do You Want to Fly?

For example, look at the case of a teenage girl who claimed to be frightened to death of flying on airplanes. When she refused in angry tears to go on a flight with her mother back East, mom decided that her daughter should get some of the latest psychotherapy. She laid down the law: "You will get therapy and ride that airplane!" With this command, daughter agreed to see a therapist. This route was a lot easier than being constantly hassled by mom. Unfortunately, as it turned out, the therapist was working on mom's problem and not daughter's. This teenager didn't want to fly and came into therapy with the unspoken attitude of, "Hell will freeze over before this behavioral jazz will work on me." She was right. It didn't.

She had allowed herself to be marched lockstep into therapy with her arm twisted behind her. This was only to prove to mom that her daughter's aerophobia was beyond help. Curiously, the therapist found out later that the only times daughter had flown anywhere were to accompany mom to family funerals back East. Did daughter have a phobia? Maybe. But until she had her own reasons for wanting to fly, nothing would change. Short of pointing a gun at your head, no one, including your therapist, can make you do something you don't want to do. No one, that is, except yourself!

Assuming you do want to fly and you have very uneasy feelings about it, or even a fully developed phobia, what can you do? First, let's determine whether you have a fear of airplanes or something else. Many people who think they have a fear of flying in an airplane are not aerophobic but claustrophobic. It's not the flying they fear but being inside a relatively enclosed airplane for several hours.

If you think you are aerophobic, walk into a small closet in your own home and see if you can sit in there with the door closed for fifteen minutes or so without feeling anxious or panicky. If you feel fine, then ask your friend, roommate, spouse, etc., to lock the door for another fifteen minutes and not let you out unless you get frightened and pound on the door. This last test is to see if you get anxious about being in situations where you can't use your primitive coping behavior of fleeing. Even though you can always tell your jailer you are frightened and then be set free, it costs you some embarrassment to do this. If you follow this procedure and are willing to suffer this embarrassment, you are claustrophobic about being in restricted places. If being in closed places does upset you, why not work on that problem right in your own home instead of flying all over the place to deal with your supposed aerophobia? The procedure is the same for either fear—evoking an orienting reflex again and again in the scary situation—but sitting in a closet is cheaper than buying an airline ticket. If, on the other hand, the closed, locked-in feeling of the closet doesn't upset you, while flying does, you probably have an aerophobic condition.

Using the Orienting Reflex to Conquer the Fear of Flying

Let me tell you about the first case of aerophobia I treated with orienting reflex methods. Then let me summarize what I did and show how you can set up your own antiphobic OR training program.

A number of years ago, Eb, a young Hollywood composer and musical arranger, came to me complaining about his fear of flying. His phobia was botching up his life. His wife, a famous popular singer, was pressuring him to fly to New York from their home in Los Angeles. She wanted him, so she said, to be there with her in negotiating the details of recording and appearance contracts.

Eb's fear kept him from traveling with his wife for several years. It all began with him being frightened out of his wits while flying over the Florida Everglades during a tropical lightning storm. During this spectacular up-and-down flight, Eb thought the plane would crash into the Everglades and the alligators would get anyone who crawled out of the wreckage. In spite of surviving the rough and scary flight, which lasted only thirty minutes, Eb felt that any plane he rode in thereafter was likely to crash. Eb was neither a drinker, nor a regular drug user. But after several more business flights, he started to get stoned on liquor and Valium whenever he had to travel by air. On his last flight, as he described it, "They had to carry me aboard." Neither the booze nor the depressant helped. (Eb's experience is not unique. Controlled laboratory studies consistently show that drugs do nothing for phobic states, and we shall see why later.) Eb finally gave up and decided not to fly anymore. That's when the problems in his marriage became directly aggravated by his phobia.

His wife was often on the road with various singing engagements for weeks on end and was lonely without Eb—just as he felt miserable in California without her. There was much bitching and moaning on both their parts over this freaky estrangement that fate had thrown them into—each of them blaming the other for being unreasonable. Except for Eb's phobia there was no practical reason for them to be separated for long periods of time. In desperation—perhaps to force Eb to do something about his problem —the wife threatened to have the vocal arrangements for her new record album done in New York by one of the young local boys there. The recording date was only four months away. Hearing that ultimatum, Eb came to me for help.

Eb and I started off using the Wolpean method of systematic desensitization of anxiety. This was the standard method in use then. I felt that the methods derived from the use of the orienting reflex were too new to try out on Eb. We were working with improvised phobic scenes of flying, relaxation and something called the SUDs level. The SUDs is another of those very complex terms we professionals use to describe something simple. SUDs means Subjective Units of Discomfort—or how anxious you get in any situation. For example, if you wanted to construct a "fear thermometer," you would call all the numbers between zero and 100 degrees of anxiety, 100 representing pure panic.

Remember when you were at the beach last summer and that big wave washed over you. You were right below the surface and at first you thought, "It can't be over seven- or eight-feet deep here. With a couple of strokes, I'll hit the surface." But those strokes toward the surface didn't do it. You were still under. You thought, "A couple more will make it." But they didn't either. That was when you found yourself in a 100-situation, experiencing real fear.

Now for the other end of the scale. It's just before you fall asleep at night. You are lying on your pillow and relaxing completely just before dozing off. Or you are sitting on the sand at the beach mesmerized by watching the beautiful surf pound the shoreline. Completely relaxed, that's a zero-situation.

You can measure your "emotional fever" in any situation by describing it with some number between zero and 100. With some practice, this can become a quick way to assess the anxiety provoked by different parts of a situation to see which is most and which is least frightening.

Eb and I worked for several weeks with me teaching him deep muscle relaxation so we could use it for counterconditioning his fears. At the same time, Eb's homework was to make up a set of note cards describing the many different situations associated with flying: "I'm going to buy a ticket over the phone or at the airline counter at the airport. I'm sitting in the flight lounge waiting for the plane. I'm sitting in the plane waiting for it to take off. The plane is going down the runway. We're taking off, etc." Eb then rated all these scenes according to the SUD level they provoked in him when he thought about them.

Starting with the lowest SUD-level card, we began ascending the scale to the most fearful situation for Eb: landing in a plane. This was a laborious process. Whenever Eb began to feel anxious over one of the flying scenes I asked him to recall, he would signal me by lifting his index finger. When this happened, I would tell him to relax; we would wait a few minutes and go back to the last card where he felt no anxiety.

A slow process. In the first three weeks, we covered four low-anxiety scenes.

On the fourth week, Eb came in and said his wife's date had been rescheduled and his timetable for flying to New York was revised. Instead of having three months left for systematic desensitization of his aerophobia, we were now left with ten days before the flight. That announcement threw the use of the Wolpean method right out the window. There was no practical way of getting through the hierarchy of scenes in ten days. After talking it over, Eb said that he was going anyway, even if he had to be stone drunk and carried aboard the plane unconscious. So we had two choices—to continue with the slow progress of the standard method to see whether it would make flying somewhat easier for him, which wasn't likely, or to stop for now and start the whole laborious process over again from scratch when Eb got back from New York. Both of these options looked pretty grim, and I told Eb so. He asked if there were any way to speed up what we were doing. He accepted neither option as limits on what we could do. He was willing to try almost anything to get rid of his phobia in a hurry. I mentioned that I was working on different ways to eliminate phobias in the laboratory at UCLA, but I made it clear that theory and laboratory research were quite different from actual practice out in the field. He then gave me carte blanche: "Please pull together what you've learned in the laboratory, and we'll see if it will work for me in ten days." I was hesitant at first. To speed up his relearning we would have to go where the airplanes were—out into the real world beyond the clinic and its safe, controlled limits. The real world had any number of dirty little details that could make things go wrong. In spite of my hesitation, Eb said he still wanted to try.

I set up an elaborate program for him—most of which, in retrospect, was unnecessary. For each of the next eight days Eb was to have either dinner or lunch in the revolving restaurant at Los Angeles International Airport. Each evening, he was to drive out to the airport and park by the side of the field for thirty minutes to watch the jets take off and land. After that, he was to go to one of the departure lounges in the airport and have a cocktail or a glass of wine. During these dinners, lunches and plane-watching expeditions, Eb was to have a sexually attractive partner who could make interesting conversation with him. If his wife were unavailable, he was to invite a secretary he knew. Every day he was to call each of the airlines that had service to San Diego out of LAX. He was to ask for the various times of departure for the morning of the ninth day, plus return times for the same morning. On the seventh day, he was to make a reservation with each airline to San Diego for the ninth day with a return to LAX the same morning with a minimum of thirty minutes between planes. On the eighth day, he was to call the airlines and cancel all reservations except the flight down with one airline and the flight back up with another. He was to choose which airlines to fly by asking friends about the different carriers and their reputations.

On the morning of the ninth day, we met outside the entrance to Western Airlines at LAX. Eb was nervous but not frightened. We went inside to pick up our tickets. I told Eb to pay for one set in cash and charge the other on American Express. After this was done, I asked him how he was going to explain this funny-looking arrangement on his next audit to the IRS. He was going to deduct his expenses for psychotherapy as permitted by law, but, you have to admit, that one set of tickets paid for by cash and the other with a charge card looked suspiciously as if it were two different people paying for these tickets. We had some time to spare before boarding, so we argued about this, with me playing the incredulous tax auditor who could see no earthly reason why one receipt was for cash and the other on a charge slip from American Express.

"Well . . . it's because my therapist told me to do it that way!"

"A likely story. Why in the world would he tell you to do that?" Eb then had to explain to me—the tax auditor—that this way of paying for tickets was only to keep him orienting to something while waiting for the flight.

We boarded the plane and I sat near the window at Eb's request. The seat near the aisle is always the more desirable one. You have a lot more room to move and stretch, and you don't feel as cramped. I always try to sit near the aisle. Eb smiled at me. He thought he had foxed me. Good for him. But I had wanted him to sit near the aisle anyway. He could orient to things and people inside the airplane much easier from the aisle seat. When I wanted him to orient to things outside the plane, he could lean over to see out the window.

During the wait for takeoff, Eb began to get nervous, so I had him play the Helen of Troy game. It's a silly game that engineering students at Cal Tech play. Helen was the legendary queen of ancient Greece who was abducted by Paris, the Prince of Troy. Helen was so beautiful that hers was the face that launched a thousand ships to the rescue. Unfortunately, Eb and I sitting in a Western 727 waiting for takeoff didn't have the fascinating prospect of conquering an ancient empire at the end of our trip to orient to, but we did have Helen's daughters. Scads of them.

The instructed orienting game was for Eb to look at each female passenger coming aboard the jet, mentally undress her, assign her a Helen of Troy rating of sexual attractiveness somewhere between zero and 1000 and then tell me about it: "This one's not bad: a 400-millihelen rating. The next one reminds me of my grade-school teacher Miss Grump. Thirteen millihelens for her. Wow! That stewardess is a real doll. She's 900 millihelens at least!" And so on. A simple mind game that maintains interest—your orienting reflex—in fearful situations for either sex.

By the time we had backed out of the jet's parking space and were trundling past the terminal toward the takeoff strip, Eb was quite relaxed. I didn't try to evoke his orienting reflex except by chatting about politics and the weather. When we came to the takeoff point, we sat there for a few minutes until one of the crew announced in an almost unintelligible Georgian drawl: "Wuhgone bactu thu termnul fucs. Wuhcotta lil trubbl wifar quipment." With that mishmash message, Eb's face fell. Silently,

I cursed myself for getting him into this situation. I cursed Western Airlines for its unscheduled maintenance problems. I especially cursed that turkey up front who'd never learned to speak English.

Well, I said to myself, let's see how effective the orienting reflex is. I turned to Eb and asked him what the crew member had said. Eb looked at me blankly and said he couldn't understand him either. I told Eb to push the stewardess call button and ask her what the trouble was. I cautioned him that the stewardess might just wave him off with a cheery, "I don't know" in passing, so he was to tell her that he got nervous in planes—especially when he didn't know what was happening. The stewardess who answered Eb's call was the one with the 900-millihelen rating. As I predicted, she tried to wave Eb off with her cheery, "I don't know." But when Eb told her he was nervous about flying, she did a really nice thing for him. All the while we were taxiing back to the terminal, she talked to him. More importantly, she sat in that sexy way that only stews can, with part of her derriére on Eb's armrest pushing into his side, one leg crossed over the other showing lots of skin, one arm laid casually over the top of Eb's headrest and the other using his shoulder for support.

Now, the ostensible reason for this physical closeness by this true daughter of Helen was to tell Eb about federal safety regulations and the philosophy of aircrew captains who never took off with even the smallest deviation in the equipment of their planes. She told Eb that we were probably going back to check out some minor thing that wouldn't make any difference in the operation of the plane anyway, but why take chances? And if it took too long to correct, we would transfer to another plane right out of the maintenance hangar. It sounded good to me. But Eb looked like he didn't hear a word of it. He was too busy orienting to her. I don't think I would have heard a word either if she had been sitting next to me like that. God bless all Western Airline stews!

When the plane reached its parking slot at the terminal, Helen's daughter left us. I wanted to keep Eb orienting, so I asked him what the problem with the plane was. He told me matter of factly it was something minor, and they were going to fix it. Feeling quite pleased that fate had given us a super-significant biological stimulus in the form of the stewardess, my pleasure was gradually worn away in the next fifteen minutes. From directly beneath our seats came a loud clank, clank, clank of metal hammering on metal. Every few minutes, clank, clank, clank . . . clank, clank, clank. . . . After a few of these series of noises, Eb looked edgy. Keep him orienting, I thought. "How is your SUD level?" I asked him. "Ninety-five," Eb said. "I'm close to getting off and going home." Let's try something physical and then use sex again to get the OR active and dominant, I thought.

"Okay Eb," I told him, "if you want to leave, we will. But first let's try something else. Stretch out in your seat, close your eyes and listen to my voice. I want you to take three deep breaths.* Breathe in when I tell you and hold it. When I say "exhale," exhaust your breath until you think your lungs will collapse. After three deep breaths, breathe normally for thirty seconds and then ask me what we do next." Eb did this with fear in his eyes. "What now?" he asked as instructed. I told him: "First lean over casually and look up and down the aisle to find the stewardess who talked to you before." (She was standing in the aisle near the pilot's cockpit, and Eb saw her at once.) "Now just feast your eyes on that gorgeous female form. Run a fantasy on what you would like to do in bed with her. . . . Now walk up to her, casually, and ask her if she knows what the problem is yet. Chat with her for a minute. Ask her

---

*See Chapter 10, page 210.

some questions." Eb did this and came back to tell me that the emergency oxygen system was off-kilter. Buckling up again, he asked me about the hammering: "Is it serious?" "No," I told him, parroting back what the stewardess had told us both. "If it were serious, they wouldn't clank it. They would unload us and dismantle it in the shop." And here I confidently added some new information, which I was only guessing at, to make Eb orient. "It's probably a spare on oxygen tank. The Feds are so full of red tape they would want us to be able to fly on emergency oxygen all the way to China even if we are only going to San Diego."

"But how come they are hammering on it?" Eb followed up.

"Normal operating procedure," I glibly replied. "What do you do when something minor doesn't work properly? You kick and whack it a few times to see if you can make whatever's stuck come unstuck."

It was clear that doing something physical while orienting to his goal—getting up and walking over to the gorgeous stew and talking to her and then asking me some meaningful questions—got Eb's orienting reflex dominant in the situation again. He sunk back into his seat and tried out the role of the bored air commuter: "I wish they would get this goddamned thing rolling again. I've got an appointment at 1:30."

With that expression of willingness to fly to San Diego, no matter what, fate smiled on us again. The clanking beneath us stopped and a minute or two later, with the door hatches closed and locked, we started our trip to the takeoff point once more. As we went along this time, I took no chances on Eb's anxiety being aroused by something I could not foresee. I gave him a small scratch pad and a pencil and kept him orienting to things outside the window as we passed them.

You see that bunch of luggage carts?
How many carts are in the whole train parked there?

The cart with the big green suitcase. How many is it from the end of the train?

How many pieces of luggage does it have on it?

You can't see the other side—well . . . how many pieces does it have stacked on this side of it?

Now, how many stacks like that could fit on the cart? Two? Three? Four? Okay . . . multiply the number of pieces of luggage in the stack you can see by the number of stacks that will fit on the cart. What number do you get?

As we turned away from the terminal, the only thing that came into view was the cyclone fence marking the end of the airport. I had Eb orient to the fence.

How wide is the airfield?

A mile? How do you know that?

Let's see if you can get a more accurate guesstimate.

How far apart are the cyclone fence poles? Hard to say. . . . Okay, let's try it a different way.

Do you watch football games?

How far would you have to go in between fence poles to make a first down?

About halfway? That looks about right to me. Okay. With a first down being ten yards, how many yards between fence poles? Okay. Now how many fence poles across the entire end of the airfield? You can't count them all? Fine. Pick out a section you can count that's about one quarter of the entire distance. How many poles in that stretch? Count them.

Now multiply the number of poles by four on your scratch pad.

Now multiply that total number of fence poles by twenty yards.

Now multiply that number of yards by three feet.

Now what do you figure the width of the airfield is in feet?

What percentage is that of a mile? Divide the number of feet you came up with by 5,280, the number of feet in a mile. What do you get?

What I was doing with all these instructions and questions, of course, was to make Eb orient—make him survey his phobic environment for specific things. When he oriented to these things, he was to obtain information about them and use this information to perform a mental and/or physical task. While running away from a feared object is a physical task, so is writing something down on a scratch pad. I could have told Eb to run back and forth along the aisle of the jet. But then the crew and the rest of the passengers would have thought he was crazy. He could have said he was a nut about jogging and physical fitness and this was his regular time for exercise, but Eb surely would have felt more anxiety over what his fellow passengers thought of his bizarre behavior than he would have about flying. Also the crew was likely to tie him to his seat or throw him off the plane. Making him write on a scratch pad or do something in the area of his seat seemed much more practical.

By this time, we were standing on the edge of the takeoff runway. I still wanted to keep Eb orienting, but we would be moving too fast on takeoff for him to see enough along the side of the runway. Also, I didn't know much about the buildings and things there to be able to give him a guided tour on all the fascinating history of the airport. Instead, I decided to have him orient to what the plane was doing itself. I told Eb we were going to see how long it took for the aircraft to lift off the runway. "Sit back in your seat and count chimpanzees," I said. Eb had never heard of that expression. I explained, "Count off one chimpanzee, two chimpanzee, three chimpanzee . . . and so on, starting when the plane begins to move down the field and stopping when we leave the ground." It takes about one second of time to say *one chimpanzee* in a normal rate of speech. The number of chimpanzees Eb would count would be the number of seconds it took for our jet to get off the ground. Since a Boeing 727 requires about 220 mph ground speed to become airborne (average speed 110 mph; half of zero mph and 220 mph), Eb could figure out on a scratch pad while we were climbing to cruising altitude how many feet of runway it took our jet to get up enough speed to lift off the ground.

In the air and cruising along to San Diego, Eb felt no anxiety at all. His SUD level was zero and he said he rather enjoyed looking out the window at the landscape scenes. San Diego is a short flight from LAX. So we were in the air for only 20 minutes.

As we approached the San Diego International Airport, I decided to resume my role of orienting reflex prompter. There is a curious paradox about San Diego airport. It has one of the worst approach patterns to its landing strips of any airport in the United States. Consequently, no matter how much the pilots bitch about it, they fly very carefully into San Diego. There is no carelessness in their landing pattern approach. As a result, the airport has one of the best safety records in the history of aviation. Another payoff for the passenger is the smoothness of landing. In the dozens of times I have flown into and out of San Diego, I have never experienced a bumpy landing or a scary takeoff. Each time the pilot's timing, touchdown and braking were slick and professional. I didn't tell Eb this bit of information though. That would have been like telling him, "There is nothing to worry about you silly fool! Millions of people fly in and out of here and don't sweat it. Your fears are foolish." That sort of exhortation just doesn't work. The primitive emotional brain does not listen to reason and inductive logic. Since landing was the greatest of his fears, I wanted his orienting reflex dominant during this most anxiety-provoking phase. I didn't want there to be any chance that he would freeze in his seat and only experience his anxiety washing over him.

I made him stretch out in his seat, get comfortable, close his eyes, pay attention to what I said and form a mental picture of what I described: "We're in the jet coming down for a landing at the San Diego airport. Instead of the runway beneath us, we're settling down on a huge, cushiony mattress. The mattress is in the shape of the runway. It's over a mile long and flat. It has sewn edges like any mattress. It has a design woven into the material all along its top surface. It has a diamond pattern woven in gold. Within the diamond there is a starburst woven in silver. Picture the mattress stretching underneath us, with us coming closer . . . closer . . . closer. . . . We're gliding right above it now. The wheels are just about touching. We're down. We're coasting on the runway mattress."

Eb finally interrupted my OR prompts by sitting up and looking out the window. "We're already down?" he asked. "I didn't feel a thing. Not even a noise." He broke into a big smile. Eb wasn't a phobic patient any longer.

We walked off the plane and headed for the coffee shop. None of the airlines serve food on the Los Angeles–San Diego run. Even though Eb was quite chipper and excited about beating his fear, airports are associated with flying and I didn't want to pass up this chance for more antiphobic retraining. Orienting to food and being worried while waiting in an airport for your next flight are incompatible. So when we found the coffee shop, I told Eb to indulge himself. After eating and chatting with me, Eb was completely at ease in the airport even though he had another flight coming up within fifteen minutes.

Each of the flights, both to and from San Diego, had its separate purpose. The flight down was to condition Eb to orienting during flying instead of anxiety. The main purpose of the flight back was to consolidate Eb's new emotional state and to finish off all those little phobic cues associated with flying and airports that Eb had accumulated over the years. I wanted Eb to go through the same routine he had experienced in flying down to San Diego, but without my having to prompt him to orient and without any anxiety. I wanted him to have the ability to walk up to the check-in counter, go to the flight lounge, wait for the plane, get aboard, etc., without anticipating nervousness. I wanted to show him that now he would fly without negative involuntary emotional responses to flying and all the things associated with it.

Eb felt just dandy flying back to Los Angeles and even made some humorous comments during the landing.

The next morning Eb flew to New York with his wife. He had no anxiety whatsoever on that trip or on the one back to Los Angeles. Since his quick *in vivo* OR antiphobia retraining flight, Eb has had no fear of flying. He has flown around the world several times for fun and profit.

seven

Retraining yourself not to fear flying with fancy foods, tight bras and games

How can *you*—preferably with the help of a friend —conquer your fear of flying? Let's break down what I did with Eb into simple ways of triggering off your orienting reflex. Then without getting too textbookish, let's set up some guidelines for you to use in your own OR retraining program.

Sneaking Up on Your Aerophobia

Work on the airport first—it's slower but surer. Many people with irrational fears say that things connected with the phobic situation upset them as well as the situation itself.

Your primitive nervous system *generalizes* its learning. When we learn that one particular thing is to be feared, part of what we learn automatically transfers to other things similar to it. For example, let's suppose you became frightened out of your wits last summer. As you were walking along in the twilight at the edge of the woods, minding your own business, this big duck leaped up squawking, honking and flapping when you tripped over it. It scared the hell out of you. If any emotional learning has taken place for you, as best we can tell from laboratory studies and clinical case histories, it is quite likely that it won't be long before a similar, but less uncomforta-

ble, feeling will automatically be triggered off by
other ducks or birds who resemble ducks. If you were
scared in a Boeing 747 and develop a phobia from
that experience, a Douglas 1011 will very likely trigger off anxiety even though you have never flown
in one before.

There is also another way that involuntary generalization of phobic anxiety can take place: by
automatic association of things having to do with
ducks themselves. If ducks were always associated
with the old duck pond back home, you would be
likely to feel anxiety whenever you saw the old duck
pond, even if all the ducks had gone south for the
winter. In the same way that ducks are associated with
ponds, flying is associated with airports, airplanes,
air terminals, even hang gliders. Patients treated for
a fear of flying have reported that they feel quite
uncomfortable just visiting a jetliner at rest on the
ground. As far as we can tell, fear of flying will
become associated with all these things automatically but to a lesser degree.

It may seem unfair that if you learn something
scary, your involuntary nervous system will generalize this fear to all sorts of related things. But remember, your primitive emotional brain is only doing this
to help you recognize supposed danger long before
you get into it. So before you curse Mother Nature,
remember that generalization works both ways. Your
nervous system will generalize its learning of a phobic
response; it will also generalize its "unlearning." In
a practical sense, this means that we can not only retrain ourselves to deal calmly with airports, airplanes,
etc., without first having to fly, but also that in doing so we automatically reduce the amount of anxiety
produced in us later by the act of flying itself.

Depending upon your own degree of anxiety about
flying, you may want to do what Eb did—work first
on reducing your anxiety level about things connected with flying—or go straight on board the plane
and work on your anxiety there. Either way can be

successful. If, however, you have a straight-out panic about flying in an airplane, I don't know of any way to elicit an instantaneous orienting reflex great enough to overcome panic short of slapping you hard on the face, thus forcing you to orient to the pain I caused. That seems to work both for fainting and hysterical panics. The pain lowers the level of the defensive reflex and calms you down. But if you are likely to panic during flying, it's also likely that being in a plane on the ground will sufficiently upset you to make you leave before it takes off. You won't be in the situation long enough to get any OR retraining started. If this is the case for you, work on the airport and things associated with flying first. Then, as Eb did, set up an inflight program for yourself with the help of a friend—both of you taking that first flight together.

When you decide to begin the flying phase of your retraining program, either with or without airport pretraining, plan on taking a short flying trip to another town nearby. It's cheaper. Why pay big money to fly to New York or Los Angeles to lose your phobia when $14 will work just as well? Also, if you misjudge your level of nervousness about flying during that first trip, remember, it's in the nature of flying that once you leave the ground there's not too much you can do about getting off early.

OR Triggers: A Quick Review

How to trigger off your orienting reflex: a quick review. There are basically five different ways to make yourself orient in any anxiety-provoking situation:

1. *Novelty.* Any new stimulus will cause you to orient. "New" in this sense means anything that changes in the situation.

2. *Biological significance.* If you are hungry, food will make you orient. So don't eat anything before you go on board, preferably for several hours, to the point of being ravenous. Also, if you haven't just leapt out of the sack with either Burt Reynolds or Britt Eckland as you dashed off to make your flight, anything sexual will be a reliable OR stimulus for reducing your anxiety.

3. *Innate stimuli* will cause you to orient. You will orient to changes in your sense of temperature, smell, light, taste, sound and touch. Touch seems to be especially significant. Someone touching you or rubbing your arm, neck or shoulders will do wonders for your state of mind.

4. *Learned interest stimuli* (acquired signal value) will reliably cause you to orient over long periods of time. (Turn to the OR Checklist on pages 301–303 and check off a half-dozen items that have held your interest in the past. Rank them from one to six with #1 being your all-time favorite topic and #6 your sixth favorite topic.)

5. *Instructed stimuli,* given during your flight by someone you trust, is one of the best ways of triggering off your orienting reflex. You will follow commands that require your thinking out something, making choices—even simple ones—and then acting them out physically with some deliberate muscular movement.

Starting on page 154, I will be giving you printed instructions to follow when you are in the phobic situation. These instructions are general and not specific to any one anxiety state or phobia. The things that the instructions prompt you to do can be used in any learned anxiety situation. They are useful in eliminating a fear of flying as well as a fear of elevators, animals, driving, heights, etc. The instructions themselves will prompt you to orient to things on the basis of novelty, biological needs, innate and learned interests, as well as *get you to orient for the sole reason that you are told to pay attention.* Now for this last method to work the instructions I give you must have *signal value*. For the instructions to have signal value, *I must have signal value for you.* How does this come about? How do you give me signal value so that what I tell you via the printed word will trigger off your orienting reflex in a phobic situation? Well, that's really up to you. I can list my qualifications as an authority, teacher, clinician, scientist and all-around hell of a nice guy, but those things don't really mean much. There are many professionals around with more impressive credentials who still don't know their ear from their elbow when it comes to making things work. What you have to do is look at what I'm saying and decide if it makes sense to you.

Unfortunately, after-the-fact validation won't help much. If you run through the retraining program and it lowers your anxiety, what I say will then have had great signal value. You will have oriented quite a bit to what I told you to do. But by then, you won't need it. So giving what I write down significance and then using that significance to lower your anxiety depends entirely upon your judgment that this retraining program makes sense. If it does, even though some of the things I tell you to do are a bit different, odd or perhaps novel to your way of thinking about yourself, the program will work for you. If it doesn't make sense and you don't see how it can help, it won't.

OR Aids to Take on the Plane with You

Now before we go into specifics on what to do on board, let's look at some things that will be helpful to take with you on your flight. First, let's assume that you are sitting at home reading this and can collect these things at your leisure. If you are sitting at the airport, waiting for a plane while reading this, we will use this list in a moment as the first part of your retraining program—right there at the airport.

1. *Food:* Pack some tempting goodies in your travel bag or briefcase. Take them along for instant snacking during the flight. Pick goodies that make you drool, delicacies you rarely indulge in and usually serve only to guests. Also take along one of those illustrated cookbooks with full-color pictures of beautifully prepared food.

2. *Sexual Materials:* Select a number of really lurid, explicitly hard-core pornographic sex novels. Certainly get more than one. When you select them, only quickly skim through them at the bookstore. Save the reading for your flight. See if you can get some good-quality erotic photography to take with you. *Playboy, Playgirl, Hustler* and about twenty-five others, are all good sources. If explicitness is not your thing, be sure to try a gothic romance novel to see it if it arouses your sexual feelings. Many of them are just lavender pornography with lace trimmings. If you have some sexual mores (or inhibitions) that are offended by pornography, think of it as a temporary therapeutic aid. "But," you might say, "that material is unnatural!" To which I would reply: "So is a cast on a broken arm. You don't wear a cast if your arm is okay. But it would seem natural enough if your arm were broken." In this case, take it as a prescriptive measure from Old Doc Smith that the use of it may help you. After you rid yourself of your phobia, you don't have to take porno on airplanes with you anymore.

3. *Innate interests:* If you are serious about losing your phobia, it may be worth your while to provide yourself with some innate stimulation during your trip. A simple way to do this is to dress *uncomfortably*. Wear an old, tight pair of pants that cut into you when you have to wear them for some time. Better still, wear one of your old bras that you know is tight and uncomfortable: the old-fashioned Merry Widow type is best. That's the kind that goes from waist to armpit with stays and wires. It's especially good if you can use one that draws up so tight your stomach feels as if it's just below your tongue. If you are male, see if you can borrow a girdle and wear it aboard. Embarrassing? Perhaps. But tell your

wife that you are thinking of becoming a transvestite and want to see what it feels like. These devices will pinch and poke every time you move, shift or breathe. And you will orient to all these nifty bodily stimuli automatically, without having to work at it. Also, if your trip is a long one, you can go into the john and take your torture device off after your fear has been extinguished.

Another source of innate bodily stimulation is touch. So take along a friend who can touch your arm, massage your shoulders or rub your back. If you don't have a friend, make one.

4. *Learned interests and hobbies:* From the OR Checklist on pages 301–303, pick a half-dozen topics that are interesting to you. Then go out to a bookstore or your public library and select at least three good books on the different topics that hold your interest. Also, go to a local drugstore with a well-stocked magazine rack. Pick out at least four pictorial magazines on different topics that have always intrigued you: horses, auto racing, sports, needlepoint, modeling, sailing, crossword puzzles, etc. But don't read any of the material you select before you board your flight. Just skim through it to make sure it is what you want.

Review your hobbies. Do you have one that can be taken aboard with you? This would be a hobby that you do with your hands as well as with your head.

If you are a nut about model railroads or automobiles, buy yourself a brand-new kit of a locomotive or a 1929 Buggati. You won't be able to construct anything in your seat, but you certainly can fiddle with the kit and that is enough to make you orient.

If art is your thing, bring a sketch pad and charcoal or drawing ink with you. You will be able to sketch the people on board, the interior of the cabin and the landscape below you at 30,000 feet in the air. If you work in, say, ceramics or sculpture, you can sketch out your next project on board. If you are into woodwork or carpentry, you can lay out your next design.

Airport Pretraining Program: Making Yourself Less Anxious on the Ground

If you are already at your air terminal waiting for your plane while reading this—*and you are nervous about flying*—let's try some things that may help reduce your anxiety even before you board the plane. The following OR instructions may seem somewhat simple-minded at times, but be assured that they are deliberately designed to be uncomplicated as well as to require you to think and make some physical response when learned anxiety interferes with your higher mental functioning. It is very important for you to follow the instructions as faithfully as you can. The instructions are to be acted upon, not just read—even to the point of writing down simple yes or no answers instead of responding to the question only in your head. Thinking is fine, but thinking and physical action together are better.

If you are sitting down at home and reading this, you may want to save it and use the pretraining section during a special trip to the airport as part of your program before you actually take a flight from there. Pick up your tickets a few days early and use that as an excuse to go to the airport. Also, have lunch or dinner there during the same excursion.

If you are at the airport now and reading this just prior to your flight, hopefully you will have some time to while away, running through the pretraining program before you board your plane.

Airport retraining program

Orienting
Reflex
Instructions
ORI 1 First of all, look in your pocket, briefcase or purse

and see if you have a pen or a pencil. If you don't, borrow one for a few minutes.

ORI 2 If you are waiting for your plane, make sure you have a few minutes to spare so you don't get involved in this program and miss your flight. Do you have some time before your flight? Write your answer in this blank.

ANSWER_____. If yes, continue on to the next instruction. If no, skip to the Inflight Retraining Program.

ORI 3 Do you have a friend with you on this relearning exercise? Not your spouse, but someone with no ax to grind; someone you trust who will walk through all these instructions with you without your having to cajole, plead or argue.

ANSWER_____. If yes, have your friend give you all the instructions from this program (including any your friend thinks up on the spot that are meaningful and are guaranteed to make you orient: Look! there's Robert Redford or Racquel Welsh!). If no, do it yourself, with me as your friendly instructor, via the pages of this book.

ORI 4 Let's take a look at your SUDs level. SUDs is an acronym for Subjective Units of Discomfort. It's a simple way of telling yourself and someone else how nervous or anxious you are at a given time. SUDs is like an anxiety thermometer with degrees of nervousness running from zero to 100. Zero on the SUDs scale means completely relaxed—about to fall asleep. One hundred means you are about to panic and run like the dickens to get out of wherever you are. Now take your emotional pulse, so to speak. As you are sitting there reading this book, pick a number between zero and 100 that roughly describes how nervous you are right now. Write it in the blank. SUDs_____.

ORI 5 What time is it now? If you don't have a watch, ask someone or look at a wall clock. TIME_____.

ORI 6 Lean back in your chair—if you are not sitting, find a seat and sit—and relax. Stretch out your legs and cross your ankles. Fold your arms across your chest. Now try to figure out how to keep reading this in that position.

ORI 7 I want you to close your eyes, take three deep breaths, then breathe normally for about thirty seconds and open your eyes again.

ORI 8 I want you to read each sentence below, then close your eyes and picture what it tells you. When you have done that, open your eyes and read the next sentence.

ORI 9 Picture yourself walking through a green meadow early on a spring morning.

ORI 10 How large is the meadow? As big as the men's room at the airport? Bigger than the lounge you're sitting in? As big as the whole air terminal?
ANSWER_____.

ORI 11 Look at the position of the sun shining on the meadow.

ORI 12 How high is the sun in the sky? (Six o'clock is on the horizon; twelve o'clock is directly overhead.)
ANSWER_____.

ORI 13 Can you see the sun (or the moon) from where you are sitting in the lounge?
ANSWER_____.

ORI 14 Look at all the budding trees, sprouting green, fresh, new leaves.

ORI 15 What kind of trees do you see? (Pine, oak, fir, chestnut, maple, birch, coconut, date palm, banana? Where does it say you can't have meadows in the tropics?)
ANSWER_____.

ORI 16 How tall is the tallest tree? Is it as high as the ceiling of the main concourse of the air terminal? Higher than the terminal building?
ANSWER_____.

ORI 17 Can you see any trees near the airport from where you are sitting?
ANSWER_____.

ORI 18 Look at the cool, green grass growing in the meadow.

ORI 19 Are you walking through it in your bare feet?
ANSWER_____.

ORI 20 Picture yourself wandering through the edges of the meadow. Look at the clothes you have on.

ORI 21 Are you standing on level ground when you start to walk, or on a slope leading to the meadow, or are you in among the trees surrounding the meadow?
ANSWER_____.

ORI 22 Walk through the meadow and look around you.

ORI 23 What shape is the meadow? Is it round, squarish, oval, kidney- or L-shaped?
ANSWER_____.

ORI 24 Does it resemble the layout of the air terminal in any way?
ANSWER_____.

ORI 25 In the far distance are high mountains on one side of the meadow. Picture them with snow on their peaks.

ORI 26 Are there any mountains you can see from the air terminal?
ANSWER_____.

ORI 27 How far are the nearest mountains from your air terminal? A few miles? Twenty? Fifty? Several hundred?
ANSWER_____.

ORI 28 How long would it take you to get to them—by car, bus, rail, or airplane—if you wanted to do some hiking there?
ANSWER_____.

ORI 29 From where you are standing in the meadow, you can just see a waterfall cascading off one of the mountain sides twisting and turning as it follows the contours of the land. You follow the water's course as it feeds a stream that enters the meadow on the far side.

ORI 30 How far is the stream from where you are standing? The length of a jetliner? Two? Three? The length of the airport's runway?
ANSWER_____.

ORI 31 Walk toward the stream. Feel the ground under your feet as you walk.

ORI 32 How does the ground in your meadow feel? Rough, hard, spongy, rocky, slippery, soft, muddy?
ANSWER_____.

ORI 33 You have walked all that distance to the stream. You stand there looking at it from the edge.

ORI 34 How warm are you from your walk? Warmer than you are right now sitting in the airport lounge?
ANSWER_____.

ORI 35 Look at the sparkling water as it splashes over the rocks in the stream bed.

ORI 36 Does it look inviting enough to bathe in?
ANSWER_____.

ORI 37 Is it deep enough to splash around in?
ANSWER_____.

ORI 38 Could you swim in it?
ANSWER_____.

ORI 39 Is the water clear enough to see the bottom of the stream?
ANSWER_____.

ORI 40 Look at the stream again and imagine its bed in your mind's eye.

ORI 41 What does the bed look like? Rocks, sand, moss, pebbles?
ANSWER_____.

ORI 42 Dip your hand into the water. Feel its swirling currents flow around your fingers.

ORI 43 Is it cold enough to be refreshing when you drink it?
ANSWER_____.

ORI 44 Could you take a skinny dip in it?
ANSWER_____.

ORI 45 Are you alone in the meadow?
ANSWER_____.

ORI 46 How many people are in the airport lounge with you? A few? Twenty? Thirty? Several hundred?
ANSWER_____.

ORI 47 Bend down and taste the water in the stream.

ORI 48 Is it colder or warmer than the water in the public drinking fountains at the airport?
ANSWER_____.

ORI 49 Now bring yourself back into the airport and take a SUDs-level reading on how you feel right now.

ORI 50 Write this SUDs in the space. SUDs_____.

ORI 51 What time is it? TIME_____.

ORI 52 Close your eyes and return to the meadow once more. You notice, there's still a trace of *eau de* cow flop in the air around you. You obviously didn't get it all off your shoe when you stumbled back up the hill to your starting point. A bit out of breath you sit down to regain your composure and to reassure yourself that a cow was responsible and there is no 2,000-pound bull pawing the ground, snorting in your direction. Completely relieved and assured by your reconnaisance, you fail to notice the giant prehistoric duck, whose private stream you muddied, as it sneaks up behind you and carries you off. Now open your eyes. Aren't you glad you are sitting in a civilized, safe airport lounge, waiting for an airplane, instead of being all alone in that freaky meadow with god knows what looking out at you from the trees.

ORI 53 Now let's orient to where you are at the airport. Look around you. Locate yourself in the air terminal. Can you see the nearest magazine and notions shop?
ANSWER_____. If yes, go on to the next instruction. If no, skip to ORI 56.

ORI 54 How long do you estimate it will take you to walk there? Write it down. TIME_____.

ORI 55 Can you walk there, spend a few minutes shopping and walk back without missing your flight?
ANSWER_____. If yes, skip to ORI 66. If no, skip to Inflight Retraining Program.

ORI 56 Can you see, or do you know where there is, a manned booth for the airline you are traveling with?
ANSWER_____. If yes, skip to ORI 58. If no, go on to the next instruction.

ORI 57 Return the pen or pencil if you borrowed one. Go to any manned airline booth and ask where your airline booth is.

ORI 58 Locate your airline booth on this clock chart: From where you are standing right at this moment, twelve o'clock is directly in front of you;

six o'clock is to your rear; three o'clock is to your right; nine o'clock is to your left.

12
9   3
6

Borrow another pencil for a minute if you don't have one. Mark an arrow from the center of the clock in the direction you will have to start walking to get there.

ORI 59 Walk to your airline booth.

ORI 60 Ask your attendant what time your flight is due to leave. Write the time down here.
TIME_____.

ORI 61 If you don't know where the nearest notions shop is, ask the attendant how to get there. On this clock chart, with twelve o'clock as the front of the airline booth, mark in which direction the notions shop is in relation to the booth.

12
9   3
6

ORI 62 What's your SUDs level now? SUDs_____.

ORI 63 What time is it? TIME_____.

ORI 64 Ask the airline attendant how long it will take to walk to the notions shop and back.
ANSWER_____.

ORI 65 Will you have enough time before your flight leaves to walk there, spend ten or fifteen minutes and walk back? ANSWER_____.
If yes, go on to the next instruction. If no, skip to Inflight Retraining Program.

ORI 66 Before you walk to the notions shop read this: Even if you don't have a wrist watch, you can time yourself in almost any activity, with some practice, to within a few seconds' accuracy. To do this, on the first step of your walk, start counting chimpanzees. One chimpanzee, two chimpanzee, three chimpanzee . . . and so forth until you reach your destination. Count chimpanzees to yourself as quickly as you can without slurring the words. It takes about one second per chimpanzee when you count at this pace. You will be a bit fast under ten and a bit slow over ten, but you can still be fairly accurate if you concentrate on saying the words clearly to yourself as rapidly and deliberately as possible. The number of chimps you count will be the number of seconds it took you to walk to the notions shop. Keep counting no matter what, even if you make any detours, such as to the john.

ORI 67 If you borrowed a pen or pencil, return it.

ORI 68 Walk to the notions shop counting chimps as you go.

ORI 69 When you reach the shop, remember the number of chimps you counted.

ORI 70 Now buy a pencil if you don't have one. A mechanical one will be fine, but anything you reliably write with is okay.

ORI 71 Now write down the number of chimps you counted during your travels. CHIMPS_____.

ORI 72 From memory, how long did the attendant (or you yourself) say it would take you to walk to the notions shop and back? Write it down. ESTIMATE_____.

ORI 73 Go back to ORI 54 or 64 and see if your memory is serving you well.

ORI 74 Take your chimpanzee count and multiply by 2. Write the answer in the blank. PRODUCT_____.

ORI 75 Divide that number by 60 and you have your practical estimate in minutes of how long it takes you to make the complete trip to the shop and then back to where you started. Write that estimate of time in the blank. ESTIMATE_____.

ORI 76 Was the attendant's (or your) estimate accurate? ANSWER_____.

ORI 77 Look at your watch or ask someone for the time. Write it down. TIME_____.

ORI 78 Do you have enough to spare before your flight leaves? ANSWER _____ If yes, go on to the next instruction. If no, skip to Inflight Retraining Program.

ORI 79   Having fun? ANSWER_____. If yes, go on to ORI 80. If no, go on to ORI 80 anyway. You won't get referred back to in-depth psychoanalysis that easy!

ORI 80   What's your SUDs level now? SUDs_____.

ORI 81   If you have not done so already, turn to the Orienting Reflex Checklist, pages 301–303. Quickly check off a half-dozen of the topics that interest you. If you have time, go through the procedure the OR Checklist suggests you use in analyzing which learned interest is your first choice, second, third, etc. If you don't have the time, just select your topics with thoughtful judgment and continue on.

ORI 82   Now turn to the magazine rack. Look for a magazine on the topic of your first interest, second interest, third interest, and so on until you have three magazines.

ORI 83   Have you found three magazines? ANSWER _____. If yes, skip to ORI 85. If no, go on to the next instruction.

ORI 84   Well so much for that. You certainly have rare interests or choose peculiar airports. No matter, pick up any three magazines that interest you from the rack.

ORI 85   Write down the titles of the magazines you have selected according to your interest in them in the following blanks:

1. _____   5. _____
2. _____   6. _____
3. _____   7. _____
4. _____   8. _____

ORI 86   Immediately pore through the magazine rack looking for a high- or low-class illustrated porno magazine. When you find one, thumb through it looking for the sexual partner of your choice, one that would turn you on right now in the notions shop. Spend at least two minutes indulging yourself in a sexual fantasy with your pictorial partner.

You are embarrassed reading a porno magazine

right out in the open? Pretend you're from the Catholic League of Decency, sent out to do a survey of what's happening in the porno market.

What if you can't find a porno magazine in the whole rack? Pity! No matter, you will just have to use your imagination. Look around you at the different people in the airport. Mentally undress each of your preferred sex as they come by. Pick out the best of the lot and run a sexual fantasy on him, her or them. Spend at least two minutes doing this, pretending to read the latest copy of *Better Homes and Gardens*, all the while peering surreptitiously over the top edge. Make sure you don't hold it upside down.

ORI 87 Go back to the rack and pick out two more magazines, both on sex. If you are flying out of a major airport, this will be no problem. If it doesn't have sex magazines, they will at least have sex novels right alongside of the magazine rack. If, however, you are flying out of a minor airport, like Tijuana, your selection may be limited to *Playboy, Playgirl,* etc. If you are really hard put to find anything naughty in your magazine rack, you may be reduced to searching through *Cosmopolitan* for some male and female skin shots. Write in the title(s) of your selection(s) in the blanks below the other magazines in ORI 85.

ORI 88 Now write down how much each magazine costs in the work space alongside of each title.

ORI 89 Now add up how much all the magazines you selected will cost. SUM_____.

ORI 90 Do you have enough to pay for them? ANSWER _____. If yes, go on to the next instruction. If no, put the magazines back in the rack and skip to ORI 92.

ORI 91 Walk up to the cashier's counter and pay for the magazines.

ORI 92 What's your SUDs level now? SUDs_____.

ORI 93 Look at your watch or ask someone the time. TIME_____.

ORI 94 Do you have enough to spare before your flight leaves?

ANSWER_____. If yes, go on to the next instruction. If no, skip to Inflight Retraining Program.

ORI 95 Can you see, or do you know, where the nearest
coffee shop or snack bar is? ANSWER_____.
If yes, go on to the next instruction. If no, skip to
ORI 97.

ORI 96 Can you walk there, spend a few minutes, walk
back to the boarding area and have some time to
spare before boarding your flight? ANSWER
_____. If yes, skip to ORI 100. If no, skip to
Inflight Retraining Program.

ORI 97 If you don't know where the snack bar is, ask
the cashier of the notions shop. Write its direction, from where you are standing in front of the
counter, in this clock chart:

12

9   3

6

ORI 98 Ask the cashier how long it will take to walk to
the snack bar and back. TIME_____.

ORI 99 Will that still allow you time to spare to go
there and back and still make your flight? AN-
SWER_____. If yes, go to the next instruction.
If no, skip to Inflight Retraining Program.

ORI 100 Walk to the snack bar or coffee shop. As you
go along, think of those foods you may find
there that you could take on board the plane
with you. Assume that you will be hungry then.
List a half-dozen foods in the spaces below
and rate them in preference from number one to
six.

1. _____   4. _____
2. _____   5. _____
3. _____   6. _____

ORI 101 As you walk into the coffee shop, look for the
menu. Go back to your food list and check off
those things you wanted that they have on the
menu.

ORI 102 Write in the price of each food item in the
work space alongside of it.

ORI 103 Now add up the cost of all the foods. SUM _____.

ORI 104 Do you have enough cash (or credit card) to pay for all or some of these foods? ANSWER _____. If yes, go on to the next instruction. If no, skip to ORI 111.

ORI 105 Order the foods you want to take on board the plane with you. Make sure you tell them: "It's to go."

ORI 106 While you are waiting, get a beverage to reward yourself for all your labors so far. Coffee, tea, milk, soft drink . . . whatever. If you like booze, lay off it for this trip. It's a waste of time to smother your cortex, along with your primitive emotional brain, with alcohol (or Valium or Librium) to any extent. What we want to do is to rid you of your uncomfortable feeling about flying—to teach your primitive emotional brain something new—not just pickle it until your next trip. With that admonition in mind, a small glass of wine would be nice, just to trim the rough edges off your primitive psyche. If you like wine, a small nip of California sherry goes very well before a flight.

ORI 107 When your food is ready, pay for it, stuff it in your pockets, purse, briefcase, or ask for a paper bag to carry it in. Don't start eating it now.

It's for inflight consumption to get the OR active on the plane. And don't eat anything else while you are on the ground. Save that hunger for the flight. A hungry person is an orienting person, and that's what we want you to be.

ORI 108 Just thinking about all that food, what's your SUDs level now? SUDs_____.

ORI 109 What time is it? TIME_____.

ORI 110 Let's get you and your snacks and salacious reading material, if any, to the boarding area. Do you know where it is? ANSWER_____. If yes, skip to ORI 114. If no, go on to the next instruction.

ORI 111 Go to the nearest manned airline booth and ask them what gate your flight leaves from. GATE NO._____.

ORI 112 Ask them how you get there if you can't see it.

ORI 113 Write the direction in which you will have to go on the clock chart below:

12

9   3

6

ORI 114 Write in your flight number here. FLIGHT NO._____.

ORI 115 Start walking back to your boarding area. As you walk along, I want you to count the number of people you pass, but I want you to pay attention to their sex and separate them in your count. For each female you pass, add plus one to your count. For each male you pass, subtract minus one from your count. If you finish up at the loading gate with a minus count, you have counted more males than females. If you finish up with a plus count, you have counted more females than males. Let's see who uses the airport most.

Start counting.

ORI 116 What is the final count? COUNT_____.

ORI 117 What time is it? TIME_____.

ORI 118 Are you within five minutes of boarding your flight?

ANSWER_____. If yes, skip to Inflight Program Retraining. If no, go on to the next instruction.

ORI 119 Now let's look at your progress in this retraining program. We are going to pictorially look at your level of nervousness as you went through this first phase of your antiphobic training. Go back through all the previous instructions and write in below the number of each ORI that asked you to take a SUDs. Then on the same line, write in the SUDs level you reported for that instruction.

ORI _____   ORI _____

ORI _____   ORI _____

ORI _____   ORI _____

ORI _____

ORI 120 Now, how many SUDs levels did you record? NUMBER_____. Double check; go back and count again. See if you haven't missed any, then go on to the next instruction.

ORI 121 What was your second count? NUMBER _____. If it's still six, you are correct; if you changed it to seven, you are orienting to a blank space that shouldn't be there!

ORI 122 And you thought all you had to do was follow directions and fill in blank spaces. Isn't this fun? ANSWER_____.

ORI 123 Now add up all your SUDs levels. SUM _____.

ORI 124 Now count the number of SUDs levels you gave. NUMBER_____.

ORI 125 Now divide the sum of your SUDs by your number of SUDs. This is your average level of nervousness during the program. AVERAGE SUDs_____.

ORI 126 Now let's look at what happened to your SUDs level during the Airport Pretraining Program. How many of the first three SUDs were higher than the average SUDs you calculated in ORI 125? ANSWER_____.

ORI 127 How many of the last three SUDs were higher than the average SUDs you calculated in ORI 125? ANSWER_____.

ORI 128 Is the number you wrote down for ORI 126 larger than the number you wrote down for ORI 127? ANSWER_____. If yes, congratulations, your trend of nervousness during the Airport Pretraining Program went down, so skip to the Inflight Retraining Program. If no, go on to the next instruction.

ORI 129 So your nervousness either went up or stayed there, or it went up and down so much that it's hard to tell what it was doing. Never mind. You can't win 'em all. But hang in there. You're still plugging away at this program and that's a much better indicator of what's really going on than a bunch of numbers plotted on a graph. (Scientists really like these numbers because they can "prove" things to other scientists with them. The only proof you need is that you can perform an activity with success. Your anxiety will sooner or later extinguish.) Let's now go on to the Inflight Retraining Program.

Inflight retraining program

Making Yourself Less Anxious After You Board the Plane

ORI 1 What time is it? ANSWER_____.

ORI 2 Isn't it about time for you to board your plane? ANSWER_____. If yes, skip to ORI 5. If no, continue with the next instruction.

ORI 3 With whatever time is left before your flight, read the introductory chapters of this book until it's time to board.

ORI 4 Is it time to board yet? ANSWER_____. If yes, go on to the next instruction. If no, go back to ORI 3.

ORI 5 Do you have a friend with you on this flight? ANSWER_____. If yes, have your friend take this book and run you through each section where you have to do something. You still answer the questions though. If no, do it yourself, with me as your friend walking you through each step.

ORI 6 Unless you have already done so, quickly check at the boarding gate and ask the attendant if your flight has reserved seats or has an open, first come-first seated policy.

ORI 7 Is your flight reserved or open? ANSWER_____. If reserved, go on to the next instruction. If open, skip to ORI.

ORI 8 Did you reserve an aisle seat for yourself?

ANSWER_____. If yes, skip to ORI 10. If no, go on to the next instruction.

ORI 9 Go back to the boarding gate attendant and see if you can get another seat on the aisle. Preferably in a section of the plane with good outside vision (away from the wings).

ORI 10 Try to get as close to the beginning of the line of boarding passengers as you can. If you haven't a reserved flight, in this way you will be assured of an aisle seat. Even if you have reserved seating, do this anyway. You will see why in a minute.

ORI 11 I want you to do a bunch of things as soon as you board the plane, so you might read ahead until ORI 18, and remember the instructions as you board. If your plane is crowded, I don't want you trampled by a herd of passengers as you pause in the aisle reading the next instruction.

ORI 12 Board the plane when the attendant signals it is ready. As you board, quickly scan the sides of the aisle as you walk into the plane. If you can't see a place to hang your coat, then ask the first stewardess if the plane has one and where it is. If you don't have an assigned seat, get one first, then come back and hang up your coat. If it's an open flight, choose an aisle seat well back from the wings so you have a clear view of things outside. If the seat you choose has poor outside vision, quickly choose another one. Right over the wings is a good place to fly for maximum comfort, but you can't see a damned thing out the window except wings.

ORI 13 Now, are you settled and comfy? ANSWER _____. If yes, continue on. If no, go on anyway.

ORI 14 Were you able to get some preferred reading material—salacious or interest-oriented—at the airport or before? ANSWER_____. If no, go to the next instruction. If yes, go there anyway for practice.

ORI 15 Look around you. Can you see the magazine rack that most airplanes have? Usually they are located near the johns in the rear of the plane or near the food serving stations.

ANSWER_____. If no, go on to the next instruction. If yes, play dumb and go on to the next instruction anyway.

ORI 16 Ask the stewardess (or steward if you are flying on a foreign carrier) where the magazine rack is located. If she says there are no magazines available, make a note to fly next time with a carrier whose registration is with a country where the literacy rate is much higher. If you are told that there are no magazines in English, no matter. You can still look at the pictures.

ORI 17 If there is a magazine rack aboard, scoot over there as quickly as possible and see what's available. If one or two look interesting, borrow them. If you are looking for a skin magazine, the best you are going to get out of the rack is *Cosmopolitan*.

ORI 18 Take your selection back to your seat and stick them in the stretch pocket in front of your knees.

ORI 19 Have you taken part in the Airport Pretraining Program?

ANSWER_____. If yes, skip on to ORI 20. If no, why not? What do you want to prove? Are you trying to be a hero? Some people never appreciate what you're trying to do for them. It took me three weeks to write that section (bitch, moan and grump!) and you decide not to use it. Okay, you're in the plane now, so let's work with what we've got. I want you to go back to ORI 4 in the preflight section and quickly read about Subjective Units of Discomfort (SUDs). When you have done that come back here and go on to the next instruction.

ORI 20 What's your SUDs level right now?
SUDs_____.

ORI 21 Now granted a SUDs level doesn't tell everything, but still, how low would it have to be on this trip for you to feel fairly comfortable?
COMFORTABLE SUDs LEVEL_____.

ORI 22   To what level would your SUDs have to rise to make you uncomfortable enough so you would want to get off the plane?
ESCAPE SUDs_____.

ORI 23   *This is a general instruction for you to keep in mind during your entire flight. If you find your anxiety level rising to a point where you are very uncomfortable or near the escape level, mark your place in the section by turning down the corner of the page you are on, then skip to ORI 128. To save time in case you forget it when you get nervous, either write it down on the inside front cover, or quickly flip backward through the pages until you orient to the italic print of this instruction.*

ORI 24   Now orient to your surroundings. What is the type of airplane you are flying on? (Boeing 707, 727, 747; Douglass DC10, 1011; Electra Fanjet; British Comet; French Mirage; Russian MIG; a Ryan open cockpit two-seater?) If you don't know, ask someone. If your fellow passengers can't tell you, ask your cabin attendant. TYPE OF PLANE_____.

ORI 25   How many passenger seats does it have? Look up and down the aisle and count the rows of seats; then multiply that by the number of seats in a row across the cabin. NUMBER OF SEATS _____.

ORI 26   How many of the seats are empty? If you have difficulty counting from where you are, get up, go back to the john area and do your counting from there.
EMPTY SEATS_____.

ORI 27   How many windows does the cabin have?
NUMBER OF WINDOWS_____.

ORI 28   In the blank space provided, draw a rough sketch of the interior of your cabin. Include seating arrangements, johns, food serving areas, water fountains, magazine racks, aisles, movie projector, movie screen, wings, exit doors, etc. Label all the fixtures you outline in your floor plan of the cabin except the seats.

ORI 29 Now mark your own seat in your diagram with an X.

ORI 30 Where is the attendant call button? ANSWER _____.

ORI 31 Locate the double audio jack where you plug in your earphones. Where is it? (On some small commuter planes, the audio and movie equipment is not installed. If you don't know where it would be, ask a fellow passenger.)

ORI 32 Look in the little stretch pocket in front of your knees. What's in there? Make a list of what you find (airline magazine, cabin safety diagram, rent-a-car hype, barf bag, some old chicken bones from the last passenger who brought his own goodies on board and went through this retraining program, etc.).
STRETCH POCKET INVENTORY_____.

ORI 33 Now while you are wating for your plane to move away from the terminal, let's run through something to use later in flight. Who is your hero or heroine? Someone you know or know of? If this person were flying in your plane, you know deep down inside it wouldn't dare do anything but fly perfectly! Mine, oddly enough, is Prince Philip. The emotional six year old inside me *knows* that He and I could sit down inside the caldera at Kilauea Volcano for lunch, and it wouldn't dare rumble until we finished dessert. Now be honest with yourself. Can you really picture Prince Philip—or Queen Elizabeth—being afraid in any situation? Not likely! If either of them were around, everything would be safe and under control—or brought under control by their authority.

ORI 34 Could you really feel any anxiety about flying if Prince Philip were seated beside you? Of course not, and, besides, under that circumstance who would care about a petty annoyance like aerophobia? We would be too busy being interested and fascinated by the prospect of getting to know Him as a person to give much of a damn about flying. "Flying you say, Your Highness? Why, regularly, every Shrove Tuesday, of course! Never miss a crack at it." At any rate, let's call your Prince Philip your emotional head of state, the anchor person, the one you know deep down inside you who will always come through unscathed, no matter what happens.
YOUR ANCHOR PERSON_____.

ORI 35 Has your plane begun to pull away from the terminal yet? ANSWER_____. If yes, skip to ORI 37: If no, continue on.

Making Yourself Less Anxious During Takeoff

ORI 36 As you sit there waiting for the plane to move, read the other chapters of this book (particularly the earlier ones, if you have not done so already) until your flight starts. Then continue on with the rest of the instructions.

ORI 37 What is your SUDs level?
SUDs_____.

ORI 38 Is it near your escape level?
ANSWER_____. If yes, skip to ORI 128: If no, continue on.

ORI 39 Can you see out a window? ANSWER_____.
If yes, skip to ORI 41. If no, continue on.

ORI 40 Can you move temporarily to a seat where you can see out a window? ANSWER_____. If yes, continue on. If no, skip to ORI 47.

ORI 41 Assuming your plane is now moving on the

ground and headed to the takeoff point, list the different airline carriers, United, Pan Am, etc., whose planes you can see in the spaces as you taxi along. Rate each plane as you go along with respect to its esthetic appeal. How nice does the airplane seem with all its insignias, letters, smiling faces, etc., on a scale from 1 to 10. 1 is yuk. 10 is fantastic-looking. Start rating and then go on to ORI 42 at the same time.

1. _____   6. _____
2. _____   7. _____
3. _____   8. _____
4. _____   9. _____
5. _____   10. _____

ORI 42 Can you see the airport control tower (the highest building in the airport, a circle of picture windows around its top) from your window? ANSWER_____. If yes, skip to ORI 46. If no, continue.

ORI 43 Can you see it through anyone else's window from where you are sitting? ANSWER_____. If yes, skip to ORI 46. If no, continue on.

ORI 44 Can you see the highest building in the airport? ANSWER_____. If yes, call that the control tower and skip to ORI 46. If no, continue on.

ORI 45 Can you see any structure out of your window? A lounge building, a coffee shop, a hangar? ANSWER_____. If yes, call that the control tower and continue on. If no, skip to ORI 47.

ORI 46 On the clock chart below, with an arrow mark the direction in which the control tower lies with respect to your plane as it moves toward the takeoff point. Twelve o'clock is always the direction the nose of your plane follows, no matter how it turns—this way or that. To plot the direction you are traveling every thirty seconds, simply keep the top of this page pointed toward the nose of your plane, and note what number on the clock chart points at the control tower. Number each arrow you draw pointing at the control tower, 1, 2, 3, etc.

12
9   3
6

Do this at thirty-second intervals as you travel along. Remember, you are doing two things at once here: plotting the course of your plane and rating all the other planes you see on your niftyness scale. Use your watch to count each thirty-second interval. Or count chimpanzees if you don't have one. (You don't know how to count chimpanzees? Then quickly go back to ORI 66 in the preflight section and find out how.)

ORI 47 What's your SUDs level? SUDs_____.

ORI 48 Is it near your escape level? ANSWER_____. If yes, skip to ORI 128. If no, continue on.

ORI 49 Are you facing down the runway yet, waiting for control tower permission to take off? ANSWER _____. If no, continue with ORI 41 and ORI 46 until you are. If yes, skip back to ORI 66 in the preflight retraining section and read how to count time without a watch. Do that quickly and come back here. Now count the number of chimpanzees from the time your plane starts moving down the runway until you can feel your plane lift off. Pay attention to the sound of the wheels and the vibrations of the plane as you travel over the runway. Pay attention to the sense of heaviness (and lack of it) in your body as the plane picks up speed. When it lifts off, you will feel a sense of freedom in its motion, as if it's not locked on the ground. A quick change in sensation is the best way to describe this sense of freedom if you have never flown before. Pay attention while you are counting, and wait for this sensation.

ORI 50 Has your plane lifted off? ANSWER_____. If no, keep counting. If yes, write down the number of chimps it took to lift off. NUMBER OF CHIMPS_____.

ORI 51 It takes about 220 mph ground speed for the average jetliner to lift off the ground. Average speed during takeoff is one half that (0 plus

220/2) or 110 mph. Divide 110 mph by 60 in the margin to the left. ANSWER_____.

ORI 52 Divide your answer by 60 seconds. Do your calculations in the work space to the left. ANSWER _____.

ORI 53 Now multiply the number of chimpanzees you counted by your final answer (.03055 mps) and you have the number of miles of runway it took for your plane to lift off. MILES_____

ORI 54 You think better in terms of feet? No problem. Just multiply your answer in miles by 5,280 feet. FEET_____.

ORI 55 How about yards? Just divide that answer by 3. YARDS_____.

Making Yourself Less Anxious In Flight

ORI 56 Now you are up in the air flying along. Is there enough light outside the plane so that you can see things in the sky or on the ground? AN-SWER_____. If yes, continue on. If no, skip to ORI 58.

ORI 57 What do you do now to countercondition your fear of flying? Again as always, orient. But let's try a simple method that has worked for eons for reducing fears. Mothers do this all the time with young children when they get anxious about their first trips out into the world. It also works for nervous adults. My good colleague, Dr. Zev Wanderer, and I have used it to help nervous fellow passengers we sit next to on trips. What Zev and I do—and what you might ask a friend or fellow passenger to help you do—is to scan the clouds and the terrain below for natural configurations that look like something else. A cloud might look like a person's face or an animal of some sort. A field far below with creeks and riverbeds crossing it often will form letters or abstract signs. Mountain ridges that jut out from the slopes often present a face in profile. We scan the environment from the window and when we see an interesting shape, we ask the nervous person to look for it: "To the rear there is an interesting cloud. It looks like something. Can you tell me which cloud it is and what it looks like?"

Make a game of it. Your partner in orienting first scans the outside environment and then asks you to locate and describe the interesting feature that resembles something. After you have located —perhaps with a little bit of help—the feature, you reverse roles. You then do the scanning and your partner must orient to the flying environment to locate the feature and describe it to you. A simple child's game that works and works well in reducing anxiety about flying. If you have to do it all yourself, so be it. It will still reduce your anxiety if you locate a particular feature *and then* sketch it roughly in a notebook.

Now you may be saying to yourself as you read this: "But to orient to something on the involuntary level—where my anxiety is—the stimulus must have signal value. It's not so significant if you're not here to motivate me and I have to search things out myself. What's to make a cloud face significant?" Here's your answer: "By looking for cloud faces and then sketching them *you are going to feel better about flying.* That's what gives them significance! Play this orienting game for at least fifteen minutes or more. After you finish playing it, go on to the rest of the program. Then if your anxiety begins to rise once more, you can turn to cloud orienting to lower it.

ORI 58 Now let's trigger off your OR by working on a mental puzzle. Can you work out the last three letters in the following sequence? H I J K L M N __ __ __ The answer, of course, as you have figured out is, O P Q, the next three letters in the alphabet. All coded sequences of this sort are dependent upon some number base. For the alphabet, it's 26 letters, so if I gave you T U V W X Y __ __ __, you would know that the three missing letters are Z A B. For the sequence B E I N __, the next letter would be T, since the sequence is made up by skipping 1, then 2, then 3, then 4, and finally 5 letters in between the ones chosen. The sequence could have a binary base, for example: 0 1 0 1 0 1 0 where the only numbers are 0 and 1 and the sequence base is 2 and must repeat. A number sequence based on eight is another, i.e., 5 6 7 8 1 2 with the next numbers being 3 and 4. There is another type of sequence with an arbitrary base, for example O S C Y S B T D E L _ _ _ _ is based upon the opening lines of the national anthem of the United States of America. The missing letters are, of course, W S P W. Now with this information on how sequences are made up and perhaps juggled around to be clever, figure out what the next three letters are in this sequence: O T T F F S S _ _ _. Clever men with doctorates behind their names have puzzled over this one for days. Graduate students have spent weeks trying to figure it out. But I know of at least one five-year-old child who got it within a minute—and that child was not a young Einstein. When you have figured out those missing letters, go on to the next instruction.

ORI 59 Let's look at your learned interests, hobbies, things that you pay attention to consistently (whether you say you really like them or not) and use them to make you feel better about flying.

ORI 60 Have you brought some OR activity like a hobby or special interest or at least something to fiddle with in your seat?
ANSWER_____. If yes, skip to ORI 63. If no, continue on.

ORI 61 Have you an interest, like art, ceramics, music, carpentry, or a special project coming up in the future that you can make sketches, diagrams, layouts, experimental plans, etc., for?
ANSWER_____. If yes, skip to ORI 73. If no, continue on.

ORI 62 Have you brought any reading material about your special interests on board? ANSWER_____
____. If yes, skip to ORI 77. If no, skip to ORI 80.

ORI 63   Take out your activity right now and fiddle with it. Don't perform it unless you can do it without arousing the ire and dirty looks of fellow passengers and attendants. Trumpet playing aboard a 747 is not too smart. You are likely to cause a visible start in your fellow travelers with your first blast of the racetrack call.

ORI 64   Now time yourself as you open the container holding the apparatus of your OR activity. Fiddle with it for one minute.

ORI 65   Now sit back in your seat, look around you at the other people in the airplane. Write down the activities they are engaged in on the margin. Orient to all of them in the three rows in front of you, your row, and the three rows behind you.

ORI 66   Go back to your OR activity and fiddle with it again for two more minutes.

ORI 67   Put your activity down and orient to what's going on outside your aircraft. Are you passing over a town, river, mountains, clouds, islands, ocean? Write this information down in the margin.

ORI 68   How's your SUDs? Is it on a very uncomfortable level? ANSWER_____. If yes, skip to ORI 128. If no continue on.

ORI 69   Go back to your OR activity and study it again. Do this for another two minutes.

ORI 70   Close your eyes, stretch out in your seat as much as possible and picture your plane flying high in the sky, skimming over and through clouds with the sun reflecting off its wings. Do this for one minute.

ORI 71   Go back to your activity and fiddle with it for as long as you feel comfortable and are not bored with it. Every two minutes, look around the interior of the plane and see what's going on. Keep a log of what six different people, picked at random, are doing each two minutes in the space below: #1 reading, #2 talking with somebody new, #3 still sleeping, etc.

1. _____   4. _____

2. _____   5. _____

3. _____   6. _____

ORI 72 Keep fiddling with your OR activity until you are bored with it, or your plane begins to land. Then skip back to ORI 61 for another OR activity. If your plane is landing skip forward to ORI 250.

ORI 73 I want you to begin designing, planning, scaling, laying out, etc., any project you might be anticipating for your special-interest activity in the future. If you have brought a scratch pad on board, use it for your scribbles and notes. If you haven't, use one or two of the blank pages in the back of the book.

ORI 74 Begin your experimental design and time yourself. After one minute, sit back and look around the airplane.

ORI 75 Begin making a log of the activities of six of your fellow passengers or continue the one you're using already. Update it every two minutes by taking a break from your experimental work and sketches. Write in the seat numbers of the people you select below and then log their activities in the space below: #1 walking about, #2 still yakking away, #3 ordered more booze, etc.

1. _____   4. _____
2. _____   5. _____
3. _____   6. _____

ORI 76 Do this and continue with it until you become bored with your OR activity or you are about to land. Then skip back to ORI 62 for another OR activity or skip forward to ORI 250 when your plane begins its descent.

ORI 77 Select your first-choice reading material on your OR interest. Begin reading it, but time yourself. After two minutes, stop and go on to the next instruction.

ORI 78 While you are reading your OR material, I want you to stop every two minutes and orient to what's going on in the airplane around you. Select six of your fellow passengers at random and log their behavior in the space below or continue with the log you started already: #1 is scratching her ear, #2 still catatonic, #3 has started breathing again, #4 reading a magazine upside down, #5 looks like he needs to go to the john, etc.

1. _____   4. _____
2. _____   5. _____
3. _____   6. _____

ORI 79   Continue with your OR reading material until you are bored with it or your plane begins to land. Then continue on to the next instruction or skip forward to ORI 250 when you start to land.

ORI 80   Do you have any pennies or dimes on you? ANSWER_____. If yes, continue on. If no, get some from the attendant or a fellow passenger and then continue on.

ORI 81   Now you are going to use an orienting reflex trigger technique that is as good as sex or food in arousing the fun half of your primitive nervous system: a hand-eye coordination task. It's an old technique used to reduce boredom and a simple one—pitching pennies. Only let's make a game of it and not make it so easy that you get tired of it quickly. On page 142 you will see a layout of squares numbered zero through nine. The object of the game is to toss a penny (or dime) from your lap onto one of those numbered squares. You place this book on your fold-down tray with one page lying flat on the tray and one page held upright with your nontossing hand.

ORI 82   Now look at page 140. As you can see, it's a rough map of the world's major cities and airports. Your job is to take a trip completely around the world starting from the major airport nearest to your present location and landing back there after circling the globe using the route you choose.

ORI 83   Notice, if you will, that there are distances in between major airports on pages 143–146. For example, between Chicago and New York there are 713 miles as the 707 flies. To get from Chicago to New York (or vice versa) you have to pitch your penny first onto the 7 square on page 142, then onto the 1 and 3 squares next. Misses in between hits don't count.

ORI 84 Now your job in triggering your involuntary orienting reflex to lower your anxiety about flying is to circumnavigate the globe in the shortest distance from your starting point and to do it with the fewest number of pitched pennies. Remember, to be a hit, the penny must lie totally within the white space of the numbered square. No touching of the borders is allowed. What about the other squares, the ones marked A, B, C, D, E, and F? you may be asking yourself. A good question—you are beginning to orient on your own already. See, it's not so hard. You were built to do it automatically, you know! If you land clearly in squares A through F, turn to page 138 and see what is in store for you.

ORI 85 Without beginning the game, take a few practice tosses to warm up. If you have a partner willing to play with you, let him or her take a few practice tosses also.

ORI 86 Choose your route around the world and write in the airports you are traveling to in the spaces below. If you have a partner, allow him or her to choose a route and write it in.

	ME	YOU
STARTING AIRPORT	_____	_____
1st stop	_____	_____
2nd stop	_____	_____
3rd stop	_____	_____
4th stop	_____	_____
5th stop	_____	_____
6th stop	_____	_____
7th stop	_____	_____
8th stop	_____	_____
9th stop	_____	_____
10th stop	_____	_____
11th stop	_____	_____

ORI 87 If you have a partner, both of you flip a coin at the 9 square. The one who gets closest to its center starts first. You both alternate in pitching at the square you need; if the second toss knocks the first toss into or out of a square, you play the penny where it finally lies. If you are playing alone, you can recreate some of the fun of playing with a partner by tossing two pennies in sequence. Remember, it's a child's game, but it automatically makes your primitive nervous system orient and that lowers your anxiety. When you finish, note how you feel and continue on with the next instruction. Begin your world trip.

A1 You have just been highjacked by a sex-starved Mongolian sheepherder and your plane is now flying to Peking. Reroute your trip accordingly. You are grounded there for three tosses until the State Department can swap your plane for an undisclosed amount of yak butter.

A2 Your pilot is feeling a little airsick. He decides that he wants to go home, the place you just took off from. You are grounded for one toss until a replacement can be found to fly the plane from there.

A3 This A3 hit counts as the number you have been tossing for.

B1 Your senior stewardess announces over the PA system that she is nine-months pregnant and the copilot finally agrees to marry her. All the passengers vote to reroute in midair to Niagara Falls via New York City. Start your trip over from there.

B2 Proceed directly to Calcutta, India on a free trip, courtesy this airline. Continue from there.

B3 Sorry! You were bumped off this flight. Disregard the numbers you have already made on this leg and start over on your last stop.

C1 While peacefully flying along, the pilot announces that the principality of Tonga has declared war on the Alaskan Eskimos in retaliation for exporting plastic walrus tusks, stamped Made in Japan. Your pilot has decided to sit out the hostilities at O'Hare Airport in Chicago. You lose two tosses during this conflict while the United Nations sends peace-keeping forces to patrol the South Pacific and Bering Sea. Plan the rest of your trip accordingly.

C2 You get an unexpected tail wind and your pilot announces that right now you are over your next destination. Continue your trip with this thrown in as a bonus.

C3 You now have a choice: Get the number you are tossing for free, or toss two more times for it and if you hit it, you get the next three numbers 0–9 free.

D1 The stewardess announces that the plane is out of champagne. An emergency detour will have to be made to Paris to pick up an additional supply. You are grounded for five tosses while the stewardesses bargain with the French ground crew for more wine.

D2 At your next stop, you meet an old friend who offers to give you a free ride to your next airport in his U.S. Air Force plane. You immediately take him up on it.

D3 On the next three tosses, any number you hit that is within plus or minus one of the number you are trying for counts as your number.

E1 Congratulations. The airline has just awarded you the number 0–9 that you just tossed for.

E2 Your plane has been grounded at your next stop because of fog. Sit out four tosses on the ground until the weather clears.

E3 It's your lucky day. You get to pick two of the numbers 0–9 that you need on this leg of your trip for free.

F1 The flight attendant informs you that you are traveling on a counterfeit ticket, and you will be taken back to the last stopover your plane took off from. Start over from that airport.

B	7	3	5
1	E	9	D
F	4	A	2
6	C	O	8

DISTANCE INDEX FOR CITIES*

Atlanta	Boston	937
	Chicago	587
	Dallas	721
	Denver	1212
	Kansas City	676
	Los Angeles	1936
Auckland	Sydney	1470
	Tahiti	2470
Azores	Bermuda	2067
	Lisbon	1054
	New York	2384
Berlin	London	574
	Moscow	996
Bermuda	Azores	2067
	Miami	980
	New York	681
Bombay	Cairo	2659
	Dar es Salaam	2855
	Peking	2964
	Singapore	2429
	Tel Aviv	2529
	Calcutta	1040
Boston	Atlanta	937
	Chicago	851
	Dallas	1551
	Denver	1769
	Los Angeles	2596
Buenos Aires	Cape Town	4320
	Valparaiso	770
Cairo	Bombay	2654
	Peking	4584
	Rome	1317
	Calcutta	3506
Cape Town	Buenos Aires	4320
	Valparaiso	770

*All distances are approximate

Caracas	Dakar	4321
	Rio de Janeiro	2540
Chicago	Atlanta	587
	Boston	851
	Dallas	803
	Denver	920
	Kansas City	414
	Los Angeles	1745
	New York	713
	Seattle	1737
	San Francisco	1858
Dakar	Cape Town	4231
	Dar es Salaam	4090
Dallas	Atlanta	721
	Boston	1551
	Chicago	803
	Denver	663
	Kansas City	451
	Los Angeles	1240
Dar es Salaam	Bombay	2855
	Dakar	4090
Denver	Atlanta	1212
	Chicago	920
	Kansas City	558
	Los Angeles	831
	Seattle	1021
Fiji	Honolulu	2965
	Sydney	1998
	Tahiti	2160
Hong Kong	Manila	693
	Tokyo	1796
Honolulu	Fiji	2965
	Los Angeles	2557
	Mexico City	3920
	Seattle	2678
	Tokyo	3850
	San Francisco	2394
Kansas City	Atlanta	676
	Chicago	414
	Denver	558
	Los Angeles	1356

Lisbon	Azores	1054
	Rome	1245
	Paris	830
	Athens	1800
Los Angeles	Atlanta	1936
	Boston	2596
	Chicago	1745
	Dallas	1240
	Denver	831
	Honolulu	2557
	Kansas City	1356
	Mexico City	1542
	Miami	2339
London	Berlin	574
	Moscow	3459
Manila	Hong Kong	693
	Singapore	1479
Mexico City	Honolulu	3920
	Los Angeles	1542
	Miami	1250
Miami	Bermuda	980
	Los Angeles	2339
	Mexico City	1250
Moscow	Peking	3597
	Budapest	880
New York	Azores	2384
	Bermuda	681
	Chicago	713
	London	3459
	San Francisco	2571
	Washington, D.C.	205
Peking	Bombay	2964
	Cairo	4584
	Moscow	3592
	Tokyo	1307
	Calcutta	2024
Rio de Janeiro	Cape Town	3750
	Caracas	2540
Rome	Cairo	1317
	Lisbon	1245

Seattle	Chicago	1737
	Denver	1021
	Honolulu	2678
	Anchorage	1469
Sydney	Auckland	1470
	Fiji	1998
	Singapore	3750
Singapore	Bombay	2429
	Manila	1479
	Sydney	3750
	Calcutta	1791
Tahiti	Auckland	2470
	Fiji	2160
	Valparaiso	4240
	San Francisco	4215
Tel Aviv	Bombay	2529
	Athens	710
Tokyo	Hong Kong	1796
	Honolulu	3850
	Peking	1307
	Anchorage	3760
Valparaiso	Buenos Aires	770
	Tahiti	4240
Paris	Lisbon	830
	Budapest	790
San Francisco	Chicago	1858
	Honolulu	2394
	New York	2571
	Tahiti	4215
Calcutta	Bombay	1041
	Cairo	3506
	Peking	2024
Athens	Lisbon	1800
	Tel Aviv	710
Budapest	Paris	790
Anchorage	Seattle	1469
	Tokyo	3760
Washington, D.C.	New York	205

F2 The flight attendant says that you have been selected as the winner of the 1,000,000,000 passenger of all the world's airlines. Whether you like it or not, they are going to turn the plane around and fly you to Washington, DC to be interrogated by the Federal Aviation Agency to see how you figured out where to stand in line so you would be awarded this prize. Start your trip again from Washington, DC.

F3 This F3 hit gives you your partner's penny-tossing contract for the next four tosses. Any clean hits made by your partner count as numbers 0–9 that you need.

ORI 88 Now let's try something else that may work wonders for you in retraining your primitive nervous system not to put out waves of nervousness whenever it gets near an airplane: sex.

ORI 89 Did you bring at least one pornographic or gothic romance novel on board with you? ANSWER _____. If yes, continue on. If no, skip to ORI 96.

ORI 90 Select one of your novels and thumb through it for a particularly sexy episode. A good way to find the erotic writing in porno novels is to go to the end of a chapter and count back two or three pages. You then should be in the middle of one sort of orgy or another. Keep skipping backward, skimming through the paragraphs until you come to the beginning of the episode. If you have a gothic romance, you have to just thumb through it.

ORI 91 When you find your titillating episode, begin reading it. Time yourself. Read for a minute, then set your book down.

ORI 92 In between reading these erotic passages, I want you to orient to what's going on around you. Select a half-dozen passengers at random. If anyone looks like you, however, include that person in your list. Write down their seat numbers.
SEAT NUMBERS: _____ _____ _____
_____ _____ _____

ORI 93 I want you to keep a running log (if you are not doing so already) on the behavior and activities of these half-dozen people you have chosen. Every two minutes, look up from your reading and orient to what they are doing. Spend only a few seconds logging their behavior in the margins: #1 still sleeping, #2 putting the make on gal across the aisle, #3 still talking, etc. Also, record when and what the captain or the flight attendants may say on the loudspeakers like: "We are passing over Bad Smell, Wyoming, folks. You can see it clearly. It's that speck to the left where the two thin lines cross: U.S. 421 and 854," i.e. "Bad Smell, Wyo., 6:46 RMT." After working on your log in the margins, go back to your sex reading.

ORI 94 Have you begun to feel the physiological consequences of sexual arousal yet? Stirring of the genitals? Enlargement of the nipples or breasts? Irregular breathing? ANSWER_____. If yes, you are not very anxious right now, so orient to the passengers and the airplane activities until your sexual excitement passes. Look out the window. See what time it is. Ask the attendant for a glass of club soda. Find out if your flight will land on time or not. Then return to your book. If no, keep reading or look for a raunchier part to read.

ORI 95 Continue this procedure until you get bored out of your mind with reading about sex or until your plane begins to land. Then continue on to the next instruction or skip to ORI 250 when your plane begins to land.

ORI 96 Remember back to when you were boarding the plane. From your mental pictures of the people standing in the line, pick out your preference for the sexiest-looking man or woman or both. Is he, she, they, visible from where you are sitting? ANSWER_____. If yes, skip to ORI 104. If no, continue on.

ORI 97 Pick out your second choice from the line. Can you see him, her or them? ANSWER_____. If yes, skip to ORI 104. If no, continue on.

ORI 98 Can you see anyone around you from your seat that has even a small dribble of sex appeal? ANSWER_____. If yes, skip to ORI 104. If no, continue on.

ORI 99 Are you flying on a military troop transport? ANSWER_____. If yes, you have my sympathy and a real problem, but continue on. If no, you have my sympathy anyway, so continue.

ORI 100 Casually get up and walk down the aisle toward either the magazine rack, the pantry area, the john or the coat closet. As you walk toward the goal you have chosen, scan the passengers for sexual appeal. Pick out at least three of the sex of your choice and rate them for sexiness (0–1000).

ORI 101 When you reach the john, pantry area, coat rack, etc., conduct some business there—get a soda, wash your hands, fiddle with your coat, etc.—then walk back the other way toward your seat and sit down again.

ORI 102 Write down the seat numbers of the sexy-looking people who stirred your libido during your walk.

SEAT NO. _____   SEAT NO. _____
SEAT NO. _____   SEAT NO. _____
SEAT NO. _____*   SEAT NO. _____

ORI 103 Now write down the sex rating between zero and 1000 that you gave each of them alongside their seat number.

ORI 104 Picture your number-one rating in your mind's eye. If you can see him or her from where you are sitting, don't cheat. Do this from memory. Concentrate on the type of clothes worn. Then go on to the following instructions.

ORI 105 Is number one wearing a jacket? ANSWER _____. If yes, continue on. If no, skip to ORI 108.

ORI 106 What color is it? (Brown, blue, red, checked, herringbone, multicolored?) COLOR_____.

ORI 107 What is it made from? (Silk, corduroy, wool, tweed, seersucker?) CLOTH_____.

---

*If you are still filling in seat numbers beyond this point, you have: (a) tremendous sex drive from being lost on a desert island during the last five years with only goats for company; (b) a naive optimism bordering upon Freudian wish-fulfillment; or (c) you live either in Greenwich Village in New York or in the San Fernando Valley in Los Angeles.

ORI 108 Is number one wearing a skirt, dress, pants or jumpsuit? ANSWER_____. If yes, continue on. If no, go over and introduce yourself.

ORI 109 Its color? COLOR_____.

ORI 110 Its cloth? CLOTH_____.

ORI 111 Is number one wearing a belt? ANSWER_____. If yes, continue on. If no, skip to ORI 113.

ORI 112 What type is it? (Leather, cloth, colored, white?) TYPE_____.

ORI 113 Is number one wearing a tie? ANSWER_____. If yes, continue on. If no, skip to ORI 115.

ORI 114 Describe its color, type cloth, etc. TYPE_____.

ORI 115 What sort of shirt, sweater, etc., is number one wearing? TYPE_____.

ORI 116 What sort of shoes? TYPE_____.

ORI 117 When you rated number one before, what was he or she doing? (Sleeping, chatting, reading, drinking, eating, nothing?) ACTIVITY OF NUMBER ONE_____.

ORI 118 Close your eyes now and picture number one walking down the aisle toward you.

ORI 119 As number one gets to your row, he or she asks if the empty seat next to you is taken. You say no and number one sits down alongside you. You smile at each other and nothing else happens. Then you realize that you have fallen asleep for a bit and when you wake up, number one is asleep with an arm casually thrown around your shoulders. Still sleepy, the next thing you know is that number one is just waking up and stroking your neck and mumbling sexy phrases in your ear. By this time you are definitely interested in what number one is telling you. When number one is awake, you are looking at each other with lust. You can just barely see each other, because it has gotten dark and the overhead lights in the airplane are not on yet. Looking out the windows, all you can see are moonlit clouds in the distance. You look around the plane and see all the other passengers are peacefully (check A, B or C):

    A. Stroking themselves.

    B. Looking for someone to stroke.

    C. Sleeping.

Then you bend over your arm rest and (check A, B or C):

    A. Your partner gooses you.

    B. You fall off your seat.

    C. You look up and down the aisle.

Everything is quiet. The aisles are empty except for (check A, B or C):

    A. A drunk snoring on the floor as one of the stews rolls him.

    B. Four married couples from San Fernando playing swap the seat stub.

    C. The attendants sipping coffee and whispering to one another in the pantry.

Your sexual number one reaches up to the overhead rack and pulls down a blanket. Then your number one (check A, B or C):

    A. Wraps it around number oneself, sits down and begins to feel himself.

    B. Throws it over his shoulders like a cape, leaps over you and runs up and down the aisle screaming like a chicken.

    C. Tucks it around both of you.

You and number one begin simultaneous teasing, petting, feeling and necking under the blanket where no one can see what is going on. If someone were to look at you two, all he would see is something that looked like (check A, B or C):

    A. Two cats and a dog in a burlap sack.

    B. A portable oil-well pump under a tarpaulin.

    C. Two people trying to keep warm.

After a few minutes of this, number ones says (check A, B or C):

    A. "You're taking too much of the blanket."

    B. "Do you smoke after sex?" and you reply, "I don't know. Next time I'll look."

    C. "Let's both go to the john where we can have some privacy."

Leading you down the aisle by the hand, you

both stop in front of the john and look back down the aisle. No one sees you slip in and lock the door behind you. Then number one says (check A, B or C):

A. "Let me in too, stupid. I didn't bring you here for that."

B. "For God's sake, close the john before you step in it."

C. "Let's make out."

ORI 120 Now, you thought this was going to be a sexual fantasy, didn't you? Well, one other thing that we only touched on, which is connected with orienting, is novelty. When you get something else from what you expect, you orient!

ORI 121 Now run through your mind's eye what is going in the john. Close your eyes and picture each detail. Where does number one put the jacket? The belt? Do you sit on the john while number one stands up? Does number one stand on the john? What do you do then? How long does it take for the tie to fall in and get flushed down? What does number one say when he leans back against the door and is hung up by the knob? Do the crew then have to pry the door off the hinges to get you both out? Get all these details in your mind and then continue with the fantasy of your choice. Then continue on to the next instruction.

ORI 122 Close your eyes and imagine the following situation. I give the rough outline, you fill in in the detalis. Your plane has just made an unscheduled stop and who should walk on board but your anchor person—the one you know deep down in your heart who will always come through, no matter what. Your anchor person walks down the aisle and even though there are other empty seats, he (she) walks up and asks if it would be all right for him (or her) to sit next to you. What do you say? REPLY TO ANCHOR PERSON _____

ORI 123 Your anchor person introduces himself (or herself) and apologizes for inconveniencing you and the other passengers with the unscheduled stop made expressly to pick up (him) or her. What do you say to this apology? Write in the actual words you would use. RESPONSE _____

ORI 124 Your anchor person casually asks: "Do you fly often?" What is your truthful response? ("What do you think these wings sticking out the back of my jacket are for?; Every chance I get; As little as possible; Only when someone kidnaps me; This is my first time and it scares the hell out of me; Never! I'm not really here. I sent a cardboard replica in my place.") RESPONSE

ORI 125 What would your anchor person say when you told him or her that you are nervous about flying? RESPONSE _____

ORI 126 Your anchor person then asks you to do him or her a favor. What does he or she ask of you? ("Loan me a cigarette; Will you buy me a drink? I left in a hurry without any cash; Can I tell you about my problems? Sometimes I get so uptight I think I'll go bananas; Can I borrow your blanket?") REQUEST _____

ORI 127 You and your anchor person start to chat. What would you ask him or her about? ("How do you like flying?" Do you have any phobias too? Where are you going? What are you going there for? Who will meet you?) Decide which way you want to lead the conversation. Write down each statement you make in the conversation in your scratch pad. Decide how your anchor person would respond and write that down also. For lowering your anxiety, writing things down instead of just using your head works better. Spend at least fifteen minutes doing this task. The next section of the Inflight Retraining Program has a number of OR subprograms used for high-anxiety states. You might want to go through them selectively and use one or several that meet your needs. If you brought some food aboard, run through the food section. Or go through the subprogram on sexual material. If you later find that you are getting anxious, come back to the high-anxiety section and begin with the first subprogram again. If in the middle of any of these subprograms your plane begins to land, skip to ORI 250.

Making Yourself Calm Down If Fear Strikes

ORI 128 Each time you come to this section, write in the ORI number you just skipped from.
WHEN DONE GO BACK TO ORI_____.
WHEN DONE GO BACK TO ORI_____.
WHEN DONE GO BACK TO ORI_____.
WHEN DONE GO BACK TO ORI_____.
WHEN DONE GO BACK TO ORI_____.
WHEN DONE GO BACK TO ORI_____.
WHEN DONE GO BACK TO ORI_____.

ORI 129 You have just skipped to this section because your SUDs level was getting high enough to make you wish you never decided to get on this damned plane. Let's see what we can do about that. Is your anxiety about flying near the panic level?
ANSWER_____. If no, skip to ORI 171. If yes, continue on.

ORI 130 Well, well! You're about to go bananas and run screaming up and down the aisles or wet your pants and then faint from sheer mortification. Besides getting off the plane, what would you like to do about it? Check off your answer.
A. Crawl into my seat and disappear.
B. Run screaming up and down the aisles.
C. Go to the john.
ANSWER_____. If you checked A, you are prone to wishful thinking. If you checked B or C, you are doing some constructive thinking. Running up and down the aisles would definite-ly help by burning off some of the adrenalin that

your primitive brain is pumping into your system. Unfortunately, the aircraft crew take a dim view of such behavior and they will throw you off, if on the ground, or tie you down, if in the air. But their motivation is understandable at least. Every time a passenger engages in this normal and healthy behavior prompted by his innate physiology, ticket sales drop and the crew get worried about their jobs. Simple rice-bowl economics, but what can you do about it? Nothing. The airlines are not ready for a jogging track in the pub lounge. Maybe in ten years, but not now. On the other hand, getting up and walking down the aisle to the john will help. It's also a *goal-oriented activity* where you have to orient to get a job done—to purposefully move somewhere instead of just running around in circles.

ORI 131 Can you get up and walk along the aisle? ANSWER_____. If yes, skip to ORI 143: If no, continue on.

ORI 132 What can you do now in the face of this panic? You can try a few tricks that may work. First, fold your arms across your chest with your hands under your arms as if you were trying to keep them warm. Close your eyes and take three deep breaths. Then breathe normally. Pretend that you have to stretch. Arch your back, extend your legs under your seat, skrunch up your shoulders and bend your neck back at the same time. Flex your biceps with your arms still crossed. Stretch like that for at least five seconds. Remember one chimpanzee, two chimpanzee, etc.? Now let your body settle back into your seat. What happened to your SUDs level? Did it go down? ANSWER_____. If yes, skip back to where you came from before getting so nervous—the ORI number is the last one you you wrote down in ORI 128: If no, continue on.

ORI 133 Do you want to give mild physical pain a try as a way of arousing your orienting reflex in a highly anxious situation? ANSWER_____. If yes, continue on: If no, wait until you can go to the john and then skip to ORI 143.

ORI 134 Try giving yourself a good slap on the left cheek with your right hand: one that will make you tingle but not leave you unconscious. Keep your forearm and hand stiff when you slap. That way you won't poke yourself in the eye. Pretend you are slapping at a mosquito—a really big one that requires a healthy wallop to bring it down.

ORI 135 Does slapping your own cheek lower your anxiety?
ANSWER_____. If yes, skip back to where you were before you came here: If no, continue on.

ORI 136 Still sitting where you are with your arms crossed and hands folded under each arm, take your thumb and index finger (the one you point with, not the one you use for obscene gestures) and grab a little bit of that loose skin on either the side of your body under the armpit or on the underside of your arm. Now apply pressure until you feel that sharp pain from a pinch. Keep it up for a few seconds. Now move to a slightly different location and do it again. Which pinch was more painful? ANSWER_____.

ORI 137 Now you know how elusive the sensation of pain is. If you expect it, since you cause it yourself, you have to search around for a spot with a goodly amount of pain receptors. If your friend does it for you sneakily, and you have little control over it, the pain seems more intense. Try this pinch procedure in a half-dozen spots and compare which spot produced the most intense pain. Now if you have a medical problem with bruising, clots, or are descended from eighteenth-century European royalty, it's not too smart to try this. If you bruise easily, you are going to have to pay the price of a few sore black-and-blue marks in order to lower your anxiety this way. Remember, especially if you have long fingernails, don't pinch so hard you draw blood. When you pinch, orient to this sensation. Where is it coming from? How far away from the top of your armpit? An inch? Two, three, four? DISTANCE_____.

ORI 138 Does the pain cause a deep throb when you pinch? A sharp superficial pain? A burning sensation? Think of it and its qualities and write them down. TYPE OF PAIN _____

_____

_____

ORI 139 Is your anxiety level still near panic? ANSWER _____. If yes, go on: If no, skip back to ORI 128 and see where you came from, then go there again.

ORI 140 Can you go to the john yet? ANSWER _____. If yes, skip to ORI 143: If no, continue on.

ORI 141 Either (a) you don't like pain and choose instead to be anxious, (b) you are very brave and pain means nothing, or (c) you are quite panicky. Short of asking someone to give you a hard slap on the cheek, there isn't much more I would recommend to reduce your panic. You might try to give yourself a cramp in the arch of your foot if you are one of the lucky people who can do this upon command; or give your eyebrow hairs a few painful tugs—without pulling them out. If such masochistic activities don't appeal to you, try exercising covertly in your seat. Stretch your legs out under the seat in front of you and tighten up your toes, feet, calves, thighs and then your buttocks. This will raise you out of your seat a little bit. Then relax your muscles in the reverse order, buttocks to toes. Do the same thing with your arms crossed over your chest: fingers, hands, wrists, forearms, biceps, shoulders, then relax. Keep doing this until you are pooped or your anxiety drops. Pay attention to the sensations in your muscles as you tighten each muscle-group and then relax it. Tension, then a leaden, tingling sensation. Now if these things don't do the trick, push the call button over your seat. Tell the attendant that you are going to be sick and must go to the john. Ask her if she would help you there. If she asks you why you are carrying this book along with you, just tell her that you always read in the john when you're going to be sick. Carry on from there, and thank her. Then skip to ORI 145.

ORI 142 Look at the fasten seat belt sign. Is it off? ANSWER_____. If yes, continue on. If no, go back to ORI 132 and continue on there until the seat belt sign goes off. Then come back here.

ORI 143 Unbuckle your seat belt—unless you do this first, you are in big trouble—and get up and walk, not run, to the farthest john. If you don't know where it is, ask.

ORI 144 When you arrive at the door of the john, see if the little sign above the door says "vacant" or "occupied." JOHN SIGN_____. If vacant, continue on: If occupied, look for another john or twiddle your thumbs, tap your foot and hum: *Whistle a happy tune* until the vacant sign goes on.

ORI 145 Enter the john. Wash your hands with warm water and soap. Note the feel of the water running over your skin. Pay careful attention to it. Remember the sensation of it and describe it to yourself in words you can write down in the work space.

ORI 146 Dry your hands. (Not on your coat. Use one of those paper towels.) Note the sensation on your skin when you rub it briskly with the towel. Now gently rub and wave your hands in the air to get the remaining bit of damp off. How does it feel when you do that?

ORI 147 Write down in the work space how the water felt on your hands. _____

_____

ORI 148 Write down in the work space how the brisk drying off of your hands felt. _____

_____

ORI 149 Write down in the work space how waving your hands in the air to dry them felt. _____

_____

ORI 150 Now sit down on the john, close your eyes and take three deep breaths.

ORI 151 Now breathe normally for thirty seconds.

ORI 152 Pick a number between 4 and 6.

ORI 153 Now stand up and turn around. Touch the heels of your feet to the john door. Lean forward and place the palms of your hands against the wall over the john. Relax your arms until your body comes close to the back wall. Now we are going to do some pushups. (Or are they called pushbacks when you do them like this?) Remember the final number you picked. It was either 4, 5 or 6. Whatever it is, let's call it X. Do X pushups from this position, but in between each pushup, when you bring your nose back to the wall, rest for X seconds in that state. Remember one chimpanzee, two chimpanzee, etc. Do it.

ORI 154 Now sit back on the john again.

ORI 155 Isn't this fun? ANSWER_____. If yes, go back outside and sit down in your seat: If no, sit down on the john again.

ORI 156 Now with your rear end firmly planted on the john, raise your hands over your head with your eyes on your feet. Turn your palms down with the fingers of each hand pointed at each other. Slowly, counting up to X, bring your hands together until the tips of your fingers just touch. Make them touch when you reach the count of X.

ORI 157 It's not as easy as it sounds. Screwed up, didn't you? ANSWER_____. If yes, all you need is some practice to get your coordination perfect, so continue on: If no, there is always one smart alec in the crowd who takes pride in doing anything right the first time, so go back outside and sit down in your seat again.

ORI 158 Do it again until you just touch the tips of your fingers together when you say X.

ORI 159 Now do it again, but this time use only your index fingers.

ORI 160 What's your SUDs level now? ANSWER____

___. If lower, go back to your seat and ORI 128: If still near the escape level continue on.

ORI 161 Place the palms of both hands on the back of your neck. Now bend forward carefully to see how far you can go without banging your head on the door or falling off the john. When you level forward, exhale all the air in your lungs. When you straighten up, take in a huge breath.

ORI 162 Now do that exercise X times with an X-second rest in between each bend.

ORI 163 Anytime you feel less anxious, you can go back to your seat, you know.

ORI 164 Now, still sitting on the john, lift one knee up as high as it will go without clipping yourself in the chin. Now put that leg back down and lift the other one as high as it will go. Now put that one down and lift both knees up as high as they will go while still balancing your tushie on the john. When you lift your legs, exhale. When you put them down, inhale deeply.

ORI 165 Do that series of exercises X times with a rest of X seconds in between each effort.

ORI 166 What's your mother's maiden name?
MOTHER'S MAIDEN NAME___.

ORI 167 Count up the number of letters in her maiden name. NUMBER___.

ORI 168 Add that number to your X number.
SUM___.

ORI 169 Count that number of chimpanzees backward, for example, 12 chimpanzee, 11 chimpanzee, 10 chimpanzee, etc.

ORI 170 When you reach 1 chimpanzee, get up and go back to your seat and the ORI number you wrote down in ORI 128.

ORI 171 What goodies did you bring on board to help you orient and thereby lower your defensive reflex? Did you bring some of your favorite foods from home with you? ANSWER___. If yes, skip to ORI 177: If no, continue on.

ORI 172 Were you able to find some good food at the airport to bring on board? ANSWER___. If yes, skip to ORI 177: If no, continue on.

ORI 173 Were you able to bring anything edible on board with you? ANSWER_____. If yes, skip to ORI 177: If no, continue on.

ORI 174 Can you borrow a gumdrop from someone? ANSWER_____. If yes, skip to ORI 177: If no, continue on.

ORI 175 Look around you. Is anyone else reading this book and nibbling on a snack they brought with them? ANSWER_____. If no, continue on: If yes, go up to him or her, explain that you are both in OR flight retraining, see if you can borrow a bit of a snack (Tell him or her they can have your dessert from the meal the airline will serve —it's terrible anyway, you won't miss it.) and then skip to ORI 177.

ORI 176 Did you bring one or more of those beautifully illustrated cookbooks aboard with you? ANSWER_____. If yes, skip to ORI 188: If no, continue on.

ORI 177 Look in the stretch pocket in front of your knees for the airline flight magazine: the one with all the movie and audio schedules as well as the advertisements for what the guilty business man can order by mail for his wife sitting at home. Quickly scan it for a one-page advertisement of Air France, Alitalia, JAL, etc., where the chef stands behind a banquet of delicacies with the whole crew behind him. Can you find a food advertisement like that? ANSWER_____. If yes, skip to ORI 188: If no, skip to ORI 201.

ORI 177 Okay, now think about your number-one food. Sit back and think about holding it in your hand. Close your eyes, stretch out and then sink back into your seat. Picture that plump little morsel you are soon to pop into your mouth. What does it look like? Its surface: is it smooth, rough, frothy, glossy? Its texture: hard, soft, chewy, creamy, liquid? Its color? What will it smell like as you lift it to your mouth? Tangy, sweet, sharp, pickled, bland, yeasty, meaty, fruity?

ORI 178 Now open your eyes and take it out of its hiding place. Lay it in your palm and look at it. Does it look like you pictured it? Take it up and smell it. Does it smell like you thought it would? Run your finger over the top of it. Does it feel like you thought it would? Lick your finger where you touched it. Does it taste like you thought it would?

ORI 179 Now look around you at the other people. Do they have such a taste treat to orient to? Pick out a person who isn't doing anything in particular. What is on his or her mind? Is it worry? Fun? Boredom? Look at his or her face and read the thoughts it reflects. Now turn back to your own gustatory delight. Take a small taste. Let the sensation of it linger in your mouth. Pass the bite from side to side, top to bottom with your tongue. How does it taste? Good, excellent, poor, average? Rate this goodie on a ten-point scale of all the other goodies like it you have ever had. Zero is dreadful. Ten is ambrosia.
TASTE RATING_____.

ORI 180 Call the stewardess or attendant over and ask for a glass of club soda. When she brings it to you, take a small mouthful and wash the taste of this morsel down. Now take another taste. Roll it around on your tongue. Rate this second taste on your ten-point scale.
TASTE RATING_____.

ORI 181 Take another sip of club soda, swish it around your mouth, then take a third nibble on your treat. Remember, the whole purpose is to get rid of your anxiety about flying, not to fill your tummy, so pay attention to every crumb that you put in your mouth. Taste it slowly. Rate that taste.
TASTE RATING_____.

ORI 182 Take another sip of club soda. Wash out the taste of your food with it. Now take another small sip of club soda. What does it taste like? How does it feel in your mouth?
CLUB SODA DESCRIPTION _____

ORI 183 This is hard work isn't it? I bet you never thought eating could be so complicated. ANSWER_____. If yes, you're on your way to becoming a gourmet. If no, you're just enjoying yourself and there's not much wrong with that.

ORI 184 Give your goodie four more tastes, interspersed with sips of club soda. Rate each taste in these blanks.

TASTE _____
SODA _____
TASTE _____
SODA _____
TASTE _____
SODA _____
TASTE _____

ORI 185 Now finish enjoying and swallowing that bite. Let the aftertaste stay in your mouth. Isn't that yummy? ANSWER_____. If yes, take another bite and continue on: If no, put that goodie back in your bag, select another one and skip back to ORI 177.

ORI 186 Slowly eat the whole thing while looking around at the other passengers who are bored out of their minds trying to find something to do.

ORI 187 When you are finished with it, go back to ORI 128 and find out where you came from. If you are still hungry after this treat, save any food you have for later when you might get nervous again. Then come back to this section starting with ORI 177 and repeat what you just did.

ORI 188 Well, here you are. Uptight in an airplane with no consumable things to pop in your mouth. Let's see what we can do about making you less nervous than you are now.

ORI 189 Stick your pen or pencil (clean end first) into your mouth and gently suck on it. When you do this you will notice that your primitive nervous system doesn't know the difference between something to eat and a ball point pen. When you place something in your mouth and suck on it, you start to salivate. Dry mouth and anxiety go hand-in-hand. A salivating mouth is a sign of a primitive nervous system that is beginning to orient.

ORI 190 Now, still sucking on your food surrogate, skim through your publication on food (cookbook, magazine, etc.). Pick out the most attractive layout (or the only one you have), the one that makes you feel that your eyes are bulging while they zip back and forth taking in the sight of all that beautiful food.

ORI 191 What is the main entree (the dish in the center) of the spread? Take your implement out of your mouth, write the name of the entree down and then replace the implement.

ANSWER_____.

ORI 192 How many different dishes are there depicted? (Meats, poultry, fish, vegetables, desserts.) Count them. ANSWER_____.

ORI 193 Now how many of them have you eaten before? ANSWER_____.

ORI 194 Pick out those that look attractive in the picture and rate them for delectability.

FOOD_____ RATING_____
FOOD_____ RATING_____
FOOD_____ RATING_____
FOOD_____ RATING_____
FOOD_____ RATING_____

ORI 195 Close your eyes, keep sucking on your pencil and picture that number-one dish being brought to you by the airline attendant. See her coming out of the pantry area, walking down the aisle with all the other passengers orienting to the food she is carrying. Down the aisle she comes until she reaches your seat. Smell the delicious odor of that food you have chosen. She places it on your folding tray. Look at it. Note the color, the texture. Imagine placing it in your mouth. Think of the flavor spreading across your tongue. You chew at it gently (not your pencil; just keeping sucking on that) and swallow its goodness and delicious taste.

ORI 196 What color was the food you just pictured in your mind? COLOR_____.

ORI 197 What did it smell like? (Meaty, fruity, tangy, spicy, bland, sweet.) ODOR_____.

ORI 198 What did it taste like? TASTE_____.

ORI 199 What did the attendant who brought you this imaginary dish look like? (Short, tall, sexy, plain, beautiful, neat, sloppy, buxom, flat-chested?)

ORI 200 Now go back to your picture and do it all over again with your second choice of food. Repeat this procedure over again for each of the five food dishes you selected. When you finish, go back to ORI 128 and see where you came into this section from. Then go back there and continue on.

ORI 201 Did you bring some sexy reading and/or viewing material on board with you? ANSWER_____. If yes, skip to ORI 207: If no, continue on.

ORI 202 Were you able at least to find a copy of *Cosmopolitan* in the magazine rack on board? ANSWER_____. If yes, skip on to ORI 237: If no, continue on.

ORI 203 Look in that stretch pocket in front of your knees again for the airline flight magazine. Rapidly pore through it looking for semiskin pics of sexy-looking people.

ORI 204 Are there any semiskin pics of sexy-looking people in there? ANSWER_____. If yes, skip to ORI 237: If no, continue on.

ORI 205 Are there any pictures of sexy-looking people with all their clothes on? ANSWER_____. If yes, skip to ORI 237: If no, continue on.

ORI 206 Are there any pictures of anyone there of your preferred sex(es) who look as if they may have had at least one sexual experience in their life? ANSWER_____. If yes, skip to ORI 237: If no, skip to ORI 237 and use your imagination.

ORI 207 Take out one of your erotic pictorial magazines. Preferably one of the ones that are so explicit that your eyes bulge in disbelief that such things are allowed nowadays.

ORI 208 What is the title of the magazine you selected? TITLE_____.

ORI 209 Quickly scan the feature skin spreads and pick one of them that has a written narrative that goes along with the pictures so you can understand what the two (three, four . . . whole group) are doing.

ORI 210 What are the page numbers of the feature spread you have selected? PAGE_____ TO PAGE_____.

ORI 211 Study the pornographic pics one by one. Take your time with each picture. Imagine yourself as the participant of your choice or as the photographer who is directing each scenario. Place yourself in the fantasy, not as a participant in some isolated sexual incident in the San Fernando Valley but as a member of the crew producing a porno spread for the magazine. Now to do good, believable, high-class porno shots, you know that there must be a gradual build up of actual sexual activity with photos taken at appropriate moments during the action. So connect each photo to the next one in the spread with yourself as a participant, building a sexual fantasy of what is happening in between shots. Do it until you have gone through the whole feature.

ORI 212 What's your SUDs level now? SUDs_____.

ORI 213 Is it well below your escape level? ANSWER _____. If yes, skip back to ORI 128 to see where you came from and continue on from that point: If no, continue on.

ORI 214 Select another feature spread from this or another porno magazine.

ORI 215 Write in its page numbers. PAGE_____ TO PAGE_____.

ORI 216 Look at the main sexual participant of your choice. Study her or him carefully. Then place the magazine down on your lap, cover up.

ORI 217 What color hair does the main sexual character have? HAIR_____.

ORI 218 Does the pubic hair match? ANSWER_____.

ORI 219 What color eyes does that character have? EYES_____.

ORI 220 What is the most distinguishing feature of the character? (Face, breasts, genitals, tushie?) FEATURE_____.

ORI 221 Which type of sexual act does the character seem most to prefer from your study of the picture? (Intercourse, foreplay, oral sex, anal sex, masturbation?) PREFERRED SEXUAL ACT_____.

ORI 222 Which is your preference? PREFERRED SEXUAL ACT_____.

ORI 223 Do you intend to loan this book to a friend when you are done? ANSWER_____.

ORI 224 How many pictures were there in the whole magazine spread? NUMBER OF PICS_____.

ORI 225 Which one aroused you sexually the most (that made your eyes dilate)? SCENE_____.

ORI 226 Look around you in the airplane. Which female looks most like the gal(s) in the pictures?

ORI 227 What is her seat number? SEAT NUMBER _____.

ORI 228 Are you sure it's not the same gal?

ORI 229 Which male passenger looks most like the guy(s) in the pictures?

ORI 230 What is his seat number? SEAT NUMBER _____.

ORI 231 Are you anatomically a male? ANSWER_____. If yes, continue on. If no, skip to ORI 234.

ORI 232 During any of this sexual fantasy and orienting, did you experience even a momentary erection? ANSWER_____. If yes, you are no longer anxious, so go back to ORI 128 and then skip back to where you came from. If no, continue on.

ORI 233 How's your SUDs level? Is it reduced below the escape figure? ANSWER_____. If yes, skip back to ORI 128 and then go back to where you were before. If no, skip to ORI 236.

ORI 234 You must be a female. During the sexual fantasy and orienting, did you experience even a momentary tightening of the nipples, the clitoris, or did you experience a dampening of the vaginal area? ANSWER_____. If yes, you are no longer panicky, so skip back to ORI 128, find out where you came from and go there. If no, continue on.

ORI 235 Is your SUDs level below the escape point? ANSWER_____. If yes, skip back to ORI 128 find out where you came from and go back there. If no, continue on.

ORI 236 You have one of two choices: (a) stay in your seat and continue reading your porno selection or (b) go to the john with your magazine, try a little quick masturbation or at least some self-stroking. Don't scoff. The ancient Romans relied on masturbation when the Gauls were pounding at the city gates and nobody could make them go away. They found it reduced their anxiety. If you choose option (b), make sure you lock the john door before proceeding. In either case, when your anxiety is lowered, skip back to where you were before anxiety struck.

ORI 237 So the only thing you have available for sexual orienting are some pictures of people who might make a halfway decent porno spread. No matter, half a loaf is better than none. What you must do now is to use your imagination. Orient to those pictures as if they were only the preliminary set up that precedes the actual orgy of your choice. Look at the first picture. Build a fantasy around it. If it is a bunch of airline stewardesses and crew walking together arm in arm, for example, where are they going with such determination and confidence? What do they do in all those strange cities, so far away from mom and with only one another and the male crew for entertainment? You have heard of all the hanky-panky between crews and stews, haven't you? Well, set things up in your mind that all these people are heading for a sexual rendezvous. Then close your eyes and watch them go, step by step, filling in all the little details with your mind. Do this for five minutes, then continue on with the next instruction.

ORI 238 What type of undergarments are they wearing?
(Bras or no, panties, panty hose, slips, jocky
shorts, tee shirts: silk, cotton, rayon, colored,
white, black?) If you don't know, go back into
your mind's eye and find out. ANSWER
_____.

ORI 239 What are the measurements (approximately) of
the most sexy attendant at the orgy?
MEASUREMENTS_____ _____ _____.

ORI 240 How tall is the sexiest of the crew at the orgy?
HEIGHT_____.

ORI 241 What color is her (his) hair? HAIR COLOR
_____.

ORI 242 Does he (she) have hair on his (her) chest?
ANSWER_____.

ORI 243 What does she (he) sound like? (Southern,
Texan, Californian, New England, Eastern,
Midwestern?) ACCENT_____.

ORI 244 What seems to be her (his) favorite sexual activity?
PREFERRED SEXUAL ACTIVITY_____.

ORI 245 What does she (he) like most to get turned on?
PREFERRED TURN ON_____.

ORI 246 Has she (he) reached orgasm yet? ANSWER
_____.

ORI 247 Has anyone reached orgasm yet? ANSWER
_____.

ORI 248 Have you become sexually aroused by your
fantasy yet? (Genital activity, breast swelling,
vaginal dampness?) ANSWER_____. If yes,
you are not anxious, so go back to that part of
the program you left and continue on there. If
no, continue on here.

ORI 249 Is your SUDs near escape level?
ANSWER_____. If yes, skip back to ORI
128. If no, continue on with your sexual fantasy
until you feel very comfortable and then skip
back to where you came from and continue on
there.

Making Yourself Less Anxious During Landing

ORI 250 You have made your trip and now comes what is one of the more nervous moments for many air travelers: the landing. How do we keep your anxiety level low during this phase of your flight? Simple, we keep you orienting during the landing. I want you to read these simple instructions through to the end and remember them. Then during the last few minutes of your flight, when your pilot makes his approach to the airport, close your eyes and orient to what the instructions have told you.

ORI 251 Picture the runway below you as your plane begins its descent. This runway is not made of asphalt or concrete but foam rubber. Imagine your foam-rubber runway stretching out under you for over a mile. Picture it in your mind's eye.

ORI 252 Pretend that you can reach out and touch the runway. Poke your finger at it and feel how deep and soft it is.

ORI 253 Now cover the foam-rubber runway with a mattress cover. Pick one that you know well; your own at home. Imagine the runway mattress with the same color and design—rolled edges, corners, etc. Only this mattress stretches way out in the distance under you. Imagine that in your mind.

ORI 254 Now as your plane begins to land, you can see it slowly, slowly, slowly come nearer and nearer the runway mattress.

ORI 255 Picture the wheels of your plane come down and ride just above the runway mattress.

ORI 256 Try and anticipate, from the sounds coming from around you and the vibrations in the plane, when the wheels will touch the runway.

ORI 257 Picture again the plane just coasting inches above the runway mattress, gliding along and just about to make contact.

ORI 258 Have the plane in your mind's eye land just when you think it will. If you are a bit too soon, wipe that picture out and have your plane still gliding down, almost touching the runway. Then guess again when your plane will touch down and try to match it.

ORI 259 When your plane has touched down on the runway, open your eyes and look around you at the other passengers.

ORI 260 Try to anticipate when the pilot will apply the brakes: a whooshing–whistling sound and a sudden slowing.

ORI 261 Settle back in your seat, look out the window and watch the plane taxi down the runway toward the terminal.

ORI 262 Now if you are making a return trip back soon, go through the Inflight Retraining Program once more and concentrate, if you can, on those parts of the program that you had to skip for one reason or another. Bon voyage.

eight

Retraining yourself not to fear heights
with sunflower seeds,
trashcans and back rubs

Fear of high places with sharp drops may or may not be built into us as a species. But the terror of heights that produces incredibly convoluted behaviors and nonsensical thoughts bordering on mindlessness is not. This kind of fear, called acrophobia, is learned; each episode in which it is experienced only reinforces its strength until it becomes a rope tethering the phobic person to the ground.

Fear of falling usually takes the form of the irrational terror that many of us feel near a window in a tall building. While we may not panic and retreat, we are aware of silent screams coming from deep within us. Some of us only feel safe near a window if we can creep up on it below the window frame of glass. Or we step back quickly in shock when the drapes are yanked away from a wall of glass looking out on a 300-foot sheer drop. When our business host invites us to view his beautiful city at night from his fiftieth-floor office suite, we feel sick and weak and make excuses, for, if we accept, the phobic impulses will be set loose to run in the primitive corridors of the brain and we will be able to think only nonsensical thoughts like: "The corner of the building will fall off and I will be left tottering on the edge, balancing back and forth over oblivion. I will slip from ten feet across the room and tumble into the inch-thick tempered glass window. It will shatter like ice into empty space with me tumbling after it."

This description of acrophobia, if it resembles your own experience of heights, might make you think that this irrational fear is difficult to treat. Even the common folklore associated with it is scary. Many people believe that if you fall off a high place in a dream, you must wake up before impact—otherwise you will die in your sleep. There is no question that acrophobia is a bona fide debilitating psychological problem. But difficult to treat? That depends on how you do it.

Acrophobia has been eliminated in just a few orienting reflex sessions by making the patient orient to a hand-eye coordination task in the phobic situation. For example, an acrophobic patient was taken by two of our staff to the first floor balcony in the rear of our Los Angeles County Mental Health Clinic in Long Beach. That balcony, about fourteen feet above ground level, overlooked a scuzzy alley and a row of trash cans. During this first session, the patient was given a bag of sunflower seeds and instructed to lean over the waist-high balcony wall and toss a sunflower seed into the nearest trash can. After the patient could hit it reliably, one farther away was used as the target. Then another one, even harder to hit, was used and so on. During the second session, the whole procedure was repeated—this time from the balcony on the third floor. On the third session, the patient and the bag of sunflower seeds were moved to the roof. There the patient again practiced making hits from forty feet up in the air. After that, a tall commercial building was used as a phobic stimulus. On different floors, the patient quickly learned to orient to other things in the phobic situation and lost the fear of heights.

On my first trip to a high building with a patient, I also lost my own discomfort about extreme heights, the feelings that I had acquired along with my fear of flying more than twenty years before. While I was instructing the patient to orient, I too was orienting one step ahead of him, because I had to figure out what he would orient to next. Both the patient and I came down from that building sans anxiety.

"Now, that's all well and good for both you and your patient," you might be saying, "but how am I to do the same thing for myself without your actual physical presence alongside me?" Starting on page 175, I will lay out a specific routine for overcoming your fear of heights; but first let's see what we are dealing with.

Is Your Fear Realistic or Unrealistic?

Before you get involved with any program for eliminating your phobia, I want you to answer two questions. First, what is it that you are afraid of when you are above the ground? In other words, what is it that you want to do without feeling anxious when you are finished with retraining?

Let me explain why your answer is important. Fear of heights may be rational or irrational. If someone says to me, "I can give you a good-paying job on the high iron as a construction worker," I would promptly tell him to stuff it. I have no desire to do a balancing act ninety stories above the ground on a girder, even though I could eventually learn not to be anxious about it. On the other hand, suppose a friend or colleague suggests that we take a glass of wine together at the Century Club, twenty-five stories above Westwood Boulevard, and enjoy the view. If I tell myself, "I can't do that—I would be too damned nervous," then I am talking from a phobic feeling and not from caution based on reality. I'm not going to fall off the Century Club. I couldn't find a way to jump off it if I tried!

So it's important to know what part of your fear you want to eliminate. If you only get upset when you take a high-rise construction job *where you could fall* but feel fine when you visit the top of the Empire State Building, you are in the same fix Frank Buck was in when his first boss said: "Go into that cage of lions and tigers and put on a good show for the people." Obviously, Frank mastered his scary job—by orienting to it—but we're not dealing with that kind of situation here. This program is for irrational fears of situations where you are not likely to suffer any harm—it's not for people who want to walk the tightrope without a net.

Second, I want you to ask yourself the question: "How much do I want my phobia to go away?" The answer to this question is also important. Getting rid of a phobia takes some effort. Although I can't give you a guarantee, I really don't think you will lose your phobia by just passively reading this book. You will also need to spend some time and energy setting things up logistically and then going out into the phobic situation to lose your fear of it. If you're willing to do this, then let's proceed with your retraining program.

Fear of heights retraining program

Although it's possible that you could walk cold into any tall building with this book in hand and eliminate your nervous feelings about heights, it's only sensible to make the whole experience easier on yourself by maximizing your chances of triggering off your orienting reflex in the phobic situation and, consequently, minimizing your defensive reflex. Some preliminary planning will make things less hit-and-miss and more reliable.

What You Will Need To Make Your Retraining Program Work

To start out, you must decide on your goal. How high up do you want to go and feel comfortable? If your city has no buildings over ten stories, it doesn't make much sense to travel to a skyscraper if you are not likely to visit one even occasionally. So pick a realistic height that you are going to encounter regularly in your everyday life. For some people this is the fourth floor of their apartment building. For others, it is the one-hundredth floor of the New York World Trade Center. One hundred floors of reconditioning may seem to be an impossible task to you, but remember that just as there isn't much difference between the third and fourth floors, there also isn't much difference between the thirtieth and fortieth or between the seventieth and ninetieth floors. The higher you go, the faster the training goes.

Next, you must see what resources are available to you. There are three minimum requirements for your retraining program that should be easy to meet. Most important, do you have a friend who will work with you on this project? Remember, Dr. Brunhilda Ritter eliminated a fear of heights in her patients in only minutes by maintaining physical contact—the OR to touch—during the reconditioning session. Get your friend to walk you through the whole retraining program and read this book with you so that he or she understands what is happening. It really doesn't matter what personal or theoretical outlook your friend has on psychotherapy—it will have little or no effect on your success or failure. All your friend need do is to take on the role of orienting reflex prompter by touching, instructing, pointing out things for you to orient to and, of course, by being sympathetic and reassuring. Almost all of us orient to support from a friend in a scary situation.

Second, find a low building that has at least four levels including the roof and that has access to the outside from each level—a window you can open, a balcony you can stand on, etc. If such a building is not available or is inconvenient, a set of stairs at least fifty feet high with a sheer drop and a railing on one side will do. You might find such a setup on a fire escape, in a football stadium, at a pedestrian entrance to a high bridge, at the Leaning Tower of Pisa, etc.

Third, find a relatively tall building with windows on each level where you can look out—and down. A ten-story building is fine. The windows in such buildings are typically sealed, but that's okay. You needn't throw anything out of them. Also, it's not necessary for the building to have an elevator. You will walk up from one floor to the next. In addition to being good exercise, walking up stairs gives you something to do besides getting anxious in between orienting instructions.

As you have probably gathered, the retraining program is split into two parts: the first using a low, three-story building and the second using a high building. If you don't have a low building available, it will work just as well to use a stairway, fire escape, etc., but you will have to divide the total height into three stages, equivalent to the height of the second and third floors and the roof. Figure approximately twelve feet per story. The usual step is seven inches high, so going up one story would be equivalent to walking up twenty steps. When the Low Building Program says go to the next story, simply ascend twenty steps for the same effect.

You will need to take some things along with you to complete this retraining program. The essentials are a sketch pad and pencil, some pennies, three wastepaper baskets or small trashcans and a package of salted sunflower seeds. The sunflower seeds serve two purposes: They are the missiles you will toss into the waste baskets from on high and they can also be nibbled on.

Dried watermelon seeds, peanuts, pistachios and almonds are also good, but they are more expensive —better for eating than throwing. You will need the seeds and wastebaskets only for the low building. There are some other things you might wish to take along with you to help trigger your orienting reflex in the uncomfortable situation: something to eat, preferably a taste treat, and something to look at like some downright lurid pornography. Both of these are excellent ways to elicit your orienting reflex. If you want to maximize the effects of food and sexual stimuli, don't eat six hours before or have sex a day before you take the first step in your retraining program.

Now, one of the things you might do prior to beginning your retraining program is to read the chapter on fear of flying. While airplanes may not make you anxious, the things that will trigger your orienting reflex apply to airplanes as well as high buildings. Reading that chapter may help you be better prepared for your own program.

Making Yourself Less Anxious in Low Buildings

ORI 1 Are there any physical reasons why you should avoid an anxious situation? Like a chronic coronary or high blood-pressure problem? ANSWER _____. If no, continue on. If yes, check with your physician, show him this program and have him modify its instructions having to do with anything physical—walking, climbing, eating—to suit your physical condition.

ORI 2 Assuming you and your friend have done your groundwork in planning locations for exposing you to your anxiety, proceed with the program.

ORI 3 Place one of your waste baskets on the ground directly under the second-story window or balcony where you can look down at it. Place the second basket two feet in front of the first one. Place the third basket three feet in front of the second.

ORI 4 With your friend lightly holding your arm—it's not necessary to drag you in!—walk into the building, climb the stairs to the second floor and go up to the window or balcony. Make sure the window or balcony you choose has a waist-high window sill, wall or railing that you can lean over.

ORI 5 With your friend still holding your arm, preferably skin touching skin, look out at your view from the second floor. Write down on your sketch pad a general description of what you see: people, three apartment buildings, a sleeping dog, five parked cars, an airplane in the distance, fourteen trees, a bunch of people in the nude doing something in the bedroom of the apartment across the way, etc. Then roughly draw what you see. A Grandma Moses primitive is just fine.

ORI 6 Now lean over your window sill and look down at the three baskets below you.

ORI 7 With your partner still touching your body somewhere with his or her hand, take out one of your sunflower seeds, lick the salt off it—salt makes you salivate and a salivating mouth tells the primitive nervous system to orient—and then take aim on basket nearest to you.

ORI 8 Toss your sunflower seed at the basket.

ORI 9 Did you hit it? ANSWER_____. If yes, keep taking out sunflower seeds, licking off the salt and tossing them at the basket until you get five hits in a row. If no, do the same as yes.

ORI 10 Have you gotten five hits in a row on basket number one yet? (You can just hold your arm out and drop it in, you know.) ANSWER _____. If yes, continue on. If no, go back to the previous instruction until you do.

ORI 11 Now do the same thing with basket number two. Keep licking sunflower seeds and tossing them at the second basket. When you have four hits in a row, continue on to the next instruction.

ORI 12 Isn't this fun? ANSWER_____. If yes, continue on. If no, who told you psychotherapy should be fun? Continue on anyway.

ORI 13 Repeat the whole game for basket number three. When you have three hits in a row, go on to the next instruction.

ORI 14 Now how do you feel? Is your SUDs level very high? (If you don't know what a SUDs level is, skip back to ORI 4 in Chapter 7, read about SUDs and then come back here.) ANSWER _____. If no, skip to ORI 17. If yes, continue on.

ORI 15 Did you bring something to eat with you in addition to the seeds? ANSWER _____. If yes, take a few nibbles, eating as slowly as possible until your SUDs goes down, then skip to ORI 17: If no, continue on.

ORI 16 Have your partner give you a back and shoulder rub as you lean your elbows on the balcony wall or window sill. When your SUDs goes down, continue on.

ORI 17 Try walking up the flight of stairs to the next floor with your friend holding your hand, arm, etc. When you get there, walk over to the third-story window, balcony, etc., and look down at your baskets.

ORI 18 Repeat the same procedure you followed on the second floor. Take out a sunflower seed, lick it and toss it at basket one. After five hits, do the same for basket two. After four hits for that basket, go on to basket three. Three hits there, and then go to the next instruction.

ORI 19 How's your SUDs level? Is it high? ANSWER _____. If no, skip to ORI 22; if yes, continue on.

ORI 20 Do you have any of your food left? ANSWER _____. If yes, eat it slowly until your SUDs goes back down to a comfortable level and then skip to ORI 22: If no, continue on.

ORI 21 Do you have any erotic pictures or magazines with you? ANSWER _____. If yes, take one out, scan it for the most explicit picture, one that makes your eyes bulge and your mouth want

to say, "They can't print something like that!"
Keep orienting to all its erotic details until your
SUDs goes down, then skip to ORI 22. If no,
have your partner rub your back and shoulders
while you lean your elbows on the railing or
window sill until your SUDs goes down. Then
continue on.

ORI 22 Can you get up on the roof? ANSWER_____.
If yes, continue on. If no, skip to ORI 26.

ORI 23 Does the roof have a wall around it so you can
either sit or stand behind it and be safe from
falling off the roof? ANSWER_____. If yes,
continue on. If no, forget about the roof and
skip to ORI 26.

ORI 24 Repeat the same procedure on the roof that you
followed on the second and third floors. Lick and
throw, lick and throw until you have five con-
secutive hits for basket one, four hits for basket
two and three for basket three. When you have
accomplished this, continue on.

ORI 25 Sit there on the roof for a few minutes and have
your partner give you some orienting instructions.
It's a simple little game. He or she points to something that catches the eye between "there and
there," and you have to look for it. It may be a
dog walking down the street, a peculiar arrangement of windows in a house or apartment, an unusual automobile parked in an alley, etc. Then
you orient to your environment, look for unusual things or changes and report them to your
partner until you match up with his or her observation. Then you reverse roles, you picking out
the eye-catching thing and your partner trying to
detect it. Do this for at least five minutes. Then
continue on.

ORI 26 Now go back downstairs to the bottom floor.

ORI 27 Go outside with your partner and turn around
and look at the building.

ORI 28 Now go back inside and walk up all the flights
of steps together but this time without your
partner holding your arm.

ORI 29 Do you feel any anxiety now? ANSWER_____

_____. If no, continue on. If yes, stop whenever you feel nervous and have your partner rub your arm until you feel comfortable, then continue on.

ORI 30 When you reach the roof, walk around it (if possible) with your partner for a minute, then go back downstairs again.

ORI 31 Go outside, leave your partner there and walk back up all the flights of stairs one by one. On each floor, go to the window or balcony, say hello and wave to your partner. When you get to the roof, do the same thing. Then come back down.

ORI 32 How do you feel? Do you feel comfortable enough in a three-story building? ANSWER _____. If yes, continue on. If no, wait for three to seven days and run through the Low Building Program again.

ORI 33 Do you feel like going right on to the high building and continuing with your retraining program? ANSWER_____. If no, go home or back to your office. Relax, have a drink, chat with friends about your experience, go out to dinner, reward yourself—with whatever that requires—then make an appointment to meet your friend again sometime between tomorrow and a week from now in the lobby of your tall building. If yes, go on to the tall building and the first instruction of its program.

Making Yourself Less Anxious in Tall Buildings

ORI 1 Walk into the lobby of the building. Let's assume that you or your partner has checked it out and that there are windows you can look out of on each floor.

ORI 2 Did you bring some favorite food with you? ANSWER_____. If yes, continue on. If no, take a few minutes and see if there is a coffee shop or snack bar in the building where you can get something to eat, preferably something you like. Anything will do if you haven't eaten in six to eight hours. Hunger makes us orient to junk food that we normally wouldn't give to a dog, but we still eat it.

ORI 3 Did you bring some sexual material with you? ANSWER_____. If yes, continue on. If no, look for the ubiquitous newsstand in the lobby and buy some.

ORI 4 How high (what floor) will you have to go in the building before you will feel anxious? ANSWER_____.

ORI 5 No matter what floor you picked, start with the second floor, look out a window and see if you feel anxious. If you do, go on to the next instruction. If not, keep walking up each flight and looking out windows until you feel anxious, then go on to the next instruction. Now, if you are in a skyscraper with thirty or more floors and your goal is to feel comfortable having a drink, or just sitting around, at the top, you don't have to recondition your orienting reflex on each floor. After the tenth floor, get on the elevator (unless you are an elevator phobe as well) and go to the fifteenth floor to work on your orienting reflex there. After that, work on it every fifth floor, i.e., the twentieth, twenty-fifth, thirtieth, thirty-fifth, etc.

ORI 6 Go back down one floor.

ORI 7 Are there any clouds in the sky? ANSWER _____. If yes, continue on. If no, skip to ORI 9.

ORI 8 Look out the window at the sky on that floor. Have your partner search for clouds that look like faces and figures. Then he or she is to tell you, for example, "There's a cloud that looks like Uncle Harry. Do you see it?" Then orient to the sky and look for that particular cloud. When you find it, your partner picks out another one. Do this for two minutes or until you feel comfortable.

ORI 9 Have your friend instruct you to orient to nearby buildings. Have him or her ask you things like: "How many floors does the middle-sized white one have? How many windows are on each floor in the black one? Look in between those two. Count five intersections down. What store is on that corner? How many people are in that office across the way—on the fifth floor, eight windows from the left?

ORI 10   Do this for three minutes or until you are quite comfortable doing it.

ORI 11   Now step back ten feet and sketch the view through the window frame.

ORI 12   Go up to the next floor as your partner touches some part of your body. If you feel uncomfortable again, have a little snack, eating very slowly and savoring each crumb. Have your partner rub your back lightly until you feel comfortable again.

ORI 13   Go over to the window once more, and this time, pick out something your partner will have to orient to: a commercial sign, three Volkswagens in a row on the street, a fat lady or gentleman walking down the sidewalk, etc. Look for unusual things. Do this for two minutes or until you feel comfortable and then go up to the next floor.

ORI 14   Repeat the same procedure as for the previous floor. If you feel uncomfortable, have your partner rub your back—or wherever else you like—and nibble on your snacks until you are comfortable. Then go back to the window and orient to the street traffic once more. Spend two minutes doing that or until you feel comfortable. Then step back ten feet and sketch the slightly different view you have through this window frame.

ORI 15   Go up to the next floor. Repeat the same procedure as on the floor below. This time, however, see if you can find a window with a different view. Walk around the floor and the halls for a few minutes. Then go to the window. Now, even if you feel anxious, take out one of your erotic magazines—or home Polaroid pictures—and study these sexual arousers. Depending on your relationship with your partner, have him or her touch you in some way that is sexual in nature. If your relationship is platonic, a plain back rub will do. Have your partner keep this contact up for two minutes, as you glance out the window and then back to your erotica—or keep this up until you feel comfortable. Then go back ten feet and sketch the view again.

Now, the rest of the program is the same as what you have already done. One flight up, look around; if you feel anxious, orient through scanning games, food, sex, touching and back rubs, all the while looking at what's happening around you and back on the ground. Do all these things until you feel comfortable again. Then go up as many flights as necessary to make you nervous again, and repeat all the OR triggers once more.

One other thing you can do to keep your anxiety low and your OR high is to pitch pennies against the window wall of the building. This may sound silly, but so is the phobic reaction of your primitive nervous system. Penny-pitching is a hand-eye coordination task and one of the best ways to arouse and maintain your orienting reflex. If you are afraid of airplanes, the best way to lose that fear is to learn to fly one—a coordination task of hand, foot and eye. If you are afraid of elevators, the best way to overcome your fear is to learn to hand-operate a manual elevator by practicing smooth, precise stops at each floor. If you are afraid of hypodermic injections, the best way to lose that fear is to learn how to give one—practicing on a banana or an orange—which is another hand-eye coordination task. Now, all this makes good sense from the perspective of our everyday experiences. Novice interns or nurses, for instance, will often pass out cold or throw up when they see their first auto accident victim in the emergency room. Three months later it's a different story, because they are practicing learned hand-eye coordination skills that make them orient in the same situation that had previously made them anxious. Then, you can routinely hear things like, "Thanks. Make mine a ham on rye . . . with lots of mustard," while they are busily saving the life of a similar accident case.

But in overcoming your fear of heights, it's

a bit difficult to learn how to "operate" a building, a mountain or a telephone pole. They don't do anything. They just sit there looking hostile and glowering at you. You could learn to wash windows while swinging from a rope on the outside of a building. That is definitely a learned coordination task. But that may not appeal to you for obvious reasons. It's more practical to perform some hand-eye coordination routine inside the building even though the routine's not related to the building itself. That's what you and your partner were doing with the sunflower seeds and waste baskets in the low building. So, pitching pennies up against the wall on each floor of a high building will give you the same orienting reflex result. And it's simpler to boot. You don't need a lot of apparatus—just a few pennies. Make a game out of it with your partner. See who can consistently come closest to the window wall, on each floor, from ten feet back, pitching the pennies just below the window. You will be orienting to the wall and to your hand-eye coordination task while, at the same time, looking out the window at what makes you so nervous. Pitch at least four rounds of pennies, if possible, on each floor you stop at.

If you are shooting for the one-hundredth floor in your building, you may not be able to work all the way up in one retraining session. After about an hour—or an hour and a half if you have a lot of physical stamina for walking up stairs—quit for the day and take a well-deserved break. Also, quit if it gets dark while you are still following the program. It's much better for your orienting reflex to work on your retraining program during the daylight hours when there are hundreds of things going on around you. Come back on a second or third session and enjoy the view from the windows at night.

nine

Retraining yourself not to fear elevators
and automobiles with tape recorders,
pennies and pushups

Now let's look at what you can do to eliminate your fear of traveling in enclosed mechanical devices that zoom up and down in a straight line. Right off, I should point out that the best way to "cure" this problem is to get some instruction and practice driving an elevator: making smooth precise stops at each floor, opening and closing the door, saying, "Watch your step," etc. See if you can find a helpful elevator operator who will teach you how to run the thing during off-hours. Maybe someone in your office or apartment building will help. Explain your predicament and tell him or her how you propose to solve it. If that solution is not possible, then use this OR retraining program.

First, let's see if you really do have an elevator phobia or if it's something similar to riding in elevators that frightens you. Many patients who say they are afraid of elevators are really claustrophobic or get uptight in small enclosed places. How can you find this out for yourself? Simple. Go into your closet at home, shut the door and see if you get very nervous. If you don't get anxious there, but you do in an elevator, you most likely have a simple, uncomplicated case of elevator phobia. On the other hand, if you get anxious in both places, you have claustrophobia and may or may not also have an elevator phobia. If you find yourself even somewhat claus-trophobic, run through the Closet Retraining Pro-gram on page 221 before you begin on elevators. It will make your work in the elevator simpler and less anxious.

In any case, the program for elevator phobia is a simple one and has eliminated this fear of riding in closed, mechanical devices in as few as twenty min-utes. As with all other retraining programs, plan to have a friend accompany you and go through all of the retraining, giving you the step-by-step orienting reflex instructions.

Do some preliminary scouting before you choose your elevator. Pick one that has little traffic on it. The first time, it's best to use an automatic elevator with only you and your partner aboard. Apartment houses in New York City and Chicago are often good for this purpose, especially those with no more than five floors. If the elevator is automatic, it will rarely be used in the evening after dinner. If your office building has an elevator, explain the situation to the building manager, tell him about this program and see if you can use the elevator after working hours. Remember to let the security guard know what you are doing beforehand or you might end up with a distaste for squad cars and desk sergeants who have heard every excuse but yours for trespassing after hours.

Even though what you feel about elevators may be only a "minor" fear, my advice is not to go off tracking the wild phobia with only one shot in your chamber. As with all the phobias, from minor ir-ritations to major fears, try to stack the odds in your favor. Bring along things you know will make you orient. Have you ever eaten a piece of good German strudel in an elevator? Have you ever looked at a full-length color centerfold of Brigitte Bardot or at Burt Reynolds' famous *Cosmopolitan* photograph in an elevator? Have you ever tried on a fantastically beautiful French designer scarf in a moving elevator while your friend holds a mirror for you? Have you ever worked out a calculus problem—if that's your thing—in an elevator? Solved a mental puzzle there? These are examples of activities that arouse your involuntary orienting reflex and maintain it while it counterconditions your learned defensive reflex.

First and most importantly, take a friend into the elevator with you. Remember just plain touching makes you orient reliably. Next, bring along some tempting food. Don't eat for about six hours before you take this food into the elevator. Also, bring along some sexually oriented reading material, either outright pornography, with or without explicit photographs, or a soft-core gothic romance, depending on which titillates you the most. Bring along a hand-held, battery-operated electronic calculator that you can use to figure out arithmetic problems while going up and down in the elevator. Another good idea is to take along a small, battery-operated cassette recorder with some of your favorite dance music on it. Have you ever danced in an elevator? Finally, bring your checkbook and bank statement to balance in transit. When you have all these aids at hand and your elevator logistics are completed, go on to the Elevator Retraining Program.

Making Yourself Less Anxious in Low Elevators

ORI 1 Go into the low elevator building after getting permission to ride the elevator as much as you need to.

ORI 2 Call for the elevator by pressing the "up" button.

ORI 3 Count off the seconds it takes for the elevator to reach you and open its doors from the time you press the "up" button.

ORI 4 Write down the time it took. TIME_____.

ORI 5 Get in the elevator.

ORI 6 Have your friend press a floor button at random.

ORI 7 When you see what floor your friend called for, lean up against the wall facing the push-button panel with both palms flat against the wall.

ORI 8 In your head, square the number of the floor button pressed (multiply it by itself, i.e., 2 × 2, 4 × 4, etc.). ANSWER_____.

ORI 9 Now, do that number of pushups (or are they called pushaways in that position?) by pushing out from the elevator wall.

ORI 10 When you are done with your pushups, wait for the elevator to stop at the floor your partner chose.

ORI 11 When the elevator stops and opens its doors, remain inside the elevator.

ORI 12 Have your friend rub your arm, back or shoulders, until the doors close by themselves.

ORI 13 If no one gets in with you, take out a bit of your favorite food and slowly eat it.

ORI 14 If the elevator does not ascend or descend to another floor at someone else's command, have your friend push another floor at random.

ORI 15 Repeat the same procedure as before while still slowly eating. Note the number of the floor button pushed, cube it in your head (multiply it by itself three times, i.e., 5 × 5 × 5 = 125) and then divide it by your age to the nearest whole number. ANSWER_____.

ORI 16 When the elevator gets to the floor chosen and opens its doors, remain aboard and put your food away.

ORI 17 If no one gets on and the elevator is not called to another floor by someone else, wait until the doors close, then skip to ORI 20.

ORI 18 If someone gets on, ride the elevator to whatever floor your fellow passenger chooses. Cube this floor number in your head and divide it by the last two digits of the year you were born. Ride to the floor chosen, with your friend placing his or her hand on your shoulder while you do your arithmetic. Then go on to the next instruction.

ORI 19 If the car is called to yet another floor by someone else, do the number of pushups corresponding to the number of each floor you pass in transit.

If the car just sits there idle with you aboard at that floor, continue on to the next instruction.

ORI 20 Until someone gets on or the car is called to another floor, take out some pennies. You and your partner are going to perform a hand-eye coordination task. Both of you are to stand back against one of the side walls. Take turns pitching pennies as close as you can to the opposite wall. To count as a valid toss, the penny must hit the opposite wall. So, you have to judge not only how accurately you have to toss your penny, but also how hard you must toss to make it bounce off the wall and still remain close. Do this for two minutes or until you are no longer nervous about the elevator standing still. Then go on to the next instruction.

ORI 21 Are you and your friend sexually interested in each other? ANSWER_____. If yes, continue on. If no, skip to ORI 29.

ORI 22 Did you bring your cassette tape recorder with some of your favorite dance music on it? ANSWER_____. If yes, turn it on and skip to ORI 26. If no, continue on.

ORI 23 Ask your partner to tell you his or her favorite tune.

ORI 24 See if you both can sing, hum or whistle it.

ORI 25 While making your own music, choose another floor, as far away from this one as possible. Push its button.

ORI 26 Now when the doors begin to close, start dancing with your partner. Do a fox trot, waltz, mambo, rhumba or jitterbug if you can. These dances all require physical touch, remember? If you don't know any of them, see if your partner can teach you. If your partner doesn't know any of them either, do a close boogie—with elbows and bottoms touching now and then—all the way to the floor you have chosen.

ORI 27 If no one gets on with you at this stop, go all the way back from whence you came and continue with your dancing. Spend at least ten minutes doing this or until someone gets on the elevator with you.

ORI 28 When another passenger gets on, repeat the procedure you followed before. This time, cube the floor chosen, divide by your mother's age, and wait until the passenger gets off. All the while, have your partner rub your shoulder.

ORI 29 Now repeat the penny-pitching routine—but with the elevator moving. Push the button for a floor, wait until the car starts moving and begin. When the car stops, repeat the procedure all over again. Do this for ten minutes.

ORI 30 Go back to ORI 6 and repeat the whole Low Elevator Program or continue until you feel completely comfortable in the elevator.

ORI 31 How do you feel now? Energetic enough to continue on with the second part of the program? ANSWER_____. If yes, go on to the high elevator program. If no, take a well-deserved break. You and your friend might want to go out for a drink or a good dinner, go see a funny movie or have a few laughs. Then begin the high elevator program within a few days.

Making Yourself Less Anxious in High Elevators

ORI 1 Make a date to meet your partner in the lobby of the building you selected.

ORI 2 Before you go to the high building, look around for a few small pebbles. Take them with you.

ORI 3 When your friend meets you in the lobby, walk up to the nearest elevator.

ORI 4 Before you get in the elevator, put a pebble in each shoe. Keep them there during the entire retraining program as a source of bodily stimulation to trigger off your OR with each bounce of the elevator and each step you take.

ORI 5 Does your building have a garage or basement floor? ANSWER_____. If yes, continue on. If no skip to ORI 8.

ORI 6 Push the "down" button. Get out in the garage with your friend and walk around briskly down there for a minute with your friend. Tell him or her how your feet feel walking on small pebbles. Then go back to the elevator.

ORI 7 Now you are going to ride the elevator back and forth between the lobby and the basement or garage five times. In between trips, get out of the elevator on the garage level and at the lobby and briskly walk around for a few minutes with your friend. Board the elevator with your friend to go to the garage or to the lobby only when the elevator has no other passengers. During each trip down and up, lean against one wall with palms pressing on it. Your partner will call out a number between one and five. He or she will then tell you to square or cube it. You then do that number of pushups away from the wall while the elevator is traveling. When you have completed five trips up and five trips down with rests in between, go on to the next instruction.

ORI 8 Now for a trip all the way to the top—or at least as far as you feel comfortable going. Get on the elevator at the lobby with your friend. You yourself push the button for the top floor.

ORI 9 As the doors start to close, shut your eyes for a moment and see if you can feel and hear when the elevator starts to move. Then open your eyes when you are certain you are traveling upward. Have your friend rub your back, arm and shoulder while you both ascend.

ORI 10 When and if you feel your anxiety rise rapidly, push the button of the nearest floor and get off. Now, if you do this because of intense anxiety, it may be that you have a fear of heights as well as elevators. It would be worth your while to interrupt your elevator retraining for a few minutes to check this out. Walk over to the nearest window and look out over the city. Do you feel anxious about being this high off the ground? ANSWER_____. If yes, go back down and plan to go through the Fear of Heights Retraining Program on page 175 before you continue with this program for elevators. When you have finished that program, come back to ORI 8 of this program and continue on. If no, continue on to the next instruction.

ORI 11 Were there a lot of passengers on the trip up with you? ANSWER_____. If no, skip to ORI 13. If yes, you may be a bit anxious about crowds, especially in tight places, so let's test this out by continuing on with the next instruction.

ORI 12 Push both the "up" and the "down" button and wait for the elevator. If there is a crowd aboard, wait until you get a relatively empty elevator going either up or down. Then board it and either travel to the top or the ground floor. Note your reaction as more people get on with you each time the elevator stops. If your anxiety gets greater with more people, then you may also have some agoraphobia, the fear of the market-place (where crowds are likely to be found). If this is the case, turn to the section on agora-phobia, page 226, after you complete this pro-gram using only relatively empty elevators. For the rest of the retraining, decide now how many people make you nervous in this elevator. If this number of people gets on, you get off. If you then breeze through the rest of this retraining, you probably have very little phobic reaction to elevators but a significant one to being crowded in. It is up to you to decide if you want to do anything about your agoraphobia. At least, you will be able to ride in elevators again provided they are uncrowded.

ORI 13 Okay, you are neither phobic about heights nor being crowded in. It seems your problem is only about elevators. Good. It's easier to work on one phobia instead of trying to countercondition several sources of anxiety at once. Call for the elevator again by pushing the "down" button.

ORI 14 When it arrives, you and your friend get aboard. Your friend is to keep an arm draped casually over your shoulder.

ORI 15 Tell your friend to gently massage your shoul-der where the hand comes in contact with it. If your friend is 5'4" and you are 6'5", this may be a problem, and your friend will have to be content with back and waist contact.

ORI 16 Before the doors close, shut your eyes. From sounds and sensations, try to guess when the elevator starts moving down. Keep your eyes closed, and when you feel the elevator stopping, tell your friend what floor you think you have stopped at. Count the seconds in your head from the time the doors close until you feel the elevator stop, and guess how many floors it has traveled. Do this for as many stops as it takes to reach the ground floor. Get out there and walk around for two minutes. Then go back to the elevators.

ORI 17 Press the "up" button.

ORI 18 Wait—if possible—until you can get on a crowded elevator. It will make more stops than an empty one.

ORI 19 Get on board with your friend still touching you. You will ride up as far as the last passenger wants to go. Follow the same procedure you used when you came down: your friend rubs your arm, shoulder, etc., and you close your eyes as soon as you get on and turn around to face the door. Try to get to the back of the elevator. Using only the sounds and sensations of the elevator, try to tell when it's moving and when it stops. Again, count the time it takes to move and tell your friend what floors you stop at without opening your eyes. At each stop, your friend will then tell you where you are. When you reach the floor where the last passenger gets off—this may be the top floor—you get off also.

ORI 20 Spend two minutes briskly walking around—if possible—and call for the elevator again by pushing the "down" button.

ORI 21 When the elevator arrives, push the button for the lowest floor.

ORI 22 Did you bring your last unbalanced bank statement with you and a hand-held electronic calculator?
ANSWER_____. If yes, continue on. If no, skip to ORI 31.

ORI 23 Do you know how to operate a calculator?
ANSWER_____. If yes, skip to ORI 25. If no, continue on.

ORI 24 Ask your friend how to use the calculator, or read the instructions. Do a simple multiplication problem: $2 \times 3 = 6$.

ORI 25 Do a simple division problem: $9 \div 2 = $_____.

ORI 26 Do a simple addition problem: $33 + 12 = $_____.

ORI 27 Do a simple subtraction problem: $56 - 13 = $_____.

ORI 28 Do a simple addition and subtraction problem: $14 + 12 + 24 - 3 - 7 + 10 = $_____.

ORI 29 Do a similar set of additions and subtractions, but but this time with decimals: $3.58 + 7.99 + 243.22 - 15.01 - 33.40 - 3.22 - 18.99 = $_____.

ORI 30 Now take out your checkbook and your bank statement, and balance them. If you reach the bottom floor before you are finished, push the button for the top floor and travel up again. Keep traveling up and down until you have balanced the checkbook and bank statement. When you have done this, continue on with the next instruction.

ORI 31 Did you bring any food along with you?
ANSWER_____. If yes continue on. If no, skip to ORI 33.

ORI 32 Get on the elevator again, go up or down, it doesn't matter which, lean against the back wall and nibble on your food. Pay attention to its taste. Note the saliva that runs into your mouth. Pay attention to how wet or dry your mouth is. If it is dry, get off on the next floor and find a water fountain. Have a few good swallows, then resume nibbling on your food and get back on the elevator. Keep paying attention to your food; its taste and how much saliva it causes to flow in your mouth. If your mouth gets dry again, get off on the next floor, find a water fountain, have a few swallows, resume nibbling and get back on the elevator. Do this until your food is consumed or your mouth salivates readily when you put food in it *while you are riding on the elevator.* Because when you salivate readily, it is likely that you will be at ease on the elevator. ORI 33 If, at the end of this program, you still have some residual anxiety about traveling in elevators, run through the entire high elevator program again a week later. But this time, make yourself walk up four flights of stairs each time the elevator stops. Then board the elevator again—your leg, back and chest muscles sending you all sorts of protests which will *make you* orient.

Automobile retraining program

Autophobia: What It Is and What It Isn't

Some of us have learned anxieties about cars and driving. Sometimes what makes us nervous is not cars and driving but something else that may be happening when we are in a car or driving it. For instance, I had a middle-aged lady referred to me for treatment of autophobia. She was no more autophobic than I was. She was divorced, had little self-confidence and a great deal of irrational anxiety about her fourteen-year-old son. Aside from his attendance at school, she virtually kept him a prisoner with her at home. She openly said that whenever he wasn't with her, she was afraid that he was going to get into trouble, get hurt, maimed, killed or seduced by some fifteen-year-old chippie in the evening hours after school. Consequently, whenever she had to drive anywhere without her son, her anxiety went sky-high. If she took a bus to visit a friend the same thing would happen.

Her psychiatrist said she had a phobia about driving. She didn't. It was her concern about her son being a potential victim that was not in touch with reality. From all the information she gave me, I concluded that the boy was only doing the routine things that most fourteen-year-old boys do. He talked and flirted with girls, played ball after school and tried to get involved with the school's social activities. Why did mom treat him as a psychological basket case? One thing became clear both to the patient and me during the six weeks we talked about her problems. As long as she continued to play the role of the self-appointed Florence Nightingale to "nurse" her "helpless" son, she would be far too busy to concern herself with other areas of her life. And these were the areas of her life where anxiety was at a peak. As far as she could tell, she felt most anxious driving away from her son. Her analysis of the problem was that she had developed an autophobia because this fear kept her near him to care for him. Curiously enough, while she was willing to look at who she was driving away from (her son), she seemed hesitant to look at who she was driving to meet. Most of the times when high anxiety struck, she was on her way to see either a lover with whom she was not too comfortable or well-meaning friends who put uncomfortable pressure on her to visit them.

I'm certain that her psychiatrist's labeling of her problem as autophobia made Freud roll over on the big couch up in the sky with an audible groan. The psychiatrist's analysis of mom's problem was twice removed from reality. The patient was anxious in her car, but her anxiety was really centered on her son. So it wouldn't do much good to treat her "autophobia" when it was "sonophobia" that she was suffering from. Right? Wrong! Her anxieties were neither related to her car nor her son. Instead, they were about *her own social life* which—if she had any— would take her away from this supposedly nincompoop offspring who desperately needed her care. Now that was a really neat dodge that kept her from looking at where she was really hurting—with other people.

Luckily, this was a mom whose time had come. She was fed up with her anxieties, both in and out of cars, her worries about her son—whom she suspected

deep down might just be a regular teenager
regular problems—and, most of all, she wa
with the depressive periods she underwent,
about by her habit of classifying herself as a lo   a
self-fulfilling label.

With my prompting and her motivation to change,
she sweated through two more months of forcing
herself to explore new things. She made new friends,
got a new lover and started new activities. No treatment was made of her "phobia." At the end of two
months of *her treating her own problem* of social
isolation, she was driving continually with no anxiety.
Needless to say, her son felt better about this new
arrangement.

The main point of this story, of course, is that
mom *thought* she had a phobia about automobiles,
but she didn't. And it was useless to try to get her
to orient while she was driving, because she didn't
have a learned anxiety about cars to eliminate. She
had anxiety about her life-style and its negative consequences for her. She did learn to orient in that
sphere with new friends, new activities and new sexual partners, and then her anxieties decreased. So, if
you get nervous in cars—or in any other situation
—first try and find out what you are anxious about.
If you are like this lady, no amount of treatment—
self, professional or otherwise—will help you eliminate a phobia you don't have.

Now, if after thoughtful consideration, you still decide you have a phobia about cars, you may then
want to think specifically about whatever it is that
makes you anxious. To find this out, it does little
good for you to ask yourself general questions on
why and *what*, such as, "Why am I afraid?" or "What
am I afraid of?" The usual, useless answers you get
back are: "I may get hurt . . . or killed . . . or embarrassed . . . or faint . . . or make a fool of myself
. . . or even show that I am afraid." It's better to ask
yourself questions about *when* and *where* you get
anxious. You are then more likely to get answers

like: "Only when driving on the expressway at high speed in heavy traffic, but not when I'm backing into my driveway at home."

Now, perhaps some of your fears are in touch with reality rather than phobic. Perhaps you aren't too sure of your driving skills in dangerous situations. Or even, if I may be so blunt, your skills are not so hot in most driving situations. If this is the case, then I strongly recommend you enroll in a driving school. Either take a beginning course to brush up on fundamentals or an advanced course to learn things like double clutching, slipping the gears, gearing down, power slides, spinning out at high speeds and reversing without coming to a stop on a two-lane highway. If you can do these things with some proficiency, however, and you still get scared on the expressway, then I would say you are phobic in that situation.

If you are a skilled driver *and know it* and you have anxiety about driving, it would be worth your while to invest some time in eliminating your phobia. One way would be to get the help of a professional behavior therapist who will *get in the car with you* and use his skills and therapy experience in planning a behavioral program for you. If that option is not practical, then you might, with the help of a friend, try the general orienting reflex program outlined in this section. It is not broken down specifically into detailed instructions, because no program can foresee what is going to happen while you are moving along in a car. Also, it would be a bit difficult for you to drive and read at the same time. So the program is broken into five general steps: driving on side streets; driving on main boulevards with light traffic; driving on main boulevards with heavy traffic; driving on expressways with light traffic; and driving on expressways with heavy traffic.

In preparing to use this program, it would first be a good idea to take your friend along for a trial run and see where your anxiety strikes on the road. Drive along the side streets first. See what your SUDs level is there.* Then find a main street with little traffic. Then find a main thoroughfare where the traffic is heavy. Next, find an expressway with light, and then heavy traffic. As you drive along, tell your friend what it is *about the situation* that makes you nervous. For example, one former patient said that he didn't realize until he tried this that he only got really nervous on side streets where kids were playing. Several years ago, he had almost run over a small boy who had rushed out in front of his car after a ball. The whole experience had shaken him up. As it turned out, he only needed a few sessions of orienting while driving in the back streets where children were likely to cause problems for his anxiety to disappear. No driving on freeways or in heavy traffic was necessary. So test out your anxiety with a friend, and see if there are any special situations that are the cause of the anxiety and that *are not related to driving a car in general.*

One result of your test drive that may surprise you is that you probably won't feel as anxious as you usually do. That's the result of going out in the phobic situation with an *instructed task.*

Now, some general preparation for the program. First, don't eat for at least six hours before the session. Then you can bring some food along with you and eat it while driving to make you orient. Your favorite foods are best, but any foods that satisfy your hunger will do the trick. Second, wear uncomfortable clothes: a girdle, a tight bra, a tight belt, tight pants, even shoes with pebbles in them. These things all cause bodily stimuli—pressure, pinches, pokes, jabs, irritations, etc.—that your involuntary nervous system will orient to. If you can't find a girdle before you leave home, roll up the edges of your undershorts or panties into three ropes: one at the waist and two at the legs. Then pull them up as high as

---

*See ORI 4, Chapter 7.

they will go, tucking them in between your buttocks. With this arrangement, your peripheral (bodily) nervous system will signal both your cortex and your primitive nervous system for quite a while that something new and unusual is going on down there. If you are in good health but out of shape, it would help to jog in place for about ten minutes before you leave home to work on the program. If you are in good shape, do some exercises that you haven't done in a while. These will make your muscles sore. Your muscles will constantly protest any movement you make while driving, increasing the probability that your orienting reflex will be triggered off.

Take along a battery-operated cassette tape recorder. Spend about an hour a few days earlier recording the following sequence of clicks or finger snaps on it, spacing each group of clicks about thirty seconds apart: 3–6–5–7–2–2–4–6–3–7–5–8–2–9–2–4– 4–3–6–7–4–3–7–8–2–6–7–8–9–4–6–9–9–6–3–4–5–3–7– 2–4–6–3–2–4–8–5–9–3–4–7–9–3–5–2–7–3–6–4–8–9–5– 2–5–7–8–9–4–3–6–5–2–5–6–7–5–4–7–3–8–9–6–4–6–8– 2–4–2–8–4–7–3–2–6–8–4–3–6–7–6– You can do this simply by tapping your fingers lightly on the microphone the required number of times for each grouping of signals. Start off with thirty seconds of silence, then three distinct clicks or finger snaps; thirty seconds of silence, then six clicks; thirty seconds of silence then five clicks, and so on. You don't have to be absolutely accurate in your timing of the thirty seconds. Anywhere between twenty-five and thirty-five seconds will do. As a matter of fact, it's a good idea to toss in a few fifteen-second spaces between groups of clicks. Also, if you make a mistake in the middle of recording, you don't have to start all over again. If you tap out the wrong number of clicks or record an occasional noise, like a cough or someone flushing the john, it's no big deal. The tape program will work just as well— maybe even better spiced up with a bit of natural irregularity.

This tape recording is an orienting reflex programming device that you will listen to on the road. You will perform various tasks depending on what number of clicks you hear. So, when you use it in the program, don't always start at the beginning. Hit the fast-forward button for a few seconds before you play it so the tape starts in a different place each time. Otherwise, by the middle of the training program, you will have the first ten numbers or so committed to memory and you will no longer orient to them.

If you get uptight on the freeway, it's best to start your counter-conditioning on the side streets where you are not likely to feel much anxiety. Then go onto the main streets, crowded boulevards and finally, after those experiences, onto the freeway to orient there. You could go straight onto the freeway and work there, but your chances of success would be lower. Also, if you complete a low-anxiety session on the side streets and take the freeway back home, without having first worked up to it, you will probably wipe out the therapeutic effect of that first low-anxiety session. Remember, this type of therapy doesn't require heroism, just good odds and percentages. The motto of OR retraining is: "All I want is an unfair advantage."

Here's one more precaution before you use this program. It requires that you orient to things other than the conditions of the road ahead of you when driving. It is unnecessary for me to say that accidents can and do happen when driving a car—*but I will say it anyway*. So if you are a person who, for example, cannot stand to play the radio while driving because it distracts you from attending to the road ahead, this retraining program is not for you. Instead, I urge that you see a behavior therapist about your problem.

If you decide to use this program, remember that the instructions are general ones. You follow them if it is safe to do so. You can always bend an instruction and use the third off-ramp instead of the second one for reasons of driving convenience and safety. The program will work just as well if you interpret it casually instead of strictly. *Do nothing that is unsafe or a real hassle, no matter what you think the instruction tells you to do.* As a matter of fact, that might be a good general rule for driving after you rid yourself of your autophobia.

Making Yourself Less Anxious Driving on Side Streets

Remember, this is a general program. You and your partner will have to fill in the details to make it work in the different driving situations you encounter. Have your friend drive to a side street in the area selected. Check your clothes for maximum stimulation. Check to see that you haven't forgotten to bring some food along. If you have, stop in a coffee shop along the way and order a sandwich and a soft drink to eat in the car. Make sure you have your recorded series of finger snaps. Turn on your tape recorder and set its volume to a comfortable, distinct level. Put it on the dashboard in front of the steering wheel (if possible). That way, you won't keep automatically turning your head to look at the recorder every thirty seconds. Now, you begin to drive along the side street you are on. *All* the time you are driving, pay attention to what your friend is doing. He or she is to continually keep a hand on your shoulder, gently squeezing and releasing it. Also pay attention to your recorded finger snap clicks. Count each number of clicks as it comes on and keep it in your mind while waiting for the next one. If you come to an intersection and the number in mind is four or below and even, turn right (if possible). If the number in mind is six or above and even, turn left (if possible). If the number is odd, continue on ahead (if possible). If you make a mistake in counting or in directions, your partner will correct you after you

are through the intersection. Keep your speed down
to 15 mph or less. As you are counting clicks, voluntarily orient toward the direction you are traveling.
Keep up a running commentary with your partner
as you go along. "There are one, two, three . . .
eleven cars parked on the street ahead. Two cars are
coming toward us on this street. I will have to slow
down here to make a left turn. . . ." Do this for
fifteen minutes, head back where you came from if
you are not going in that general direction already.
Do exactly the same things as before, but this time
take your food out and nibble on it as you drive
along. Tell your partner what it tastes like. Sip some
liquid in between nibbles. When you have been driving around for a half-hour, pull over to the side, turn
off the recorder and let your partner drive you home.

Making Yourself Less Anxious Driving on
Uncrowded Main Boulevards

Pick your boulevard and time beforehand so you
know the road will be relatively empty of traffic
when you drive on it. Set everything up before as you
did in the side street program: food, clothes, physical exercises, tape recorder and partner. Turn on the
tape recorder and pay attention to the finger snaps.
Start out from the side street and enter the main
boulevard heading north, if it runs north–south, or
west, if it runs east–west. With the number of clicks
you have just counted in mind, turn off the boulevard within three blocks to the left (if possible) if
the number is six or above and even. Turn off to the
right (if possible) if the number is four or below and
even. Keep going straight ahead (if possible) if the
number is odd. After you make the turn and are back
on a side street, the next finger-snap number you
count determines if you get back on the boulevard
heading in the same direction or the opposite one. If
it is even, go opposite. If it is odd, go the same way as

before. Travel in any direction you wish to get back on the boulevard. Do this for fifteen minutes, then turn around and head in the opposite direction and repeat the same procedure. For the next fifteen minutes, nibble on your food. When those fifteen minutes are up, pull over to the side and have your partner drive you home.

Making Yourself Less Anxious Driving on Crowded Main Boulevards

Time your session so the boulevard will have moderate-to-heavy traffic on it. The program in this section is identical to the two previous ones except you will not use the tape recording for the first fifteen minutes.

Drive off the side street onto the main boulevard in either direction you choose. Take the easier one, which is usually to the right. Then have your partner pick out a particular automobile—any one will do. You are to figure out which one he has chosen. He will tell you the number of people in it, or its color scheme, or its make, and you are to scan for it in front of you or through the rearview mirrors. When you think you've located it, point it out to your partner. Then *you* pick an automobile and have your partner locate it.

When you have done this, make a left-hand turn (if possible) at the next intersection or the one beyond it, double back around the block and get in the traffic flow heading in the opposite direction. Repeat the car-orienting game again. Then make another left-hand turn at the next or the following intersection (if possible), double back and head in the opposite direction. Do this for fifteen minutes. Then get off the boulevard, double back and again head in the opposite direction. Now keep traveling in that direction for seven minutes (if possible). During this time you will drive in the slow lane and nibble on your food. After seven minutes, turn off the main boulevard, double back again and head in the opposite direction. Regain your position in the slow lane and keep nibbling on your food. During this last fifteen-minute period, turn on the tape recorder and listen for the finger snaps again. Every thirty seconds, when you hear the group of clicks, shift your body slightly, or hunch your shoulders, or stretch your left leg or rotate your head slightly in a circular motion. At the same time, count the clicks you hear. If the number is even, tell your friend what sensations you are feeling from your uncomfortable clothes. If the number is odd, tell your friend what sensations you are feeling from your sore muscles. At the end of the fifteen minutes, pull onto a side street and let your friend drive you home.

Making Yourself Less Anxious Driving on Uncrowded Expressways

Get on the highway, expressway, turnpike or freeway at a time when it is relatively empty of traffic. All the preparations for this program are identical to the ones preceding it: clothes, food, tape recorder, exercise, etc. Have your friend drive you to a side street near the entrance ramp you have picked beforehand. Go in either direction you choose. When you're on the expressway, turn on the tape recorder. Begin listening for and counting clicks. After you pass the next exit ramp, listen for the next two groups of clicks. Multiply the numbers by each other and tell your partner the product. If the product of both clicks is forty-three or greater, stay on the expressway and repeat the whole procedure again after you pass the next exit ramp. If the product is forty-two or less, get off using the next exit ramp (if safe). Drive to the closest entrance ramp going in the opposite direction, get on the expressway again and repeat the whole procedure. Do this counting–multiplying game for fifteen minutes.

During the second fifteen-minute period, drive for seven minutes in one direction. When you have seven minutes left in your half-hour session, get off the expressway and get on again, this time traveling in the opposite direction. During this last fifteen minutes, take out your food treat and slowly nibble on it. Make it last the whole time you are driving on the expressway. Listen again for the finger-snap clicks coming from your recorder. Each time you start counting, shift your body, stretch, move around slightly, etc. If the count is odd, describe the sensations coming from your sore muscles to your friend. If the count is even, describe the sensations coming from your uncomfortable clothing. When the fifteen minutes are up, drive off at the nearest exit ramp, pull up at a side street and let your friend drive you home.

Making Yourself Less Anxious Driving on Crowded Expressways

As in the previous program on the expressway, pick your time and place: preferably the same stretch of the road, only this time with heavy traffic on it. All the preparations are the same as before. Because of the crowded conditions on the road, plan on working a full hour on the expressway instead of thirty minutes. When you get onto the expressway, your job will be to change lanes depending on what the taped program tells you. Turn the tape recorder on and begin orienting to the clicks. Start counting clicks as soon as you pass the next exit ramp. Again, count in groups of two sequences. Subtract the smaller of the two counts from the larger. If the remainder is two or less, shift one lane to the right as soon as it is safe to do so. If the remainder is three or four, stay in the lane you are now driving in (if possible). If the remainder is five or greater, shift one lane to the left as soon as it is safe to do so. After you have made your lane change (or stayed where you are), begin your count again with the next two sequences of clicks. Do this for fifteen minutes, then get off the expressway, drive to the nearest exit ramp and head back in the direction you came from.

Repeat the same procedure you followed in the first fifteen minutes, but this time do it for money. Each time the tape program instructs you to shift to the right, your partner must pay you a nickel, dime or quarter, depending on how wealthy you both are. On the other hand, for every time you shift left, you pay your partner a similar sum. Have your friend keep tab of the wins and losses on one of the blank pages at the back of this book. Do this for fifteen minutes, then get off at the next exit ramp, change directions and get back on the expressway again.

During the next fifteen minutes, break out your food and begin nibbling on it, but only when the count on the tape program is even. When it is odd, your partner gets to nibble. Drive with the traffic on the expressway, neither fast nor slow. At the same time, both of you keep your eyes peeled for cops. The first to see one and to call "copper" gets paid a dollar in cash by the other. At the end of the third fifteen-minute section, double back on the expressway in the opposite direction.

During the final fifteen minutes, orient to the cars ahead of you. Comment to your friend on any apparent driving skill or lack of it in your fellow commuters. Rewind your tape recorder so that it has about half of the tape to go. Begin counting the number of sequences, not the number of clicks in each sequence. When you have counted thirty sequences, get off on the next exit ramp and drive home.

ten

Retraining yourself not to fear animals
by reading, fantasizing
and breathing hard

Fears of animals such as dogs, cats, horses, sharks, snakes, spiders and insects are considered minor phobias since most of the time we can happily lead our everyday lives without coming into contact with any of these stimuli if we choose. For many people with these minor phobias there comes a time, however, when the phobic object cannot be effectively avoided. Your nextdoor neighbor buys a Great Dane (or perhaps a poodle), and there it is with its head resting on the top of your fence staring at you each morning. Or you want to take that vacation trip to the mountains of California or Arizona, and your friend laughingly tells you about the snakes he missed stepping on last year during the same trip. Or you have put off that trip to Hawaii for six summers because you get light-headed just thinking about "jaws" lying in wait for you personally off the beach in Maui.

Why do many of us have minor fears like these that only rarely restrict our activities? The simplest assumption is a behavioral one: We had some bad experience(s) in the past with animals or situations, either in a real or very active imaginary way. For instance, I was always uneasy about sharks when I was diving off the California coast. And there was no valid reason for me to be afraid. Shark attacks there, especially on scuba divers, are so rare that they can practically be discounted. Even if I had met a shark underwater, it was not likely to attack. Sharks are notorious cowards and easily frightened off—or so I was told by my more experienced diving companions, all of whom were either active members of naval underwater demolition teams or fellow scientists trained by the UDT branch of the Navy. Still, I often felt uneasy, especially when it was my turn to watch over the others as they fished the incredibly rich deep-water abalone and lobster spots that lined the outer reef off La Jolla. If there were no danger, I used to ask, then how come I'm twenty feet above you? And what am I looking for? Just routine safety precautions, they assured me. It's done on every dive —safety first and all that.

I don't even know why I was nervous. At that time, I had never seen a large shark except in the movies.

If I had complained about this anxiety to an old-time Freudian analytical type, I surely would have been told something like: "Herr Doctor Smith. You are suffering from an unresolved Oedipal complex with fears of castration. The abalone is your mother's vagina you still covet, and the shark is your father. You are afraid the shark will bite off your dong. In-depth analysis is indicated."

Fear of Animals: Part Reality, Mostly Ignorance

Asking the question—*Why am I nervous about certain animals?*—is much less productive than asking: *How do I go about getting rid of my nervousness?* In reality, the "why" of it all may simply be—as it was with my nervousness about sharks—that unfamiliarity with the feared animal causes negative imaginings and emotions to mushroom.

Let's look at snake phobia, for example. Most of the people who say they are afraid of snakes are women. Yes, this is true, even though you knew a girl in college who kept a pet boa constrictor under her bed. Why do more women than men fear, or say they fear, snakes? The fear of snakes is not instinctual. We are not born with it. Children will readily play with snakes and show no fear of them. Most of the fear of snakes appears after puberty. There are several theories on why this is so. The Freudian explanation is obvious. The snake represents the phallus, and females are supposed to be frightened of it. On the other hand, classical analytic theory makes a big point of supposed "penis envy" existing in the psyche of women. So you would think that instead of avoiding snakes, women would collect them to satisfy this desire to have a penis. So much for the Freudian interpretation.

Another theory on why women reportedly fear snakes is that young girls learn social ways of behaving as girls. Part of this feminine life-style is to act as if they were repulsed by earthy things such as spiders, snakes and sex. This theory claims that these fears are not real fears but only conforming behavior.

A variation of this same theory claims that all of us are afraid of snakes, but only women are allowed to express it. In other words men are just as fearful as women, but they don't show it. In effect, this theory says that if you behave as if you were afraid, you will be phobic. And if you don't show—or won't allow yourself to show—fear, you will not be phobic. This theory isn't much help either. I haven't met a patient yet who was helped by me or anyone else telling them: "Don't be afraid and you won't be phobic."

A third theory may be of more help. This theory states that most men are not as afraid of snakes as most women, because men are rewarded throughout their lives for taking action; in other words, they orient to the snake as a momentary problem for which they will find a solution, not as a snake per se. If you put a rattlesnake in a man's front yard and told him to get rid of it, chances are he would have a pretty good idea on how to go about it from past experience in working with his hands. Just for fun, I asked the people in my various therapy groups how they would deal with this hypothetical snake. With few exceptions, the women gave answers like: I would call my husband, father, boyfriend, neighbor, the police, the pound, etc. On the other hand, the men came up with direct solutions, such as doing it in with a hoe, shovel, rake, a two-by-four, etc., driving over it with the car, or chasing it away with the water hose turned on full blast. One aerospace engineer came up with an original solution. He said the best way was to squirt a liquid carbon-dioxide fire extinguisher on it and freeze it solid. Then you could walk up, tap it on the head with a hammer and watch it shatter like glass.

It makes sense, therefore, that one way to reduce your anxiety about phobic things is to actively learn more about the thing that makes you anxious. Now, I'm not suggesting that you undergo a male task-oriented retraining program in which you learn the best ways to dispose of snakes—although that wouldn't hurt. I am suggesting that you study the phobic animal—its habits and habitat, what different types look like, its genetic history, etc.—from both books and observation of the real thing in the pound or the zoo.

I did not deal very effectively with my fear of sharks. In fact, I retreated. I stayed away from the ocean for close to ten years. I always told myself it was only because of the pressures of graduate school, research, work, clinical training, and so on. But deep down inside, I always felt wistful when I saw a boat-load of scuba divers or fishermen cruising off to Catalina, Anacapa or Baja. To this day, I'm not sure what caused my ocean activities to taper off. Per-haps it was a combination of nervousness about sharks and the middle-class pressures to succeed. And I still don't know, because both of these possible causes of my retreat from the ocean changed about the same time. I lost my nervousness about sharks in the same year my clinical internship finished. Since then, my old passion for the Pacific Ocean and fishing has reasserted itself to the point of incurring the displeasure of my wife whenever it is mentioned.

Deep Breathing: Another Trigger of the OR

What rid me of my nervousness about sharks? A year of in-depth analysis? No . . . about three minutes of inhalation therapy when I was on the staff of the Center for Behavior Therapy in Beverly Hills. Inhalation therapy is another name for artificially induced hypoventilation, which fools the body into thinking it has just run up and down a flight of stairs without breathing. Now don't confuse *hypo*ventilation (*under*breathing or blood acidosis) with *hyper*ventilation (*over*breathing or blood alkalosis). The first results in too much carbon dioxide in the blood stream, a condition that occurs when we exercise or when we hold our breath for as long as possible. The second, hyperventilation, is caused in some people by anxious feelings which trigger off a preparatory flight response. The person then simply breathes too much. But the person does not take to his or her heels to burn up energy and set things right physiologically. Instead, he or she just sits there as if nothing is happening and continues with heavy breathing. This results in a lowered carbon-dioxide level in the blood stream and consequent dizziness. The most common and effective clinical method used to reduce hyperventilation is to place a paper bag over your head. This increases the amount of carbon dioxide taken back into the lungs with each breath until the required balance of carbon dioxide in the blood stream is achieved.

Artificially induced hypoventilation makes clever

use of our adaptation reflex that eliminates excess amounts of carbon dioxide from our body. Carbon dioxide is the by-product of oxygen and blood sugar (a carbon compound) which combines in our body to produce the energy that we need. When we do heavy physical labor or run up and down stairs, even for a short period, we start to breathe heavily because our primitive brain tells the rest of our nervous system there is too much carbon dioxide in our lungs and blood stream. So we automatically breathe quickly and heavily to take in more oxygen and expel more carbon dioxide. This rapid-breathing cycle can be artificially induced within a second or two by breathing a special mixture of air that has a higher than normal concentration of carbon dioxide. The percentage of carbon dioxide added is just above the amount that will trigger off the body's automatic hypoventilation response.

Now, going through inhalation therapy—even as a teaching lark—is an experience. After two breaths of the special mixture, I thought I was having a heart attack. My breathing was not my own. I huffed and puffed for about thirty seconds, and then my breathing went back to normal on its own accord. I can definitely tell you that I was not relaxed. *I was exhausted!*—both in the muscular and the respiratory spheres. It scared the hell out of me! My body and limbs felt waves of tingling sensations rise up and subside for at least two minutes after the inhalation of the gas. It was during this time that my teacher and colleague, Dr. Zev Wanderer, asked me what things had made me nervous in the past. I told him sharks, and he said think of yourself swimming and a shark coming up close to you. In all truth, I could not conceive of anything frightening me while in that brief tingly state. I thought of a shark coming up and circling me in the water, and without forcing my mind to work, I saw my hand reach out and touch the shark's nose. To my mind's eye it was soft and fuzzy, like that of a gentle moo cow. That was the end of my nervousness about sharks. Since then, I have been close to sharks often, and no involuntary shudders have raced down my spine, nor have I experienced any nervousness or anxiety. And I have not yet had a single impulse to touch a shark's nose to see if it's soft and fuzzy!

This incident, using artificially induced hypoventilation to reduce a minor fear, may be connected to the orienting reflex. We do know that deep breathing —the spasms at the start of hypoventilation—is tied into the orienting reflex. Deep breathing triggers off the OR quite reliably, while regular breathing does not. We have seen this happen thousands of times in the psychophysiology laboratory.

Using deep breathing and deliberate muscular movements to trigger off your orienting reflex can be done in private, where you won't worry about looking silly to others and thus compounding your anxiety. With minor animal phobias, much of the work can be done in private, because you will have to use substitutes for the real phobic situation. These creatures—sharks, snakes, spiders—are not readily accessible to most of us. You will have to substitute pictures for them, reading material and your own imagination, etc. It makes little difference what specific object or act frightens you. The procedure for reducing your fear is the same. Break up your program into two parts. First, study the source of your probia at the library or at home. Then go to where the phobic object is found: dog pounds, kennels, riding academies, zoos, natural history museums, aquariums, the ocean.

Making Yourself Less Anxious About the Animal You Fear

The animal phobia program is quite simple and is outlined in the following steps.

1. Take your SUDs level* by imagining yourself opening a book on the animal that makes you anxious. On the first page you see a full-color illustration of the animal. If this gets you so nervous that you think you will faint, ask a friend to pick up a couple of illustrated books for you on this animal at the library. If you find that you are relatively calm thinking about it, pick up the books yourself. Use books that give some information about the animal as well as those that only have illustrations or photographs.

2. When you have the books, plan on spending at least an hour or two every day (you may need much less) for a week to study them. Start reading from page one and make notes as you go along. Copy each illustration or photograph of the animal on a small sketch pad in pencil. If you find your freehand sketching is poor, keep at it and try to improve as you go along.

3. To assure yourself that your Animal Retraining Program is working for you, go through the entire book and give yourself a SUDs level on each picture of that animal—before you begin reading and sketching the phobic animal. Then, after finishing your sketch and reading the accompanying information pages, rate that illustration again for SUDs. Do this as you proceed through the entire book. When you are finished, go back to the beginning and rate all the pictures once more to see how much lower the SUDs level is this time—after having learned to orient to them.

4. If you find yourself getting highly anxious or panicky just looking at pictures, sketching them and reading about the animal, do any of a number of things that will also make you orient. Keep a salty or acidic snack handy like oranges, plums, tart apples, grapes, salted nuts or meat, etc. When you find your anxiety going up, place some food in your mouth and begin to eat it, but also pay attention to how the food tastes as you look at the phobic object. If you find your mouth dry, reach for a glass of water or soda that you should keep near by.

---

*See Chapter 7, page 102.

5. If you find your anxiety still going up, place the illustration of the animal on the floor in front of you and do a variety of physical exercises while still looking at it: pushups, situps, bendovers, etc. Do this for at least two minutes and you will find that you will also be taking deep breaths automatically in the presence of your phobic object. You can use deep breathing alone to force your nervous system to orient, but if you do this without exercising you may find you're hyperventilating—breathing too much—and consequently getting dizzy. A simple way to eliminate hyperventilation is to hypoventilate voluntarily. In other words hold your breath until you feel an involuntary "choking" sensation in your upper throat. This will take from between 15 to 30 seconds. When you feel that uncomfortable protest from your primitive nervous system, wait 5 seconds longer and begin to breathe again. You will find these breaths are deep involuntary ones resulting from your body's reflex to expel excess carbon dioxide from your bloodstream. By hypoventilating this way when you get phobicly anxious you will orient and lower your anxiety.

If you have never paid attention to what sensations you feel when you hold your breath, limit your breath-holding experimentation to approximately thirty seconds at the most. Physiology performance laboratories have studied voluntary hypoventilation and found a surprising result. Athletes swimming underwater can hold their breath for just over two minutes before the involuntary reflex to expel carbon dioxide from the blood stream ceases. Then the swimmers can hold their breath indefinitely, but they soon pass out—still holding their breath—and sink slowly to the bottom as they vainly try to swim through the wall of the pool. As with everything else in life, let your common sense be your guide. If you have any respiratory tract problems like emphysema, consult your physician and see if he or she has any recommendations for helping you to use these active methods in reducing your phobic anxieties.

6. In the second step of your "library study," go

through the set of pictures of the phobic animal you have available. For each picture make up a story about it and you. Jot down the bare outlines of your imaginative tale on the back of each sketch you have drawn from the illustration. The story will increase your orienting to the phobic animal if you include three things in its plot: (1) the location of the animal—Borneo, the Cincinatti zoo, your back-yard, (2) how you came to be involved with the animal—by chance, job, involvement with other people, curiosity, etc. and (3) how you instruct other people on the characteristics of the animal— its place in the ecological food chain, its benefits to the animal world and mankind, its dangerous quali-ties, its imaginary attributes, etc. In making up your story, use your creativity fully, with you being the central character who is also a bit of a hero or heroine. Incorporate all the knowledge you have acquired from your library study. Don't write down a com-plete novel on the back of your sketch page, just a brief outline sequence as you think your story out.

Now after the fifth or sixth story, you may be say-ing to yourself: "My God! This is getting boring and dull. I keep telling the same story over and over again." And when you say that to yourself, think back to your initial reaction to the first picture in your library book and compare your feelings of anxiety then to your present feelings of boredom with the whole subject. When that happens, you are ready for the second half of the Animal Retrain-ing Program: working with live animals.

7. Locate where your phobic animal can be found in your area. It may be as simple as taking a trip to the dog pound or a kennel or to a nearby farm with horses or a riding academy in the city park. Some animals, however, might be a bit difficult to find. Sharks are hard to locate in Midwestern America and Central Europe. You might have to wait until a movie about them comes to town or a lecture on them is scheduled at your local museum of natural history. Spiders are also difficult to work with logistically unless you live in the American South-west or Western Mexico. Also, there seems to be

no standard on how you "should" behave toward these and other insects. What is a nonphobic response to the spider? I would really be tempted to ask, "Why?" if you told me that you wanted to feel no anxiety when a spider walks up your bare arm. This feat has been used by some researchers as a dramatic demonstration that their antiphobic training works, but frankly, who needs it? I think you are not phobic if you can zap them with a rolled up newspaper or a squirt of insecticide, and then calmly go about your daily business. You do have territorial rights like the other animals, no matter what the effete Eastern literary establishment says!

8. When you have located your kennel, stable, zoo, aquarium, etc., do a quick reconnaisance of the place. Ask an attendant how many different breeds, variations and subspecies of your phobic animal can be found there. Sketch the pen or cage floor plan from a window or door before going in, if possible. Then again use your imagination and make up a story about each of the subspecies or breeds available for you to view. After you sense that feeling of boredom about your stories, go into the viewing area. Proceed cage by cage and sketch the occupants. Don't worry if your sketches look like stick figures drawn by a falling down, drunk Piccaso. Fit in as many details as you can from the particular animal on your sketch. After you have sketched the animals, you might want to ask the attendant if you can pet them, particularly if they are dogs or horses. Explain your problem to the attendant and see if she or he will show you a gentle animal you can touch.

9. During your field trip, remember to bring along your orienting aids such as tasty foods, etc. Also, remember to use deep breathing as you have before when your anxiety rises in the presence of the real thing.

eleven

Overcoming your fear of four walls and fun city with sex, walking sticks and sore muscles

Feeling trapped by four small walls and then feeling the surges of panic rising in you is silly. But then so are many of the other scary feelings we picked up somewhere along the way and continue to incubate in our minds and memories.

I still remember the time my younger brother, Phil, rolled a ball underneath the wooden steps in front of our house and then proceeded to get his head stuck between the steps and the ground when he reached in to retrieve it. He was terrified. I got him to calm down, and then I helped him get out by working backward the same way he had wormed his way underneath. I then showed him my superiority in solving problems by doing the same damned stupid thing when I tried to retrieve the ball. Phil called our neighbor and he freed me with a crowbar. I remember the panic that surged up inside me when I was trapped under the porch. Also, it didn't make me feel any better when dad came home and asked, "What happened to the porch step?"

Although I haven't the slightest bit of learned claustrophobia from that incident, every so often I think back upon it and shudder. Both my feeling of panic at the time and the embarrassment I felt after being freed are typical reactions reported by many phobic patients. Many of them say that part of their anxiety is over what may happen if they enter the feared situation again. *I will show my fear. Maybe my hands will begin to shake uncontrollably. Or my face will get chalk white. If I panic I feel like I'm going to die . . . or have a heart attack. And I will look so stupid behaving this way in front of others.* These reports don't adequately tell of the panic in the phobic situation—the frightening sensations of a pounding heart, lungs that can barely get enough air, a sick stomach, jellied knees, shaking hands, dizziness and fainting. Some of these patients report that it's not really the things in the phobic situation that make them uncomfortable, but their own reaction to it. They are afraid of fear itself; afraid of panicking and having their mind shut off with no one there to help them.

What's Claustrophobic and What's Not

Let's look in this chapter at two different situations in which people experience panic: closed-in places and wide-open spaces. Some people seek help because they feel uncomfortable going into small, enclosed rooms. This problem may be claustrophobia or it may not. In some cases, such anxieties are caused by something about the room besides its closeness. For instance, I saw a dental technician who complained of claustrophobia in the clinic darkroom but who never felt anxious in her small underground wine cellar. She was not claustrophobic. As it turned out, she was uncomfortable—but not panicky—about processing the dental X-ray negatives. She felt unsure of her skill in developing them. Her anxiety had nothing to do with small enclosed rooms but only with what she was doing in one of them, the darkroom. The "cure"? She took an advanced course in photography, consulted the X-ray manual and thoroughly questioned other X-ray technicians. Then she lost her "claustrophobia."

If you think you are claustrophobic, first, before

you do anything about it, see if there is something in particular about what you do in enclosed places that makes you anxious. As in the case of the dental technician, it does little good for you to work on your fear of being enclosed if what you really fear is something else entirely. If you are claustrophobic, you will get very anxious when you go into a closet at home and the door is locked from the outside. If you don't get anxious under those conditions, it's likely you are not claustrophobic, so you want then to look elsewhere for the source of your anxiety. If you do get anxious in the closet, the "cure" is to orient while you are in there. The following short program is designed to get you to orient while closeted away, so that you can break this learned anxiety habit.

Making Yourself Less Anxious About Close Places

ORI 1 Find a small closet in your home. Empty it of clothes, suitcases, toys, etc., for the time being.

ORI 2 Enlist the help of a sympathetic friend to be your "jailer" and/or helper.

ORI 3 Spend a little time collecting retraining aids before you begin: a little hard-core porn, with or without pictures, or soft-core, paperback gothic romance —whatever turns you on sexually. Get in some of your favorite food snacks and put them in the fridge with a note, "Hands off. For retraining only!" If you have a hobby or a burning interest in something, get some material on that hobby or interest: either reading material, a cassette recording or the real thing. If you are a woman, find one of your old girdles—if you ever wore one—and one of your old, tight, uncomfortable bras. If you are a man, dig around and get that tight pair of shoes you really hate. A pair of tight, uncomfortable pants that cuts into you when you sit down is also fine.

ORI 4 Don't eat anything, if possible, for six to eight hours before you begin your session.

ORI 5 When you are ready to begin, move a small table near the closet and place on it your OR aids: food, sexy reading, hobbies, tight clothes, etc.

ORI 6 Put a small, upright chair—the metal, wood or cane type—inside the closet. Don't make it comfortable by putting a cushion on it.

ORI 7 Go into the closet and sit with the door open. Strip nude, then reach out and get your uncomfortable clothes. Put them on there in the closet. If you are modest, decide which makes you more anxious: dressing in a closet with the door open or the door closed. Close or open it accordingly.

ORI 8 After you have dressed uncomfortably—and make sure it feels uncomfortable—reach out for the sexually stimulating material. Pick something that you know already has really made your breathing change, your genitals active and your pupils dilate. Sit in there for five minutes going over the most explicit passages you can find. Then close the door halfway. Reach out and get one of your food goodies. Nibble on it while you continue to read the sexy material for another five minutes. Close the door fully after you get another food goodie. Sit in there for a half hour with the door closed, reading about lurid sex and nibbling on your food.

ORI 9 Take your aids outside, sit back down inside and close the door. Turn off the light and sit there for five minutes. Count the seconds off by saying one chimpanzee, two chimpanzee, three chimpanzee, etc., until you reach 300 chimpanzee. Are you anxious? ANSWER_____. If no, skip to ORI 11. If yes, you may be either still a bit claustrophobic or afraid of the dark. In either case, run through the program again using food, sexual material and hobby or interest material. This time, turn off the light first and then close the door in six steps, each after a five-minute orienting period.

ORI 10 Now with the door fully closed and the light off, count up to 300 chimpanzees. Are you still a bit anxious? ANSWER_____. If no, go on to OR 11. If yes, repeat the last five-minute period with the door just open a crack. Sit with your back to the crack so you can read your material and nibble on your food. Then check your SUDs level with the door closed. Repeat this step as often as you need to eliminate this last bit of nervousness.

ORI 11 Ask your friend to lock you in the closet with the lights on, walk out of the house and come back in five minutes to release you. Before he or she does this, take your food, sexual material and hobby-interest material into the closet with you. Sit there doing three things: counting 300 chimps, reading your sexual material or working on your hobby, and nibbling on your food.

ORI 12 When your friend comes back, step out and chat about a few things, then have your friend lock you in for a fifteen-minute period. Orient to sex, hobbies, food and count 900 chimpanzees.

ORI 13 When your friend comes back, step out and walk around to stretch before being locked up again for a half hour. Repeat all the orienting procedures during this period. By now, your tight clothes must be killing you. Orient to all the bodily pinches, jabs and twists that your clothes give you.

ORI 14 When you come out, wait one day and then go back in the closet—close the door and paint it the color of your choice.

ORI 15 On the third day, sit in your freshly painted closet and read the newspaper for fifteen minutes.

This orienting reflex program was originally developed by my colleague, Dr. Zev Wanderer, at the Center for Behavior Therapy in Beverly Hills. Only Zev made things much simpler. The patient was willingly locked in a closet in the clinic. He or she sat down for one hour on a canvas chair and was instructed to search through the various three hundred hard- and soft-core porno books that were in there to find one that turned him or her on. This method has been very successful with patients willing to try it. It typically takes the patient only one to two hours in the closet, orienting to sex, to rid himself or herself of the claustrophobia.

Agoraphobia: The Fear of Wide-Open Spaces— Or Is It?

Claustrophobia (the fear of closed-in spaces) and agoraphobia (the fear of wide-open spaces) are not related to each other theoretically or practically. While claustrophobia is fairly well defined and relatively easy to eliminate, agoraphobia has about as many definitions and treatments as there are people suffering from it. Some agoraphobics say they cannot tolerate open fields. Others say they become psychologically immobilized and panicked in crowded stores. For some it's city streets that upset them. For others, it's walking alongside tall buildings. Many of them say their uncomfortable feelings are triggered off by just being with crowds of people in restaurants, theaters, airports, railway stations and the like. The only sensible generalization we can make about the anxieties which agoraphobic patients report is that these feelings all take place outside of their own homes. A more accurate description of agoraphobia—if indeed it is a single phobia and not a collection of them, or something else entirely—would be *the fear of being away from home* or *of something happening while away from home*. Now that's an awfully big chunk of human life to write off as a phobia. So this label may not be any more useful than the other ones used in such profusion by clinicians to describe agoraphobia.

The Agoraphobic Housewife

The typical agoraphobic patient is adult, female, married and a homemaker with few outside interests. But there are other major characteristics of the typical agoraphobic patient that point at one link in the chain on how the patient became agoraphobic and also what can be done about it. The typical agoraphobic patient is middle class and white. Minority women in Western society don't seem to be as susceptible to becoming agoraphobic as their relatively affluent white counterparts. I'm sure it has nothing to do with genes and skin color. Minority women do have a much greater amount of stress placed upon them than do white women, both in growing up and as adults, because of their social environments and economic disadvantages. We have learned a great deal about the effects of stress from examining the awful effects of German concentration camps upon their survivors. During their incarceration in these camps, indications of poor mental health, such as phobias, compulsions and obsessions, dropped out and disappeared. The only evidences of mental problems that remained unaffected by the stress of the German concentration camp were the psychoses. Neurotic disabilities—and here I'm interpreting these as learned disabilities—suddenly cleared up when they threatened the inmate's survival.

Sticking It Out Until Fear Fades

Women in our society are not more prone to become agoraphobic because they are white but because their middle-class life-style and relative affluence allow them to become phobic. The life-style of women in the lower socio-economic brackets, white or minority, is not likely to permit them to become agoraphobic. Agoraphobia doesn't seem to strike women who *must* work for a living. With few exceptions, agoraphobics are people who have the resources, usually working parents or spouse, or an occupation at home, that permit them to avoid the business marketplace and its crowds of people. Think about this for a minute. What do you think the typical reaction of, say, a longshoreman would be at the end of a bone-bruising day at the docks when he found out there was no dinner waiting because his wife said she was afraid to go to the market? My guess is that he would give her a choice such as: "Who scares you most—me or the market?" And she would go to the market. In this direct way, the husband would have provided the motivation for his wife to undergo a self-help version of what professionals call "implosion" therapy.* Treated according to this method, the patient agrees to go into the phobic situation and stay there for up to eight hours at time, no matter how anxious he or she gets. At the end of several of these sessions, patients who stick it out typically report that they feel twinges of anxiety but nothing they can't handle. And the longer the patient stays in the agoraphobic situation, the better it works.

If the OR is involved in eliminating phobias, then it must be triggered off in some way by this method. But what does the patient orient to for all those hours in the city streets?

Let me describe a little scenario of agoraphobic treatment for you. The patient agrees to go out in the city, shopping or just walking about in the crowded streets for eight hours. During the morning, nothing much happens besides getting anxious. Then about eleven o'clock, the patient begins to notice two things that penetrate the phobic anxiety: one is hunger; the other is tired feet and legs, and a

---

*Implosion therapy is a fancy name for a method of treatment that *floods* the patient with anxiety. It simply means that we don't sneak the phobia up on the patient as Mary Cover Jones did to little Peter when she brought in the white rabbit. Think of it as tossing a hydrophobe bodily into the deep end of the swimming pool rather than letting him or her gradually wade in step by step from the shallow end. As the name implies, present-day psychotherapists are still as fond of ideas borrowed from eighteenth-century physics as were Freud's followers. To implode something means to increase the external pressure on it until it collapses into itself, (much like what happens to a submarine when it dives beyond its rated water-depth-pressure level). Explosion is the opposite of implosion; (the submarine explodes when someone dynamites it from inside). Psychotherapy has little relationship to eighteenth-century physics. The theory that anxiety builds up so high that it implodes the phobia is sixth-grade thinking—but the method called implosion is one of the best clinical treatments.

sore back. During the next hour, the patient orients to these bodily sensations in the phobic situation, instead of just responding physiologically to anxiety. Then the patient has lunch for an hour—also in the phobic situation. At one o'clock, it's back to the streets for the patient feeling somewhat rested. The afternoon is a repeat of the morning, anxiety builds up until the body begins to protest—this time more strongly than before. By three o'clock, the patient is getting stronger signals from the body on how tired and achy it feels than fear signals from Fun City. For the next two hours, these strong orienting reflexes blank out anxiety about open streets, market-places and crowds. That's what I see happening in the counterconditioning procedure.

Although I can't actually look into the nervous system of the patient and tell you for sure that this type of OR generation occurs, I'm willing to bet that it does. *Muscle tension and bodily stimuli are the OR triggers that overcome agoraphobic feelings.* If you feel that this analysis of the treatment is a bit too simple-minded for your taste, consider some other obvious things staring us in the face.

Implosion doesn't work for aerophobia. How do we know this? From the first-hand reports of patients who have tried this method themselves before seeking professional treatment. Many of these patients try to stick it out for hours in the air, and all they get for their bravery are more anxious feelings until they decide to stop flying altogether. Why doesn't this self-administered implosion therapy work? Most flights are too comfortable and too short. About the only flight I know personally that would produce enough uncomfortable bodily sensations is the San Francisco to Sydney, Australia run. That flight over its various stages takes almost twenty-four hours to complete. After eighteen hours in the air without sleep, your body will be protesting so much that an aerophobic impulse hasn't a snowball's chance in hell of getting through to your primitive nervous system.

Let's look at the results of another relatively unsuccessful way of treating phobias—with drugs. Valium is primarily a muscle relaxant. It is the most widely prescribed and used drug—except for simple aspirin—on the market today. That statistic might tip us off right away that it would be of little use in eliminating a phobia. There are so many of us using it that you would expect to see the number of phobic patients drop off sharply if it "cured" phobic reactions. There is no indication, from populace or professionals, that this is happening. Some years ago Valium was tried as a quickie substitute for the progressive relaxation used to countercondition phobic anxieties. It was a total flop. My guess is that if increased muscle tension and other bodily stimuli *help* reduce your fears, because your nervous system orients to these things instead of letting anxiety wash over you, then a muscle relaxant is totally inappropriate. The kind of drug that might work would have to produce the aftereffects of something like a tetanus or a typhoid shot—where for hours the patient would feel sore all over. That would be a cheap, chemical method for reducing learned anxieties.

This talk on the why and how of agoraphobia is just fancy theorizing. But it makes a reasonable argument for looking at agoraphobia as something that can be learned like any other phobia and can also be "unlearned." For some patients, what we call agoraphobia may not be a single phobia but a variety of different specific phobias. On the other hand, the problem for many agoraphobic patients may not be a specific fear response to crowded theaters, streets or department stores. Instead, it is more likely a general anxiety or nervous apprehension that a severe "panic attack" will strike them while away from the privacy of their home. Many patients, but not all, report that their agoraphobic reaction started with a panic attack, and, at that time, they didn't realize it for what it was—just a sense of panic, albeit intense.

Some thought they were severely ill or dying. Others thought it was a heart attack.

Sufferers respond differently to this apprehension. Some never leave their homes. Others always travel by private automobile, because they feel secure in it. Some will travel only if friends or relatives live along their route. They feel they can duck in to these "safe" places if a panic attack strikes them along the way. I recently consulted with an agoraphobic woman who only has her panic attacks while waiting in line at the supermarket. She is a golfing nut and the supermarket line is one of the few places where she feels she can't take along her putter and practice a few (hand-eye coordination OR triggers) strokes. So it's clear from patient reports that *for some people* agoraphobia is not a specific fear of city crowds, open fields, public buildings and streets but a *sense of nervousness that they will experience a frightening and humiliating panic attack in those circumstances.*

Let me give you a hypothetical example of the degree to which this sense of nervous apprehension, this fear of panic, can disrupt a person's life. Once upon a time, there was a wealthy millionaire industrialist named Howard Hughes. Some people even said he was the richest man in the world. Howard was born to wealth and inherited the Hughes' oil-tool company when his father unexpectedly passed away in his mid-fifties, a victim of a heart attack. Howard took over his father's affairs and did an amazing number of things to increase his wealth, mostly by doing them on his own initiative and only consulting others when necessary. Things went along well for Howard until he began to approach the time of life when his father experienced his fatal heart attack. It was said that Howard brooded long on the possibility that there was some genetic problem in his bloodline that made his father die at so young an age. With his secretive personality style—not talking over things with other people—and this supposed worry about his life expectancy, Howard Hughes was set up for the inevitable: every normal ache, throb and gas pain (which most of us routinely experience at that age) were interpreted as the first signs of the problem that killed his father. His misinterpretation that his normal bodily protests were going to kill him began the process that would eventually lead to panic attacks. Now, as far as is known, Howard never told anyone what his problem was or that he had panic attacks. We do know that he followed a typical agoraphobic behavioral pattern, staying indoors as much as possible. Some people thought him paranoid because of this behavior. Others thought him the wealthy eccentric who did things oddly just because he could afford to. His wealth did allow him to marginally cope with his agoraphobia and thereby unluckily avoid seeking help for it. He had the luxury of never being outside without a vehicle of some sort. He even could afford a constant supply of male assistants to carry him between hotel and automobile in a chair or gurney. If while being carried along, panic struck him even to the point of fainting, who could tell he was afraid while he was sitting or lying down? Howard Hughes' phobic fear for his health was also generalized to morbid thoughts and behaviors about being physiologically made vulnerable to infection. He showed identical behavior patterns with other people with similar irrational fears of germs, such as wearing gloves constantly and isolating himself from potential germ-carriers by insisting they talk only on the telephone or wear white gloves also.*

---

*The phobia of germ infections has been eliminated relatively quickly in a number of patients by having them imagine situations with germs that are not frightening to them and then working up to more anxious situations. It was necessary for one patient to imagine only a single germ being dropped into the other end of the city reservoir before he could feel comfortable about dipping his hand into the water supply or not having to boil water before drinking it. From that point on, his irrational fears of germ infection and his compulsive sanitary behavior yielded quickly to behavioral methods.

This story about Howard Hughes is pure hypothesis. Was Howard Hughes himself an agoraphobic? Given the details of his private life that have come to public attention, he probably was. And if he were agoraphobic, then these stories we hear about him tell us that Hughes did all the things that would have made his condition worse: avoiding the phobic situation, avoiding contact with other people and not sharing his personal worries and fears, avoiding muscular exercise and orienting in the phobic situation, and probably using drugs to calm his anxieties.

Social Fears and Panic in the Streets

What does my own experience in working with patients tell me about agoraphobia? I see two things defeating many people: a combination of general social anxieties about people and anxieties about things and places outside the home. When you or I leave the house, we have to do one or both of two things: socialize and enter specific situations. We meet people, talk to them, joke with them, negotiate with them, chastise them, relate to them, do business with them, work with them, even eat with them outside our homes. And we do these things in city streets, markets, office buildings, theaters, department stores, transportation terminals—the places vaguely specified by most agoraphobics as where their anxiety is triggered off. A sound treatment plan for yourself, if you have agoraphobic tendencies, is to look at your feelings about both interacting with people—even with strangers—and where you interact with them. You might then consider doing two things: working on your social anxieties as well as your phobic reactions to crowds, markets, streets, etc.

Social anxieties are general ones and not easily remedied with anti-anxiety retraining methods designed for specific phobias. In my experience, most social anxieties are caused primarily by a lack of self-assertiveness in the individual. It would take another whole book* to describe in detail how we become socially anxious and nonassertive. Briefly, our personal insecurities prompt us to give up too soon and too often when telling other people our wants. Our fear of personal criticism causes us to withdraw into a shell. Our simple lack of basic knowledge about social communication and conversation cuts us off from social rewards. And, perhaps most importantly for the agoraphobic patient, our fear of making social gaffs or mistakes inhibits our social freedom and motivation. Making social mistakes, looking foolish or odd, and showing embarrassment are all part of the social fear of the agoraphobic. The patient knows that when panic strikes out in the public place, he or she will have heart palpitations, sweating or clammy skin, a flushed or blanched face, shaking hands and weak limbs; the patient will perhaps even swoon. Besides anticipating the unpleasantness of this extreme anxiety—fearing fear itself—the typical patient seems unable to cope with appearing sick, disabled or just making a scene in front of other people. The patient usually feels that one panic attack would make an outing so unpleasant it would not be worthwhile to even attempt it. So learning to cope with the possibility of being socially odd is a great help to these patients—cultivating an attitude of: "So I get panicky sometimes. Don't we all have problems?"

The lack of assertiveness in agoraphobic patients also causes some of them to use their phobic feelings as a social crutch. These phobic patients use their anxieties as a lever to get their spouses and families to do things for them. It's a side effect of: "What do you expect from a person with a phobia? I can't do that. You'll have to do it with me." This type of payoff from a phobic condition makes the patient into a "wheelchair" phobic who is "obviously" crippled and needs special consideration from the people around her or him. With a small dose of assertive re-

---

*See Manuel J. Smith, *When I say no, I feel guilty* (New York: The Dial Press, 1975).

training, the patient typically finds that it's much simpler and a lot less strain to ask for the same help—and get it—without having to rely on a phobia as an excuse.

If you are agoraphobic, what can you do to effectively eliminate your anxious feelings? First, you want to eliminate your specific anxieties about leaving home and going into the city. After that, you can work on your social anxieties by learning to be more assertive with other people. The best and quickest method is implosion therapy—where you promise yourself to go into the frightening situation for at least four hours at a time. There is a harder way to do this and an easier way. The harder way is to go into the city and let yourself be passively bombarded with things that make you anxious. The easier—and smarter—way is to set up your own program in which you maximize the number of things that will make you orient while in the streets, crowds and market places.

Now let's look at some guidelines set up to make the retraining experience as short and effective as possible.

Making Yourself Less Anxious Away from Home

1. This set of orienting reflex retraining guidelines is designed to help you reduce your anxieties about being in a metropolitan environment with all its crowded public streets, places, stores, theaters and restaurants. It is designed to help whether or not you experience panic attacks in public places, because the trigger of anxiety—the city environment—is the same for both kinds of agoraphobia. So, in either case, panic or nonpanic, follow the suggested guidelines to make yourself orient in places that are phobic for you.
2. Determine your SUDs* level when you step out your front door. If you panic at this point, take the basic program and break it up into at least a half-

---

*See Chapter 7, page 110.

dozen substeps, leading up to the most fearful part—when you are actually in the crowded city. Instead of flooding yourself with anxiety downtown, do it in stages: first, step out in front of your house; then onto your street or road for fifty yards on either side of your house; next go two, three, four, five, etc., blocks away from your house, and repeat the method until you are functioning in the middle of a crowded area.

3. Make a commitment to yourself that *no matter what happens,* you will not give up until the appointed hour.* This means that you will stay in the phobic situation even if you are afraid you will faint, look silly or get so weak you might wet your pants. Without this promise to yourself, the OR program is not likely to work for you. There is one variation on this commitment that works just as well, but it takes a lot more of your time. See Guideline 11.

4. Prior to each foray into the field spend thirty minutes doing exercises. Now, this suggestion is most critical for making the program as short and effective as possible. If, indeed, tired legs, feet and back muscles are what make agoraphobic implosion work, then you might want to be clever about the whole thing and get the results of some healthy exercise to boot. Remember the motto of OR behavior retraining: "All I want is an unfair advantage." So before each excursion, run through any standard set of exercises: jogging in place, deep-knee bends, sit-ups, pushups, bend-overs, hula-hooping the hips, etc. Take advantage of your sedentary life: Doing these exercises before you go out into the field will be the equivalent of about three hours of walking in the city streets. Why spend time there just to get your muscles tired if you can get the same effect in the privacy and comfort of your own home or apartment? If you are in good physical shape and exercise regularly (I suspect you are not. I haven't met one patient yet who couldn't benefit from more exercise.), add some other exercises, which you

---

*Eight hours per session seem to give the best results; anything under four hours seems to be ineffective.

don't normally do, for your legs and back, such as yoga routines. If you haven't done them before, I guarantee that you will ache for some hours afterward.

When you finish your exercises, cool down to your normal body temperature and then rest in a cool part of your house until you feel slightly stiff. When you notice that your body protests with movement, that's the time to begin your implosion session. Then you will be automatically orienting to your body, which is protesting your sudden desire to become an active person again. You may also want to be a bit clever in maximizing your advantage over your phobia. A week or so before you schedule your first retraining trip in the field, it would be a good idea to do the exercises to get your body tired and then time yourself to see how long it takes for your muscles to cool down and become stiff and sore. The time it takes for this to happen will depend upon the type of exercises you do, how much you exercise and your general physical condition. You may find that it will take several hours of rest before your muscles will protest strongly. It would be smart to do these exercises in the morning and see what happens during the rest of the day. If you do them at night, you will probably find it difficult to go to sleep because of your aching body. If you are under treatment for any physical condition, it would also be a good idea to ask your physician about the extent to which you should exercise. Talk the problem over with him or her, explain this program, and its demand for physical exercise; see what modifications and limitations are recommended.

Remember, no matter what variations you make, it'll be easier on your primitive nervous system if you *set up conditions that will force you to automatically orient* in the phobic situation. And the best way to do that is to make your muscles sore beforehand.

5. Set yourself a task to do before you step out your front door. You are to visit at least three places during your stint in the streets. Also pick out three other places as backup tasks if you run out of places

before your time is up. If you are using a step-by-step variation of the program, pick out specific places or things to do in each step of your program. It's better not to just walk around aimlessly, picking your phobic places at random.

6. If you are going downtown, begin with places that would normally pique your interest if you weren't phobic: concert halls, museums with special exhibits, parks where artists display their creations. Then if you have time left in your schedule, go to places that are less interesting, such as airline terminals, and railway stations.

7. Depending upon what you are doing already, the rest of the guidelines must be fitted into your own method of operating in the streets. If you can already walk around the city with a friend, then go only by yourself. If you can't travel because of your fear of panicking under any circumstances, then take a trusted friend along during the first session. Your spouse might tend to make you anxious. Your friend can chat with you about anything except your phobia and lay a hand on you whenever your anxiety rises. The presence of a friend will make you feel more comfortable about such things as, "What happens if I faint?" Your friend, of course, will see that you don't faint by making you sit down and put your head between your knees and by telling you to push your head up while he or she holds it down. This will forcibly increase the blood pressure to your brain, preventing you from fainting. Also, as a result of your friend just being there, you will not be as likely to faint, no matter what your anxiety level.

8. During your first session in the city, have your friend drive you there by automobile. If you are like many agoraphobics, you may feel that the auto is like an extension of the home—a place safe from anxiety. If private transportation is unavailable to you for the first session, set a goal of walking to a populated center and back during the four hours. Walking in this program is very important, so it doesn't matter much whether you walk to the crowded spots or are transported there and then begin walking.

9. If you rarely leave the area around your home, during the first retraining session, use all the OR triggers that other agoraphobics have discovered. Bring along a bag of a sweet or acid candy or a bag of salted nuts. During the entire session, keep popping something into your mouth for your nervous system to orient to. Also, take along a walking stick, umbrella, baby's pram, luggage or grocery cart on that first trip. These are all mechanical devices that force you to use hand–eye–foot coordination. All of them require you to orient in a very simple way while walking. Take along your monthly bank statement and checkbook, and balance them on a park bench, in a restaurant or in a crowded hotel lobby. That mental task will force you to orient in the scary situation. Gradually discontinue using these OR aids as you progress, until, on the final session, you are able to travel the crowded streets orienting only to yourself and the activity around you in shops, meeting places, etc.

10. When you go out in the city, wear uncomfortable clothes. Wear a tight, uncomfortable bra, girdle, pants, etc. These clothes will cause bodily sensations that will automatically make you orient.

11. If you find that you honestly cannot make a commitment to yourself to remain in the scary situation for at least four hours at a time, you might want to try a variation of the implosion method that works just as well but takes longer. In this variation, you agree to go only as far away from home as you can without feeling anxious. When you begin to feel anxious, you turn straight for home. When you get there, you wait until your anxiety level drops, and then you head right back out again. You keep following this procedure for at least four hours a day. Now, if you are honest with yourself in determining when you are no longer too anxious to be out in the world, the trips will merge into one another: You will be spending more time outside than at home. That is why this treatment is considered a variation of the implosion method. Also, you may notice that this variation keeps you walking all the time except for brief rests in your home.

And, if you want it to work faster still, you keep
walking while you're at home in between trips instead of flopping out on the sofa.

12. Now is the time to give you an important tip on
coping with your agoraphobic feelings. You will
experience anxiety outside your home; even using
the suggestions outlined here cannot totally prevent
that. Getting your muscles sore and bringing things
along to help you orient are just ways to stack
the odds in your favor. Remember: "All I want is an
unfair advantage" is the motto of orienting reflex
retraining. However, doing these things will not
make your anxiety disappear completely outside
your home, and if you do panic, *roll with it.* Don't
fight it, just say to yourself, "Another panic attack.
My nervous system is running like hell inside me and
I'm just standing here." I'm not agoraphobic and I
often get nervous away from home (as well as in it).
So you will not eliminate anxiety right away. Also,
good feelings will not come immediately just by
going through this program. They will come later,
in the same way as for all of us, when we interact
with other people outside our homes. Keep a
jaundiced eye, then, on your emotional expectations. Being nonphobic about crowds, streets and
marketplaces does not mean that you will necessarily feel good or happy about these things. All it
means, at first, is that you will be able to interact
with other people without panicking. Keep in mind
the reality of the world we live in by thinking of
Gahan Wilson's cartoon of several men, decked
out in angel's suits and halos, standing just inside
of Heaven's walls. One fellow is looking around at
the panorama of cracking plaster, the "v" in the
sign, This is Heaven, having fallen off to the ground.
One of the angels is picking his teeth; another is
standing there, hands in his pockets, wistfully looking out Heaven's entry gate. He then says to his
companion angel: "Somehow I thought It would
be classier." The commercial city world outside our
homes is much like Gahan Wilson's cartoon. Somehow we all think it much classier than it really is.

twelve
Orienting to sex and orgasm

Just by definition—if we consider how we are built to
orient to the things in the world around us—the
words *sexual* and *phobia* seem to be contradictory
and therefore impossible to pair. Ah! If that were
only so, life would be a lot simpler. Unfortunately,
sexual phobias with learned anxiety at their base play
a large part in many of the sexual problems that people bring into the psychological clinic. *These phobias
can be treated like any other phobia.* This reality was
not always recognized by the various disciplines of
psychotherapy. Even though I shouldn't point too
long a finger at the classical, old-time Freudians,
these most rigid analytical types were a source of
misinformation on the subject for many years. "Don't
touch the phobia," they warned us. "It's only symp-
tomatic of something lying in wait underneath."
What they really were saying was: "If you fool
around with the phobia, the boogie man will get
you." This ultracautious, hands-off attitude, under-
standably, was the result of a lack of information on
the subject of sex. But since it was expressed by the
practitioners of the then most prestigious discipline,
it's not surprising that the study of sexual problems
was for many years considered the province of neurologists in monkey and rat laboratories, monks with
dispensations from the Vatican, classical art collectors
and a few academic weirdos with a personality fixa-
tion in this area. Not until the 1960s, when Masters
and Johnson published their investigations into sex-

ual function and dysfunction, did it become generally known that there was an alternative treatment for sexual problems besides looking for some libidinal boogie man under the classical analytical couch.

It was also about this time that a new therapy was created, behavioral sexual treatment, wherein the patient engaged in sex under controlled conditions. Although these methods worked very well for many of the problems, the behaviorists were initially just as guilty of enthusiastic overstatement in staking their claim to this treatment area as the old-time analytic types had been. Consequently, and because of the simplicity of the behavioral methods, many amateur sexual "clinics" were opened and then, within a few years, closed. They didn't close because of legal problems with the local authorities. Most legal authorities were and still are quite sympathetic to the problems of treating bona fide sexual problems. One eminent clinician in the field at UCLA suspects that after a few years enough professional people were trained so the amateurs could no longer compete for the business. But the demand for such clinics is widespread. If we can believe the statistical magnitude of sexual dysfunction estimated by Dr. William Masters and Virginia Johnson, approximately one quarter of the population of the United States has had, does have or will have some sexual problem. That seems enough people with problems to employ another quarter of the population as therapists. So the argument that the pros are driving out the amateurs doesn't make much sense, numberswise. My bet is many of the amateur clinics closed when they saw that the behavioral methods—typically the only thing they knew, or thought they knew—had no relevance for clients with sexual problems that were not phobias. As I see it—and this is only my guess—amateur surrogates saw themselves operating as prostitutes and not as sexual therapists for a goodly proportion of their time with patients who were not phobic. And they didn't want to operate that way. Sexual Surrogates, with a capital *S*, yes. Prostitutes, no. Scientific sex is one thing; sex for pay only is another. Even though many of the sexual problems that people bring into psychological clinics are caused by learned anxieties, a great many of them are also caused by anger, which requires an entirely different treatment.

Let me give you an example of what can happen when successful behavioral methods are used without the therapist really knowing which sexual problem is being treated: anger or anxiety. A few years ago, I was supervising a therapy case that three graduate students were working on at UCLA. The identified patient was a man who proclaimed himself impotent with his wife. She concurred with her husband's self-diagnosis. We gathered all their history, analyzed it and came up with a treatment plan based upon the behavioral portion of the Masters and Johnson method. The couple was very cooperative and went through the behavioral routines and talked with us every week about their practice sessions and what was happening. What was happening was *nothing*. This (pardon the pun) was screwy! For other patients, these same therapy routines produced dramatic positive changes within as few as three weeks. At the end of two fruitless months of therapy, we found out why. The husband came in one day and asked for an unscheduled appointment without his wife. When we saw him, his whole story about what was going on had changed. During this period of "impotency" with his wife, he had been regularly making it with his secretary and just yesterday she had told him that she was now in a family way. That bit of information ended the treatment for his impotence! This particular information—his impotence was limited to his spouse—was denied to us by him in both individual and conjoint sessions with his wife when it was questioned as a possibility.

During that last session, we again went over the physiological details of his sexual behavior toward his wife. His story changed. The problem did not seem to be a lack of erection at the appropriate time but a lack of interest at the appropriate time. The behavioral methods didn't work, because he didn't have a behavioral problem caused by anxiety. Instead, he had a motivational problem caused by marital conflict with his wife. He bore her a smoldering, passive anger and didn't really want to have sex with her. After that therapy session, the patient declined our offer to work on the marital conflicts with his wife, and we never saw either of them again.

Now, how is this example of a nonbehavioral anger problem connected to the closing of amateur sexual clinics? What do you think the reaction of the amateur female surrogate would be after collecting a history similar to this man's—with or without his wife participating—if on the first sexual reconditioning session there was no sign of the sexual problem? And no sign on the second? After a number of coital experiences in the name of "curing" this patient's sexual problem, how long would it take for the therapist to feel that she was providing not sex therapy but sex for a fee?

I use this example to point out to you that while there are sexual phobias aplenty, there are also other causes for sexual difficulties besides anxiety; and the methods used for anxiety don't work for problems not caused by anxiety. If you, or someone close to you has a sexual problem, how can you tell what is likely to be causing the problem and what can be done about it? To briefly answer these questions, let's look for a moment at the information on which professional treatment of sexual problems is based.

There are three valid treatment models for sexual problems: the Anxiety Model (as practiced by behavior therapists); the Anger Model (as practiced by traditional "talk" therapists); and the Mixed Model (a combination of the Anxiety and Anger models as typified by the practice of Masters and Johnson). The clinicians who successfully use any or all of these three treatment models assume two things about the sexual problem they intend to treat. First, they assume that the problem is not caused by some physical or neurological deficit, injury or trauma. A neurologist is often consulted before treatment if the patient's history shows any indication of these problems. Second, the clinicians assume that the sexual difficulty is the result of some form of psychological learning acquired through negative experiences with sex or sexual partners. Let's very briefly look at what each of these treatment models says about sexual problems and then come back and concentrate on the Anxiety Model, the one that deals exclusively with sexual phobias.

The Anxiety Model of Treating Sexual Problems

The Anxiety Model of treatment is based upon the physiological and clinical observation that sexual performance is impossible in the presence of anxiety. In simple words, the Anxiety Model tells us that we can't have fun sexually and worry at the same time about the IRS being after us for fudging on last year's tax return.

Over the past two decades, clinical researchers have teased out and isolated a number of sexual difficulties that have been successfully treated using the Anxiety Model. For men these problems take the form of:

1. Impotence with a sexual partner but with no problem of sexual arousal or potency in another context, such as solitary masturbation. This impotence is characterized by either lack of erection prior to sex or loss of erection during foreplay or intercourse of some sort.
2. Premature ejaculation, typically defined either as consistent ejaculation within one minute of penetration or as ejaculation prior to intercourse with or without full erection during foreplay.

For women, the anxiety-based sexual problems are:

1. Vaginismus, the *involuntary* closure or contraction of the vaginal sphincter (the circular muscle at the opening of the vagina) thereby preventing intercourse.
2. Lack of orgasm with either a specific sexual partner with whom there had previously been no problem or with any sexual partner but where orgasm occurs regularly in another situation, such as solitary masturbation.

In using the Anxiety Model, the general strategy has been to introduce sex or sexual stimuli in very small doses while something else is going on: usually a friendly interchange between a possible or past sexual partner where physical and sexual stimulation is gradually increased over periods of time and in various ways—all of which, not so incidentally, trigger off the patient's orienting reflex. This type of anxiety treatment has a good probability of clearing up sexual difficulties with relative speed—within several weeks to several months.

The Anger Model of Treating Sexual Problems

The second major method of treating sexual problems is the use of the Anger Model. With this model it is assumed that the problem is not one of anxiety but of anger at a mate, spouse or lover. The sexual problem is typically not generated or learned on the bed, couch or bearskin rug but during the everyday conflicts between two people living together. The problem is one of unresolved, typically passive, anger at the sexual partner. It is built up over time into a silent grudge composed of all the putdowns and cuts exchanged in the process of "winning" conflicts about who should do what, when and why. The grudges that are expressed during treatment for this type of sexual problem are generally unrelated to sex itself. Over a period of time, one partner has pulled back from sharing any private part of himself or herself—including sex—with the mate. In contrast to the multiple signs of sexual difficulty caused by anxiety, there has been only a gradual, slow decline in the frequency of sexual contact with the partner over a period of months or years. Typically, the frequency of sexual contact does not bottom out at zero but bounces back and forth between zero and low frequency over long periods of time. And this drop in frequency, along with the social problems between sexual partners, is the only indication of sexual difficulties caused by anger.

The case of the couple seen by the graduate students at UCLA, given earlier,* points out this characteristic of sexual anger. The male patient complained of impotence, but he had no problem having sexual relations with his secretary at work on a regular, ongoing basis. The onset of his problem with his wife was not sudden. It did not even happen within a few weeks or months, with sex then becoming impossible because of a lack of erection in his wife's presence. Instead, it happened gradually over a period of years, with none of the indications of sexual difficulties pointed out by the Anxiety Model present. When he had sex with his wife, he performed with no difficulties. The real problem was their frequency of sex declining over a period of time to near zero. Other theorists and practitioners of sexual behavior therapy, even prominent ones such as Zev Wanderer, Joseph Wolpe and William Masters, all point to the difficulties in treating sexual dysfunction if anger or lack of caring is also present—especially if it is not recognized before treatment begins.

The treatment proposed by the Anger Model is not as straightforward and as simple as the treatment used for sexual anxiety. Typically, a couple is seen together for traditional "talk" therapy in the hope that this exploration will allow them to work out

---

*See page 243.

their conflicts without resorting to the attempt to "win" at all costs through put-downs, manipulation, personal cuts, chops, slams and assorted other degradations. One recent addition to the armamentarium of the talk therapist has been the introduction of assertive training programs, which systematically teach couples how to cope with and extinguish such personal verbal attacks from their lives—and with less personal pain.*

The Mixed Model of Treating Sexual Problems

The third method of treating sexual dysfunction, the Mixed Model, tells us that sexual problems can be compounded by the presence of both anxiety and anger. It does seem to matter, for all practical purposes, which emotion appears first. Lack of sexual performance caused by anxiety can become the source and subject of marital conflicts outside the bed that produce resentment and anger. On the other hand, marital anger and resentment that derive from nonsexual conflicts can be brought into the bed and thereby produce anxiety about sexual failure—a self-fulfilling prophecy. Whichever way these emotions run, the existence of anger and anxiety together will effectively complicate sexual difficulties. The Mixed Model attempts to deal with both the anger and anxiety problems at the same time but through different means—counseling for the anger and behavioral programs for the anxiety. It does little for the patient to work on one aspect of the problem and ignore the other. If only the anxiety portion is dealt with, the anger will very likely preclude successful sexual contact. If the anger alone is treated, the lack of sexual performance will continue and probably be a source of further anger.

---

*See *When I say no, I feel guilty* and George R. Bach and Peter Wyden, *Intimate Enemy* (Avon: New York, 1969).

This model of treatment points out the absolute necessity for a *cooperative sexual partner* in resolving sexual difficulties. And getting a truly cooperative partner for sexual behavior therapy can be difficult. A partner may appear cooperative but have his or her own hidden motivations for taking part. And these hidden reasons are probably responsible for the occasional failures of sexual therapy. The so-called cooperative partner may have his or her own sexual insecurities. For this person, a sexually crippled mate poses less of a threat than a fully operative one who could suggest—God only knows what—kinky sexual twists. Prostitutes are generally not very cooperative. Prostitutes are mainly interested in collecting the money from turning over as many quick tricks as possible. Any slowdown of their production rate for "therapy" purposes is not accepted sympathetically either by the women themselves or their pimps. So, prostitutes are generally not a good resource in sexual therapy unless they are supervised by an experienced therapist who is willing to be an observer of the actual sexual therapy session. The angry or disgruntled wife or husband is not likely to be a cooperative partner—unless they see themselves as part of the sexual problem. How about pickups, one-night stands, and such? Patients who try this route don't report much success with it. The universal impression given to me by patients is that quickie sex enthusiasts aren't much interested in the patient's problem; they're just out for their own sexual gratification of the moment.

In treating both males and females for a variety of sexual problems, I have made some casual clinical observations about cooperative and noncooperative partners in sexual retraining. They may not be representative, but they are observations from personal experience and, for whatever they're worth, here they are. A person who is younger than thirty or older than forty-five is a good bet as a cooperative partner. Partners between thirty and forty-five are less likely to be fully cooperative, although I can think of exceptions. The partner who is somewhat detached from the problem, who doesn't take it as a personal affront, and yet is concerned about its resolution, is more likely to be cooperative. The partner who doesn't complain of his or her own sexual frustration puts no pressure on the patient and therefore is a good choice. The partner who is loose in both his or her expectations and judgments helps greatly.

I remember the wife of an impotent, homosexual pedophile who openly stated that she would rather her husband molest young boys than cheat on her with another woman. As you might expect, his treatment was as short lived as her expectations of his fidelity. Perhaps the most common characteristic of successful cooperative partners is their ability to communicate a lack of personal nervousness and worry about the patient's sexual problem, as if they have been through this whole sexual-problem routine before and found nothing frightening in it.

The Mixed Model represents, in a sophisticated and advanced form, the casual advice traditionally given patients in the course of general psychotherapy when sexual difficulties are mentioned: "Try a different place and/or a different partner." With this bit of advice, the traditional therapist has recognized through practical observation that sexual difficulties are caused by a lack of novelty or by negative feelings about where and/or with whom sex takes place. The common therapeutic observation that there is nothing mystical about sexual problems or their treatment is amply borne out by cases of spontaneous remissions. Most therapists have incidents of such "self-cures" in their case portfolio which they delight in telling about.

One patient's problem, on which I was consulted several years ago, and the story of his "cure," is a classic example of this clinical folklore. Bill was a blue-collar worker in his mid-forties. He was married to the same woman for twenty years and, during the

third year of their marriage, he became first a premature ejaculator and then impotent. During the fifth
year of marriage, he took a business trip to San
Francisco for two weeks. On the plane up, he met a
stewardess who obviously liked him as a person.
They had dinner together that first night. By the
second night they were in bed with each other. Feeling embarrassed, Bill told her that he wasn't much of
a lover and had some difficulties in the sexual area.
Her response to his cautions? "It's no big thing. We
can still have fun." And that's exactly what happened.
Over a period of one week, Bill's problem of premature ejaculation and impotence disappeared when
he was in bed with the stewardess. For the next week,
they engaged in various forms of lovemaking with
no hint of difficulty. At the end of the two weeks,
Bill went back to his wife and found that, indeed,
there seemed to be no problem sexually with her
either. But during the next two weeks, his premature
ejaculation and finally his impotence with his wife
was relearned.

Fifteen years later, Bill was asking me if he could
go through some behavioral program with his wife to
achieve the results he had gotten with the stewardess.
I asked him if his wife was interested in taking part;
would she be a cooperative partner? Bill thought for
a few moments and then said no, he doubted she
would be interested. But then he asked me if he
could be retrained by a surrogate and have that effect
transfer to his sexual performance with his wife. I
replied that unless things had changed in their marriage relationship, I wouldn't want to give him even-
money odds that such a program would work. I
reminded him of what had happened when he went
into his marriage twenty years ago without any sexual difficulties and then of what happened when he
came home from San Francisco fifteen years ago without his sexual problem. He thought about it for a
few moments and then told me, with some trace of
sadness, that his relationship with his wife was the

problem all along. After saying that, he seemed to re-solve something in his mind and brightened up. He told me he was going on lots of separate vacations to San Francisco. Clearly, Bill recognized the problem of not having a cooperative sexual partner—one without her own ax to grind in the sexual relearning process —because he opted for the simplicity of finding someone new (the Anxiety Model) instead of the complexity involved in dealing with his wife (the Mixed Model). With this distinction in mind, let's look in detail at a case that illustrates the basis for the workings of the Anxiety Model in dealing with sex-ual phobias.

Sexual Failure: A Built-In Response of Our Primitive Nervous System

When Cedric first came to see me, he was twenty-four years old and had been unable to have an erec-tion for the last three years, since getting out of the U.S. Navy. Cedric had become impotent during his enlistment, but prior to his military service he had had good sexual relations with several women. His only negative sexual experience before becoming impotent occurred when his mother punished him as a young child for masturbation. Although Cedric never learned about the birds and the bees from his parents, he gathered from their attitude about it that "there was something wrong with sex."

During Ced's last year of his tour in the Mediter-ranean command, he lived with a local girl in Italy while he was on shore duty. Up to that time, Ced had never had a sexual problem with women. During the first six months of that year, he lived with his paid mistress in an apparently satisfactory manner. Then something changed in their relationship. Ced couldn't put his finger on what it was, but gradually his mistress began complaining that he didn't care for her as much as he used to, he wasn't with her enough, he didn't show enough affection for her. . . . Evidently, Ced's protests and denials of his lack of affection were not what his mistress wanted to hear, because in the last two months of their relationship she began to *criticize him during their lovemaking*. As he recalled, she began to make remarks such as: "You're not as good as Charlie," (the last sailor who kept her), or "You're not a man. A little boy could do it better," and similar cuts to his male ego. Ced stated that after about two weeks of this criticism, the time it took for him to have sex with her shortened considerably. After about a month, he began to lose his erection during intercourse. At the end of the last two months he was unable to arouse an erection in her presence. That was when he decided he needed this woman like he needed another four years in the navy.

During the next three months, he attempted to have sexual intercourse with other women. He picked up a prostitute a month after he left his mistress. With her he lost his erection shortly after penetration and did not regain it. A month later, he tried again with a second prostitute, but with her he was completely impotent. For the next three years and a bit, his only sexual outlet was masturbation. Over that period of time, he began to worry about whether he would be able to have an erection under any circumstance. By the time he came to me for treatment, he was unable to have an erection when he tried to masturbate.

Ced's history seems like a page out of a clinical textbook on sexual phobia. Over a period of two months, he had been conditioned, right in his bed, to become impotent by his sexual partner and her anxiety-provoking assessments of his sexual prowess. During the next two months, this negative learning was strengthened by Ced's anxiety about failing to perform adequately with other women, which produced exactly what he feared—lack of a potent sexual response. Now what Ced had learned, he could unlearn in therapy that used behavioral methods to evoke his orienting reflex. But before we look at how Ced's OR eliminated his sexual phobia, let's briefly look at how it was possible to condition his involuntary nervous system to be indifferent to sex—and in much the same way that Pavlov's dogs were conditioned to salivate to the sound of their keeper's footsteps at mealtime.

We could argue that Ced was conditionable because of his own self-doubts about sex that were set up by his parents' attitude toward, and their punishment of, his early sexual experimentation. But there is a flaw in thinking of the problem that way. I suspect there has not trod upon this earth a man or woman completely sure of his or her own sexuality, appeal, responsivity or potency. Every indication—clinical, literary, historical—supports this belief. The experience of sexual self-doubts is universal; so attributing sexual phobias to self-doubts is not much help in understanding how we learn them. Furthermore, this line of thinking begs the real question: Why do we all seem to have these doubts? There is only one meaningful answer: *Because the basis of these doubts is wired into our primitive nervous system.*

"Now that makes sense," you may be saying, "for things like breathing and sleeping, but are you saying we are genetically designed to have sexual anxieties? Are you saying that they are neither a screwup, a fluke nor the product of a personality disorder but the direct result of our innate design?" If you are thinking this, you are absolutely right. We have sexual phobias because we were built to have them. I don't blame you if you find it hard to believe that Mother Nature was so mischievous eons back. But let's look at the evidence and you decide.

If we can trust the facts of human sexual neurology, put before us by physiologists and sexual researchers, it appears our sexual arousal pattern is regular, straightforward and a bit mechanical. The whole sex act up to orgasm can be looked at in three phases: arousal, plateau, and orgasm. Chart any measure of how we are aroused sexually (see the descriptive figure in the Appendix, page 304) from start to finish, and you will see a rapid buildup of sexual excitement during the arousal phase. This feeling of excitement matches the activity of the blood supply in the genitals for both men and women. During the arousal phase, the blood rushes to the genitals producing the penile erection in men and the engorgement of the vaginal tissues, including the vestigial penis —the clitoris, in women. The arousal phase may last from a few seconds to a few minutes. After the arousal phase, sexual excitement—as well as blood flow to the genitals—tapers off to a steady level as we reach the plateau phase. This phase may last from several to many minutes. Finally, when the orgasmic phase is triggered off, sexual excitement again rises to a peak, and for women there is another massive increase in blood flow to the vaginal tissue.*

"Okay," you tell me. "So you have just described in technical terms how I make love. What have you said that I don't already know?" To answer you I have to ask another question: What parts of the primitive nervous system activate and control each of these three phases of sexual arousal and performance?

---

*We, incidentally, know an awful lot more about the sexual function and dysfunction of men than we do of women. This bias in the history of sexual research has come about for two very practical reasons. First, the male provided the researcher with an obviously simple means to measure degrees of sexual arousal: the presence or absence of an erection—or a condition somewhere in between. With the male, you can tell just by looking if he is able or unable to engage in sex. With the female, it hasn't been so easy. What do you measure for a woman, how do you measure it and how do you even know there is a problem besides what the woman tells you?

Second, the administrators of universities and research centers frowned upon faculty members fooling around with the vagina in their laboratories. The professors kept telling the regents, "It's for research and science," while the regents kept thinking, "You're only doing it for fun and there will be a big scandal." So most of the information collected on sexual problems and treatment has been taken from male cases simply because they have been easier to work with.

"Why naturally the 'fun' half of the primitive nervous system," you respond.

Not quite. The arousal phase is under the control of the parasympathetic, the fun, half of the nervous system. That makes sense; arousal is fun. The plateau phase is also under control of the fun half. That too makes sense; while we make love, we feel good. The fun half controls the blood supply to the penis and vagina and that is necessary—for the male, at least—for us to continue with the sex act. But how about the orgasmic phase, where the peak of fun and pleasure is involved? It only makes common sense that the fun half of our primitive nervous system should be in control there too. . . . *Wrong!* The orgasmic phase—wherein many of us think lies the most fun—is under control of the "fear" half of our primitive nervous system.

"Now this crazy arrangement doesn't make sense," you might be saying to yourself. "You mean to tell me that sex wasn't designed to be fun all the way—that fear is also involved? What a rotten idea!"

I'm in complete sympathy. When I myself found this out, I harked back to the embarrassment and self-induced shame of the first time I could not perform sexually upon command. I thought I, or it, should be like the old comic book hero, Captain Phallus—"Shazam" and up it goes—and cursed God, Mother Nature, the Evolutional Design Committee or whoever was responsible for this stupid, wasteful, yes even criminal, arrangement I was supplied with.

On the other hand, I tried to look at the situation dispassionately. This crazy system explains why the male automatically loses his erection after ejaculation. I felt much better when I counted up on one hand the number of times during my life I remained erect after ejaculation. I could even see some advantages—however dubious—in this arrangement. The fear half, coming into play at the end of sex, solves a problem for the male who would otherwise be walking around afterward with a protuberance likely to get caught in cracks and branches. Also, if we were genetically designed to be responsive to anxiety —via the fear half—during sex, then sexual failure wasn't really my personal fault, was it? The cause was not something twisted or lacking in my personality or sexual appetites (but external and unpropitious circumstance). So the next time I was sexually lacking, I told myself: "Self. Don't worry. You are only behaving in strict accordance with your evolutional design parameters laid down eons ago." A lot of help that was. Why did He, She, They or It do this to us? This physiological arrangement of our sexual responsivity still didn't make sense. The more I thought about it, the more interesting the *why* question became. What grand purpose does it serve to make us sexually anxious by switching a basic mechanical connection in our primitive nervous system? There must be some usefulness to it. Everything else in our design is functional.

I haven't come up with a sure answer, but the most intriguing speculation is that our sexual neurology, with its anxiety switch, has evolutionally evolved so that it—over any other possible arrangement—fits best with the rest of our physical and psychological makeup: our size, behavior, thinking brain but most of all, to balance our outrageous preoccupation with sexual orienting.

The sexual neurology of a species—ourselves included—is dependent upon the total makeup of the species: what it does, how it copes, its physical strengths and limits, its size, its intelligence, etc. Let me point this out with a simple example from another species, the rabbit. Now the single, most obvious characteristic of rabbit sex is its speed. And speedy sex for the rabbit is dependent upon its makeup, primarily its small size. If you see two rabbits mate, you might at first be amazed to see how quickly they do it. With a minimum amount of foreplay the buck mounts the doe, thrusts for about fifteen to thirty seconds as if sex is going out of style and falls off to the ground upon ejaculating into the female, where he lies quivering and twitching for a few seconds in an epileptic-like seizure; and then, typically, he gets up with a start, often running a few feet away from the scene of the sex act.

That sexual behavior of the rabbit is quite stereotyped. You can observe its simplicity time after time. It seems like instinctual behavior wired into the rabbit's nervous system. Why do I say this? How many times have you seen a male rabbit sitting around smoking a cigarette after sex and communicating the rabbit equivalent of: "That was just great. We'll have to try that again." You don't see anything like this because the rabbit is wired to get sex over with quickly and get on with other things like staying alive.

Why is a rabbit designed this way? Because the rabbit's sexual nervous system is placed in the physical frame and limits of a rabbit. To get perspective on this result of eons of evolutionary *why*, let's place ourselves in the position of someone on the Evolutional Planning Committee for a moment.

Suppose Mother Nature sent a memo down to you and me from the big administrative office in the sky. The memo says that you and I are temporarily appointed to the Evolutional Design Subcommittee to work out the sexual construction details for a new species with the following ecological characteristics:

This design is to be a vegetarian animal able to convert leafy grasses of many types into high-grade protein. It should be plentiful and spread throughout the continents. It should be able to provide meals for a wide variety of other animals like wolves, foxes, birds of prey, etc., requiring an ample supply of inexpensive protein. It follows then, it should not be too clever in the ways of evasion, forcing the expense of much energy to catch it. It should of necessity, therefore, be relatively small, about a foot long and a quarter as much wide, thus precluding a huge size provoking many lost battles and meals. Give it big ears, with which it

can hear well through tall grass, and large rear feet to provide both balance in sitting up to attend to danger as well as strength in leaping from it. Because of the need for small size, provide it with speed of escape as its natural coping. This prototype design is to be called *rabitus rabitus vulgaris,* or the "rabbit" for short.
Get with it,
Mom

How do we go about designing a sexual nervous system for this tasty, small, defenseless, speedy, animal? One that will fit in with these characteristics over the long haul. First, we make it prolific and spread throughout the land. We do that with this new species by not giving it the seasonal mating instincts of other animals. Make the male orient to sex all the time. As soon as one litter is dropped, make the female sexually receptive again. A year-round sexual interest and large litter capacity will make the species flourish and spread throughout the land.

But its strong sex drive raises another problem. If we make its sex drive dominant so it will mate as often as possible, what happens if a male and female meet in unsafe circumstances? If we build in such a strong orienting reflex to sexual stimuli, might not this great response block out danger signals, as we know it will for other stimuli? What about situations where the male and female rabbit may get eaten if they hang around having sex too long. Do they forget about the danger signals and say, "To hell with it, the EPC says this is much more important"? That doesn't sound like an intelligent design philosophy. Herd animals could get away with it. They are surrounded by their own kind and typically mate once a year. But the members of this new species are to be on their own and mating as many times each year as possible. One sexually active male rabbit could conceivably mate 365 times a year if new females kept passing his way.

One possible solution to the problem of balancing the rabbit's conflicting need to orient to things sexual as well as to things dangerous would be to couple sex to something else the rabbit does well: get up speed. Why can't we make it fast of sex as well of foot? A high sex-orienting drive that blocks out perception of danger could be counterbalanced by a sex act lasting only a few seconds: sort of a primeval, "Hello, Sam . . . wham . . . bam . . . thank you, Ma'am." We could have the species attuned for sex to insure a high reproduction rate but make the sex act short to reduce the chance of the helpless pair being eaten because of not orienting to a nearby predator during the sex act.

Following the eminently practical notion expressed by the old joke, "How do porcupines mate? Very carefully!", Mother Nature, it seems, has evolved a sexual design for the rabbit much like this hypothetical one. The rabbit's style and mode of sex are very well fitted into its physical and environmental requirements.

You might object and say this is all sheer speculation. Perhaps it is way off the mark, but think about it for a moment. How many times have you seen a bull elephant mimic the rabbit's copulatory pattern? Can you really imagine that four-ton beast having sex with his mate for only fifteen to thirty seconds and afterward falling off onto the ground in a dead faint? If I were on his Evolutional Design Subcommittee, I would make sure that he could have his fun, anytime, anywhere, for as long as it took.

So my point is this: The sexual mechanics of the species must fit in with its other evolved coping behaviors. The small and defenseless animal is not going to be around for long in a predatory environment if it adopts—for all to see and hear—the blatant and proudly proclaimed sexual behavior of the bull elephant, especially if this behavior occurs more than once a year. Irrespective of how we sexually feel at times, we are neither rabbits nor elephants. But what are we? More importantly, what sort of animal frame did we have eons ago when our sexual nervous system was being evolutionally fitted into it? Were we small and defenseless or filled with physical bravado? According to the best evidence and theory that anthropologists, paleontologists and other scientists have given us, our first human-like ancestor walked upright on the savanna in Africa between two and five million years ago, He was a little over four feet tall and weighed in, at most, eighty pounds—soaking wet. We call this ancestor *Australopithecus Africanus*, or the upright southern African ape. Australopithecus was about the size of a present-day, healthy ten-year-old boy. This size meant that while Australopithecus was not designed on the scale of the timid rabbit, neither was he or she immune from attack from predators that existed during that era.

As with the example of the rabbit, let's consider how the Evolutional Planning Committee would design a sexual nervous system to aid our early ancestors in their struggle for survival? We were few in number—a new species—and though predators ourselves, we were not very high in the aggressive pecking order of things. Like the rabbit, we should be designed to enjoy sex as often as possible—not just once a year like herd, pack or pride animals—so as to propagate the species and make it flourish. But we were not so small and helpless that one, or a pair, of us could not defend ourselves by showing our attackers we were no cheap meal. But if we were totally enraptured in the act of sex by orienting to it solely and thus made oblivious to all else, we would indeed be a cheap and easy meal. This consideration would have been especially important for our early ancestors, since, like us, they must have been ready for sex anytime, anywhere. And the sexual receptivity of the human male and female on a day in, day out basis makes us vulnerable to danger. A fundamental question for our survival then, was: How could this emerging species acquire a built-in means of protection during this very frequent sex act?

One solution for the EPC was to design a male Australopithecus with the sexual speed of a rabbit. That might have worked, except for one significant drawback. Some rabbits are slower sexually than others and mutants are thrown off by Mother Nature. The really slow ones would have a higher probability of being caught during sex. So the process of natural selection would keep the fast ones breeding more and the slower ones breeding less. The likely result? Mostly fast-mating rabbits.

But Australopithecus was a thinking animal. It could make choices, even complicated ones. How long, for example, would it have taken Ms. Australopithecus to figure out that Speedy Australopithecus from the next cave was so quick—he wasn't any fun at all. But Malmo Australopithecus from down by the river . . . he took his time. That devil really made a girl feel good about the whole thing. So natural selection in our own species would have ruled out rabbit-like speed as a sexual coping defense.

What other alternatives did the EPC have available? Probably a lot and tried them all. But one alternative had a certain elegance and simplicity. Don't make the *entire* sex act fun for Australopithecus. You really need do that only during the first part of sex, particularly when the male needs an erection to penetrate and copulate. Activate the fear half of the primitive nervous system only when you want the sexual act to end quickly in the face of something dangerous, fearful or, today, anxiety provoking. How to do this? Simple. Make the orgasmic phase controlled by the fear half of the primitive nervous system. To see what this would accomplish, picture a pair of our early ancestors mating. They are in a place somewhat secluded, really enjoying themselves, when a large hairy something or other comes rushing upon them with assorted growls, howls and gnashing of teeth. The flight–fight system then swings automatically into action and diverts the pair from sex. Neurologically, it is now not the fun thing it was a moment ago. Both the male and the female are now operating with the flight–fight nervous system dominant and are free to either attack, aggressively defend themselves or flee. The results of coupling the orgasmic phase of the sex act to the fear half of the nervous system? Whenever danger appears, the sex act is finished immediately, and without orgasm. It wouldn't do to have two limp humanoids turning to face a charging predator.

But there is one more clever twist evolved by nature. When the flight–fight system is activated during sex, the male "prematurely" ejaculates into the female, automatically increasing the chance of impregnation, no matter what the outcome from the battle or chase between the intruder and the male. For an emerging species, relatively few in number, this automatic impregnation of the female in the face of danger would benefit the species greatly. As I said, a most elegant design philosophy.

If we take into consideration that our ancestor's basic neurology of fun–fear sex could be conditioned, we may have one possible explanation for why sex has usually been—with some notable civilized exceptions ranging from Biblical orgies to those in the San Fernando Valley—a private matter. If the unwary pair in the primitive environment—or even ours today —coupled indiscriminately wherever and whenever the fancy took them, it would not be long before wide-open public spaces would have learned negative characteristics: "Dammit Austro. Everytime we try it out in the field, someone sneaks up on us and I finish off. Let's find somewhere we can get some privacy. How's about your place?" Also, if this negative experience of triggering off the fear system during sex happens quite often—especially in the arousal phase—we then see the learned sexual dysfunction of what we call premature ejaculation and impotence in men and sexual frigidity in women. This outcome is exactly what our patient, Ced, experienced in his relations with his mistress. He was a conditioned sexual phobe—impotent—not because of his self-doubts, but because his early ancestor *Australopithecus Africanus* was evolved to be sexually phobic to increase the chances for his species survival.

Unlearning Impotence

How was Ced cured of his impotence using the orienting reflex? My colleague, Zev Wanderer, and I took Ced into Irv Maltzman's laboratory at UCLA and worked out a scheme for his retraining. Ced had no cooperative partners available to him. Our services would have to be limited to less than twelve weeks since the academic year—no one works in the summer at the university—was rapidly closing. What could we do? The answer was prompted by necessity. Ced told us that he masturbated occasionally just to see if he could get an erection. So we decided to hook him up to a physiological polygraph—the fancy name for a lie detector. We used a special photoelectric device taped to his penis to measure minute changes in its blood volume. With this information, we could give Ced moment to moment positive feedback—the orienting reflex is triggered off by things positive—on the state of his erection or lack of it. The changes in his erection that could be measured with this device were so small that he would normally be unaware of them. Because he was concerned about—oriented to—the state of his erection, this feedback should be a positive counterconditioning stimulus that would combat his phobic anxiety.

We had no female to recondition him to, so we used what we had on hand: a series of over 100 full-color 35 mm slides of women in varying states of sexuality. We started with commercial bra and panty ads and progressed to full "beaver" shots of the vaginal area. These slides were projected over Ced's shoulder into a quiet treatment room where he was sitting away from all the distracting electronic apparatus.

With this relearning arrangement, we could praise Ced for his minute erectile responses using a microphone and earphones. We could also model positive attitudes and specifics to orient to during each female slide by saying things like: "Wow. . . . Look at that gal. She has a really neat pair of sex objects," and so on.

You can see the results of this sexual retraining for the first two sessions in the polygraph recording on page 304 of the Appendix. The thin, slowly changing line is the measurement of changes in blood volume in Ced's penis. As you can see, it was quite irregular over the whole retraining session, with the level of blood volume going up and down as if the primitive nervous system had difficulty in "making up its mind" if Ced should have an erection or not. The other squiggly line is a measure of the blood supply to the brain—more technically, the temporal–cephalic area supplying the right eye. The rapid up-and-down movement on the graph is the strength of the pulse —produced by each heartbeat—that reached this area of the head. The research on the orienting reflex carried out in Irv Maltzman's laboratory had previously discovered that the width of the pulse measured in this area was a good indication of the relative dominance of the tonic, or long-term, orienting reflex (a wide-pulse width) and the tonic defensive reflex (a small-pulse width). As you can see, shortly after Ced saw the first female slide, his cephalic pulse width narrowed to about 2.5 times of what it was previously. His nervous system was producing a tonic conditioned defensive reflex—a phobic reaction—to the female stimuli. When we recognized this was happening to him, we stopped the session, and I went inside to talk with him. He said he was getting nervous, so I told him to count backward from 100 whenever a blank 35 mm slide came on between female slides. With Ced doing this, we continued the session. Orienting to my blank slide instruction, his pulse width didn't seem to get much larger for the rest of the session with him—but neither did it get smaller. For that first session, we settled for a draw. The phobic stimuli were presented and, while he did not respond positively to them, his negative phobic response was minimized by making him orient to other things in the situation. What happened on the next session, one week later, is a fascinating example of not knowing what will happen in clinical research. During the week, Irv and I had gone over Ced's polygraph recording and were pleased with what we saw. Then Irv asked an embarrassing question: How did we know that Ced was giving a DR just on the basis of the female slides? We had nothing to compare his response to. So on the next session, I added to the slide series a bunch of typical tourist scenes taken in Hawaii and Europe to be shown before the female slides.

At the appointed time, we ran the second reconditioning session on Ced, and I'll be damned if Irv wasn't right—but not in a way we had foreseen. In the middle of the tourist scenes having nothing to do with females, Ced's pulse width began to slowly narrow, indicating his nervous system was responding phobically once more, only this time to seashore and landscape scenes of Hawaii and Europe. That didn't make sense. I stopped the session again and went in to talk to Ced. He said spontaneously that he was getting nervous; and the reason for his upset was the seashore scenes. Ced explained that he was in the navy when his impotence struck, and the seashore reminded him of the navy and when he thought of the navy he thought of his mistress who'd caused the whole damned problem, and he began to get uptight. I told Ced to forget about the tourist scenes and we'd begin again using the female slides. But this time, whenever a blank slide came on the screen in between females, he was to count the pulse rate in his index finger, the one with the photoelectric device taped to it. We spent a few seconds adjusting the pressure of the surgical tape on his finger until he could just feel a pulse—bodily sensations trigger off the OR—and we started over again.

What we saw this time was dramatic. The changes in his small erectile beginnings were not erratic as they had been previously. They had altered in character, being more slow and progressive—long, sweeping changes instead of more rapid ups and downs. This change prevailed during all of the remaining counterconditioning sessions. Also, during this second session, we saw our first direct evidence of a defensive reflex paralleling a decrease in erection. If you count off twenty-four (24) seconds after the second female slide (F2) in the treatment series, you will see a large decrease (upswing) in the blood volume of the finger and the temple—a defensive reflex. Just at this time, the increase in blood flow causing an erection in the penis tapers off and stops, causing Ced's penis to become less erect. At that point, the OR–DR theory of phobia was no longer theory. It was fact.

A female therapist was drafted and pressed into service for one session in which she substituted for me and gave Ced positive feedback and modeling comments: "I'll bet this one will turn you on Ced," or, "You certainly gave a big response to her. Very good Ced." Considering his sexual history, we were sure that positive feedback of a sexual nature from a female would certainly be a novelty for him.

The turning point came in the fourth session. During the entire conditioning time, Ced consistently produced large erections in response to the female slides and then just as quickly lost them. Fearing some weird religious attitude or personality quirk that he had not told me about, I asked Ced what had happened to his erections during the session. He told me that the masking tape used to hold the measuring instrument against his penis began to tug quite painfully on his pubic hairs as his penis became more erect. When a certain level of pain was reached, he lost his erection and the cycle began again. Erection–pain–loss of erection—over and over again this cycle repeated itself during the entire session. After learning of Ced's pain, we used a commercial condom with the end snipped off as wide "rubber band" to hold the measuring device against his penis. To test this new/arrangement, I had Ced try it out with no slides. I told him over the earphones to think of sexy women in his imagination for several minutes. Then I told him to stop fantasizing and think of baseball, or auto racing, etc. Whenever I told him to think of women, he gained a full erection. When I told him to think of something else, he was not aroused.

Now, after this brief treatment program—under six hours' total conditioning time—Ced was able to produce an erection simply by thinking of women. The slides, modeling, feedback, even the female therapist, were no longer needed.

How could we tell that this laboratory retraining with sexual slides had transferred to sex with real women? The first indication that it had was from Ced himself who came to see me with a big grin the week after the last retraining session. Ced got on his regular bus to go home and a beautiful young girl got on and sat down beside him. In between orienting to her beauty and sexiness and the occasional touching of thighs, Ced noticed within minutes that he involuntarily produced a maximum erection sitting alongside her on the bus. His erection was of such magnitude and duration that he missed his regular bus stop by almost a mile. He had to wait for several blocks after she left before he could get up and walk down the aisle without his erection being obvious to the other passengers. Several months later, Ced let me know that he was engaging in sexual intercourse with several girls.

Unlearning Inhibitions to Orgasm

Ced's story of success in regaining his sexual potency, with six hours of OR retraining following a hiatus of over three years as an impotent, is just short of amazing. But his case gives us little information on the general treatment of sexual phobias without the use of a laboratory full of complicated electronic devices. Can this sort of retraining be used outside the laboratory? Will it work for women? On other sexual phobias? To answer these questions, let's briefly look at two other cases of sexual phobia—nonorgasmic Gail and impotent, gay Boris—and see what was done.

When Gail asked me for help, she was thirty-two years old, a mother of a five-year-old child, divorced, dating a steady boyfriend and nonorgasmic. In checking out her history, she told me that she had orgasms regularly during masturbation but never experienced one in making love with a man. The treatment for this condition was relatively simple and straightforward—or so I thought at the time. Have Gail masturbate to orgasm and gradually, over a period of time, bring a male into the situation. First the male would only be male, not a sexual partner. Then he, or another male, could assume the role of a lover. I decided I would play the first therapeutic role of the male: the male stimulus. Then after Gail had been able to achieve orgasm in my stimulus presence, her boyfriend could carry her the rest of the way. We met for therapy sessions at my house for three reasons. For one thing, there was no need to do any involved physiological recordings—or so I thought—to determine Gail's problem. It was clear that she was an androphobe, the clinical name for one who is anxious about having sex in the presence of another person. Second, to assure Gail that I was only a male stimulus and not a sexual partner, my wife would be present in the house while we were reconditioning her dysfunction. Third, UCLA at that time was not equipped with a bed to use for sexual therapy (it has since corrected that deficit).

We set up the following treatment plan. During the initial stages, Gail was not to have sex with her boyfriend. He was to be reintroduced after she had had an orgasm in my presence. Over a number of sessions, Gail was to strip, lie on the bed in the guest room and masturbate to orgasm while I was sitting, progressively, outside with the door closed, partially open, wide open, sitting in the doorway, inside the room and alongside the bed. Gail would masturbate both by stimulating her clitoris with her fingers or a vibrator and alternately stimulating the whole genital area, including the sexual nerve endings in the vagina with a banana to simulate the erect male.

That should eliminate her androphobia, I thought, but I added a final touch. One more session where I would hold her hand or arm so the male presence would bridge the gap between "being there" and "being in contact." Thank God for that afterthought.

Gail and I went through the whole therapy procedure as we outlined it. She was quite shy at first, demanding that I pay no attention to her when the door was partially opened. I told her that I was sitting there and working on my income-tax return, which I was. As the sessions progressed, she was more at ease and felt completely comfortable being nude in my presence while we reviewed what happened or talked over what she might try to increase her sexual arousal during masturbation. During the last session I moved close up to the bed, sat on the edge and held her hand while she masturbated. For the first time I spoke to her as she masturbated and suggested she think about the sexy feelings in her genitals. After a few minutes, she asked me to rub her shoulder so she could use both hands. I did as she asked, and a minute later she went limp and said: "I did it." I congratulated her and we began to discuss what she was to do tomorrow night with her boyfriend. We agreed to meet for several more sessions to allow the orgasm with the neutral male to overlap the sexual intercourse with the sexual male. Gail came back the following week and announced that the therapy was over. She had achieved orgasm with her friend for the first time the night after we last met and had been completely satisfied upon their next three couplings also. Then she looked at me with an embarrassed look and said: "I lied to you before. I was too embarrassed to tell you the truth." "What lie?" I asked. "When I said I have orgasms masturbating," she confessed. "Until you held my hand and rubbed my shoulder that night, I had never reached orgasm in my life." Well . . . that little bit of information knocked me for a loop. So much for my traditional, well-planned behavior therapy, based on Mary Cover Jones and little Peter's white rabbit phobia. Dealing with totally nonorgasmic men and women is a hit-and-miss affair. *No one*—the behaviorists, the Freudians, the eclectics, the gestaltists, the sex therapists—really knows what they are doing in treating nonorgasmic people. There isn't even a halfway decent theory on what to do about total nonorgasmic dysfunction. It's really a case of, "Let's relax 'em . . . no pressure . . . take your time . . . and run 'em through whatever the rest of us do to enjoy sex. Maybe that will work." If Gail had told me that she was completely nonorgasmic, I would have referred her to someplace where at least *they thought* they knew what they were doing.

The only palatable psychological explanation for why people are nonorgasmic is that some previously learned anxiety about sex triggers off the fear system before they can reach orgasm—or some variation on this theme. Why did Gail have anxiety—and she was anxious—about sex and masturbation? I don't know. But my best guess would be that her mother, father or some other adult in her childhood caused it. Probably, in a well-meaning way, she was punished for playing with her genitals as a child. If I had to bet money on a reason, that's the one I'd pick. But again, the reason why we have sexual anxieties is no help in eliminating them. Gail's mother and father could have sat down and pleaded with their daughter, "We really didn't mean for you not to enjoy sex when you grew up. We love you and want you to be happy in all things, including sex. We just wanted for you to be civilized about it. You shouldn't be anxious. There is really nothing wrong with sex," and that exhortation would have had all the impact on Gail's primitive nervous system of a mouse breaking wind during the Indianapolis 500.

What caused Gail to come to orgasm for the first time during that last therapy session? Again, I have no sure knowledge, but I would bet it had something to do with my bodily touch on her hand, arm and shoulder, as well as my suggestion that she think mainly about the sexual sensations coming from her vagina and clitoris. These things would evoke an OR to compete with her learned anxiety about sex. After the treatment was over, Gail and I sat down and talked about her unsuccessful attempts to reach orgasm. We came up with a lot of vague and fancy theories on how she failed consistently, but one piece of behavior during masturbation and sex was consistent for her. Instead of attending and "tuning in" to the sensations arising from sex, Gail kept thinking of telephone numbers, license plates and street addresses; and she would add and subtract them in her mind. Now that is orienting, but to things that don't lead to orgasm. Coming to orgasm is relatively simple and mechanical. But it's not a passive activity like riding in a plane. You can reduce your learned anxiety in flight and sit back completely comfortable. But you may never really enjoy flying as a passenger. You certainly won't come to orgasm just sitting there at 30,000 feet. Most of the time it's quite boring. Coming to orgasm is not so mechanical that we can ignore it like the pilot who puts his plane on autopilot and walks back to chat with the passengers. We have to be at least minimally involved with sex before we will come to orgasm. The way Gail had learned to reduce her anxiety about sexual sensations was to avoid attending to these sensations during sex. She put her system on autopilot and left—no pun intended—the cockpit by orienting to other things, numbers, math and license plates. This would be the equivalent of keeping your eyes closed while balancing on a high wire. You would feel less anxious about falling, sure. But you would never get to the other side either.

So for at least some of us, being nonorgasmic may be the result of misusing our orienting reflex during sex to reduce sexual anxiety. "But," you may be asking yourself, "if phobias are learned and all we need do in the phobic situation is to orient, what does it matter how we orient as long as the anxiety is reduced?"

In the first part of this book, I told how my college chum, Fred, had eliminated my fear of flying by teaching me how to fly. I also said that Fred could have taught me to juggle three oranges in flight and achieved the same result—my phobia would have been eliminated. But juggling three oranges in flight wouldn't have given me the joy of flying. In sex, you don't want to feel just comfortable. I believe—and I can speak with great authority on this subject for myself—that you want something more than feeling just at ease.

The most commonsense advice tells us where to orient during sex in order to achieve orgasm. "Let yourself go," experienced women tell novices, or "accept yourself and your sexual feelings." Before women's lib, "surrender yourself to him," was popular. Lately it's more fashionable to say "know your own body and its sensations." All these commonsense statements say in other words, "Orient during sex to reduce your anxiety but orient to things sexual: fantasies, strokes; attend to sensations and parts of your body, even to your breathing and heartbeat."

Are there some other ways of orienting during sex to make things easier besides this commonsense advice? Yes, but they may not fit in with your personal life-style. The use of leathers and sado–masochism is based upon the orienting reflex. "Now that's a bit kinky," you may be telling yourself. But *kinky* is a value judgment we all have to make for ourselves. Remember, we are built to learn to like anything, even tight garments and mild pain during sex. How does this work neurologically? Leathers, or the tight garments worn by their aficionados during sex, are both a source of constant bodily stimulation—an OR generator—and an anxiety reducer. Leathers evoke the touch orienting reflex, and the OR to touch seems to poop out slower than many others. Masochism, or the affliction of mild pain—generally to the sex organs—is both a source of sexual stimulation and an anxiety reducer. You find this a bit hard to believe? Let me tell you about Boris.

Boris was referred to me some seven years ago because he could not find a psychologist or psychiatrist in the greater Los Angeles area who would treat him. He gave up after seeing four in a row face-to-face who *would not* treat his condition and got negatives over the phone from six more who did not want to be involved with his case. Why did they not want to get involved? Because Boris was impotent, masochistic, homosexual and wanted to remain being gay. I don't know whether the professional attitude about providing help for such "immoral" problems is as negative now, seven years later, as it was then, but I do know there are very few clinics that will treat such problems. Boris came to me finally, because he met a gay psychiatrist socially who suggested that I might be able to help.

When Boris and I sat down to see if anything could be done for his problem, I found very little to work with. Boris was young, in his mid-twenties. He did not have a stable relationship with any other gays. There was no option for using a Masters and Johnson method of treatment for his impotence, because Boris had no cooperative gay partner to work with. Worse still, Boris had great difficulty in reaching orgasm through masturbation. His was a complex, difficult case to treat—not because of his homosexuality or the question of its morality. His situation made it difficult.

Masochistic Impotence and the Lie Detector

I told Boris this bit of depressing news, and then he told me what he did to come to orgasm. What he said left me no choice but to try and treat his problem in any way possible. Boris' regular way of achieving orgasm was to stimulate his urethra—the interior canal in the penis through which urine and sperm flow—with various objects during masturbation. He had used a number of devices, like the refill cartridges from ball-point pens, wooden sticks, even a toy rubber worm bought at a novelty shop. This technique of self-stimulation was not novel to Boris. It has been known for centuries in central and eastern Europe and called the "hot stick." But Boris went beyond European tradition. He would insert the stick totally into the penis and work it down to the prostate gland area—where the white substance of the semen is produced—while masturbating to stimulate an orgasm. Two months before he saw me, he lost the rubber worm in his bladder and it had to be removed by a urologist. The physician recommended he see a psychotherapist. Boris declined the suggestion until six weeks later. Then he tried masturbating again. But this time he used as his "hot stick" a short, glass martini stirring rod. Boris also lost this glass rod in his urethra. It took him close to an hour lying on his bed to work it out. He said that incident scared him. It scared the hell out of me just listening to it. If Boris had bent over, squatted, gotten a muscle cramp or a stomachache during that hour, the glass rod would have broken inside of him. His life expectancy at that point would have been about twenty to thirty minutes after one of the major blood vessels in that location was punctured.

After I heard this tale, Boris and I began a therapy relationship that lasted three years. For the first three months, we just talked about his background, how he coped in general with problems and what sort of person he was. Amazingly enough, Boris had relatively good mental health. He seemed to have no severe neurotic anxieties or depressions. He had no rages or other compulsions. He just wanted to be sexually competent in the same way his friends were. There was nothing out of the ordinary about Boris. He was a college graduate and had a job on the side while putting himself through law school. Nothing in his history gave any indication of what had caused his problem or what could be done for it. During this period of exploring his background, Boris had agreed not to use martini rods, pencils, thin screwdrivers or anything else found around the house as a sexual aid. He was trying masturbation—and trying to make sexual contacts with his gay friends—to satisfy his sexual urges. Nothing I suggested seemed to work. Then Boris called me up one day, greatly excited, and said he had found a way to produce successful masturbation everytime; he twisted his testicles until it was painful. I cautioned Boris that this might not be as dangerous as the martini rod but just as scary if he injured himself. Boris rejected my warnings and insisted he knew what he was doing. At this point, I was willing to try anything in the behavioral mode to give Boris some alternative method of gratification besides having to injure himself. I suggested that we try the same technique that had worked before with Ced, the heterosexual impotent. Boris was willing, but he could not see how this would help. Neither could I, but I was grasping at straws.

To make a long story short, we went through the same procedure for Boris at the UCLA Maltzman Laboratory, using a selection of 35 mm slides of males purchased from a gay porno shop. We tried this procedure for twelve weeks: Boris making up sexual fantasies about the men in the slides and me giving him positive feedback for partial erection responses recorded on the polygraph.

The twelve weeks of treatment were a complete bust. Nothing happened. Nothing, except for one consistent observation: Boris gave his maximum erection responses to Black and Chicano males. When I casually noted this at the end of some of the sessions, Boris vehemently denied it. In my best clinical manner I "umm-hummed" him and said privately to myself: "What the hell does he know? If the polygraph says he gets turned on most by Blacks and Chicanos, then he gets turned on by Blacks and Chicanos. Why should I argue with this cantankerous son-of-a-bitch?" In retrospect, I can see that if I had argued with him, we might have shortened the time of the successful treatment for his masochistic impotence by six months. Three weeks after we gave up on the UCLA feedback treatment, Boris disappeared. He had moved and left no forwarding address. Three months later, he called me and asked for another appointment. I agreed and at the meeting he told me that for the last week he had been in the hospital receiving treatment for an injury to his testicles. He had carried his painful twisting a bit too far during his last masturbation, and it was still not clear whether his testicles would have to be removed or whether they would recover. It was clear that Boris was now motivated to listen to whatever I told him.

"First thing, no more sexual aids."

"Agreed."

"Second thing, no more twisting of the testicles or any other part of the body."

"Definitely agreed."

"Third, let's talk about why you got so huffy with me when I said you were turned on most by Blacks and Chicanos back at UCLA."

Boris gave me an exasperated look that said, *Why do you even have to ask that question?* and then amplified what his look said: "I'm not like that. I wouldn't have anything to do with them. I'm gay, but I'm not that kind of gay."

Realizing that I might have found the key to the whole problem, I said, "Boris, You are gay like you are everything else. You are an ultramiddle-class conservative gay. You even voted for Nixon. Does your mother know you are gay?" I asked. "Of course she doesn't. You're just her little boy studying hard so she can say, 'that's my son the lawyer!' What kind of gays do you openly associate with? The other middle-class gays down on the gay Riviera in Laguna. Have you ever been caught being gay? Never! You dash in and out of the gay bars with pickups as if you're Captain Midnight with whoever you can scrounge up. You have never gone to one gay bar just for an evening of fun. What do you fear most that people will call you? A *queer.* Homosexual or gay doesn't bother you, but the middle-class reprobation *Queer* with a capital *Q* does. You are no different from the middle-class spinster in the Iowa corn belt who can't stand the thought that anyone would even guess that she had sexual impulses. You're so dammed middle class, it's choking off your hard on!"

After that outburst I felt a lot better. Evidently Boris did too, for he smiled at me and said, "I guess you want me to take some chances sexually that I wouldn't want mom to find out about?" He was right. From now on Boris was to masturbate in the way males without complications usually did it. He was to fantasize about Black men and Chicanos while doing it. He was also to patronize gay bars—since he still refused to form a stable sexual alliance with another gay—and get to be known as a gay in the Hollywood area. Boris did this and found that his sexual attempts with gays were not much better than before, but at least he felt more comfortable about himself and his gayness. After about three months of this new sexual life-style, Boris came in to see me with a grin on his face. "I did it," he said. "I was worried about it for a while, but he was so attractive I couldn't resist." For the first time in his life, Boris had successful sexual relations with another human. After congratulating him, I asked casually: "Was he Chicano?" Boris looked sheepish and answered, "Yes." Since that first time, Boris has successfully made it many times with other gays, mostly Caucasians.

Now, what is the point of Boris' story? Simply this. I, and as far as I can tell, every other representative of the professional Los Angeles therapeutic community, didn't know what to do for Boris. As it turned out, the key to treating his problem was given by his involuntary orienting reflex. He oriented sexually to Black and Chicano males, yet he didn't—or wouldn't—realize it. When we found out what turned him on the most (Chicano males), he was able—even with much procrastination—to use that sexual information to overcome his anxiety about having sex with another human being. Once that initial block was overcome, he performed sexually like many gays and straights; sometimes sex was great, other times it was just okay. Most importantly, he was able to achieve a safe sex life by knowing what turned him on the most and using it.

Sexual Orgasm: What You Orient to Is What You Get

Now these three cases, Cedric's, Gail's and Boris', had a common problem: anxiety about sex and its circumstances. And their successful treatment was due to dealing with this anxiety in different ways. In each of these ways, however, the orienting reflex was involved. If you have a sexual problem related to anxiety, you may be able to use your own orienting reflex to reduce your problem or eliminate it completely. Remember, we professionals only report on sexual problems "cured" with our help for people who come into our offices. For every patient I have "cured," I have heard two stories about people who have solved their own sexual difficulties without any professional help whatsoever. I'll bet it is done everyday without our help. So let's turn to some instructions on what you can do to help relieve your own, or your partner's, anxieties about sex. As in driving a car, sex is not a passive spectator sport. Also, for most of us, at least, sex does not send us into a sheer panic that makes us feel like running from it screaming, "Let me the hell out of here!" It is more typical for us to feel a sense of shame and guilt from our lack of sexual response, and we react by withdrawing inside ourselves rather than fleeing in panic.

The most common complaint from persons with sexual anxieties is: "What's wrong with me? Why can't I be like other people and just enjoy sex like they do?" If you find yourself cursing your sex life this way, think of your sexual functioning in terms of driving a car. To get it moving, you have to do two things: release the handbrake and hit the gas pedal. Sexual anxieties are a jammed handbrake and sexual stimulation is the gas. For you to enjoy sex from arousal through orgasm, your primitive nervous system demands that there be no anxiety and plenty of sexual stimulation. So the remedy for sexual problems caused by anxieties has two requisite parts: (1) reducing your anxiety—releasing the handbrake— so your sexual neurology *is free to let you go* from arousal to orgasm, and (2) getting you to orient to sexual things during sex—hitting the gas pedal—so

your sexual neurology *will carry you* from arousal
to orgasm.

The sexual retraining programs in this chapter,
therefore, are designed to help you do both of these
things—orient to reduce your anxiety, and orient
to maximize your sexual stimulation. As in retraining
yourself to drive a car without fear, you can't be
programmed in minute steps, because only you know
where you are. So the instructions are general ones
recommending that you do this and not that. How
and when you do them must be adjusted according
to your own personal preferences. I can give you the
best ways to get your sexual car rolling again, but
you have to do the fine-tuning on your own engine
so it runs the way you want it to.

The sexual retraining program is basically in two
parts: one for the *preorgasmic anxieties* of women
and men who rarely reach orgasm, and a second set
of subprograms for the *conjoint orgasmic anxieties*
of women and men who have difficulty reaching orgasm with another person. If you find yourself in the
preorgasmic category, use that program first and
then use the sections of the second conjoint program
that are appropriate for you. If you find yourself
only with problems in the conjoint situation, you
may find it worth your while to read the first section
before you begin your program with another person.

Making Yourself Less Anxious During Self-Stimulation

If you have difficulty coming to orgasm, like Gail,
even without the added anxiety of another person
involved, a professional would probably diagnose you
as having a "primary sexual dysfunction," a fancy
(and dreary) name for what is known as a *preorgasmic* problem in many women's self-help groups.
This problem is not limited to women, however.
Male patients seen in clinics for sexual problems also complain of it. To be very honest, total inability to

come to orgasm is something not very well understood by professionals. Although, theoretically, anxiety is generally assumed to be one main cause for the lack of orgasm, the patients who complain of this problem range in character from those with few sexual inhibitions to those with rigid ideas about the dirtiness and immorality of sex to those psychotic individuals who are filled with fixed delusions that other people are transmitting evil sexual wishes to them and that God will punish us all for enjoying sex.

As you can see, what causes a total lack of orgasm may vary greatly from one person to another.

For example, perhaps you don't particularly care for some aspects of sex. You get sweaty, smelly, shaky and tired, you feel wet and sloppy, undignified, limp and vulnerable at times, you exchange germs with your partner and usually run the risk of getting —or getting someone else—pregnant. It's difficult to have sex without these things happening. As they say, it goes with the territory. How you feel about yourself—your self-image—and what you feel good doing are just as important as any learned anxieties you have. If any of these regular consequences of sex are distasteful to you, they will act as inhibitions to your primitive nervous system that will turn you off accordingly. And when you get turned off, you don't reach orgasm—even if you are masturbating alone.

Your program of sexual retraining has to get you to orient to reduce any learned anxiety you may have. Also, you have to learn to like what you are doing—or discover more things you like. To do this you have to orient to what's going on in sex. To help yourself in accomplishing both these goals, use the information and OR suggestions in the following steps.

1. You have a much better chance of being fully orgasmic with a sexual partner if you can first become orgasmic by yourself. This means masturbation—sexual self-stimulation. If you object to masturbation, ask yourself why. Was it your parent's attitude toward it? Most

clinical case histories of sexual difficulties have punishment of masturbation as an early trauma. And contrary to what most parents think and teach their children, many neurologists state that sexual play before the age of six is beneficial to infantile brain growth, which allows a healthy, normal sex life as adults. So, if you can believe the experts, sex before six is good for you. After six, it's just for fun.

2. Explore and orient to different sexual fantasies. Do this first without masturbating. Are you afraid to do this because you might find some kinky twist in your sexual appetites? Perhaps you might get turned on fantastically by some scene or act that would petrify you in real life. Fantasize to your heart's content. Take it from an old and experienced clinical type. You don't have to act out your fantasies. We see so many cases of patients unnecessarily controlling their impulses that the incidents of lack of control pale into insignificance. Being turned on by your fantasies is a reliable way to trigger off your sexual orienting reflex. Now, in trying out your fantasies for the first time, you may say to yourself: "Me do that? That's disgusting." Well, it may be disgusting intellectually, but it may also be causing your primitive nervous system to prime your sexual apparatus. Very often we use *denial* as a means of avoiding either the anxiety or the guilty feelings that accompany the true facts of a situation. Rather than experience these emotions, our intellect immediately turns them off without really exploring the situation.

Give your distaste its voice, but give your sexual orienting reflex a chance to tell you what it's doing also. Explore what turns you on sexually in the privacy and comfort of your own fantasies. And then use that sexual excitement to stimulate yourself toward orgasm.

Now there are aids to sexual fantasizing. Pictures of nude or sexy partners help. Pornographic magazines or novels are helpful too. Even soft-core porn such as gothic romance novels will aid you if that is your thing. Don't cut yourself off from these resources. If you don't like porn for esthetic or life-style reasons, you don't have to read it—that is after you are consistently able to reach orgasm.

If you are a woman, you have four direct sources of

sexual stimulation in the vaginal area: the edges of the vaginal lips, the clitoris at the top of the vaginal lips (belly up), the nerve tract endings in the vaginal walls themselves and the corresponding parallel nerve tract endings in the walls of the anal colon. The vaginal nerve endings are concentrated in two spots, each about the size of the end of your little finger. They are located about one third of the way in on the vaginal wall in a 4 o'clock and an 8 o'clock position (with 12 o'clock being the top of the vagina, belly up). Some women have a third nerve tract located in the 12 o'clock position. Examine the sensations when you stimulate each of these areas with your fingers. To find the vaginal spots, insert your fingers—or some smooth object—into your vagina with sweeping motions or you gradually penetrate deeper. First, you will feel a hump or wall. This is the vaginal sphincter, or the circular, muscle which closes the vagina. Notice the sensation you feel as you sweep your finger across the wall of the vagina. When the sensation abruptly changes, you have touched one of the sexual nerve tract endings. You may wish to do the same thing for the tracts in your anal colon. Although orgasm is generally reached with stimulation of any or all of these nerve endings, the anal nerve tract endings contribute to orgasm during anal intercourse, both for women and gay men.

3. Orient to what you are doing to stimulate yourself sexually. Experiment and explore the sensations of different ways of arousing your sexual feelings and maintaining them during masturbation. If you are a novice or a fumbler, get some of the many "how to do it" sex books on the market today. There are a flood of them, giving all sorts of advice on different ways to stimulate yourself. One of the best I have seen is *Making Love*, by Patricia Raley.* Investigate the use of mechanical aids in stimulation. Phallic-shaped vibrators or ones that slip over the hand are very simple to use. If you don't believe in using such mechanical aids, that's okay too. After you are consistently orgasmic, don't use them anymore.

---

*The Dial Press, 1976.

4. Pick your own time and place to be sexual. If you are going to be distracted, cancel your time and choose another one where you can be at ease. At first, make it a totally private matter even if you applaud exhibitionism. Don't bring mom or her psychological presence into the bedroom with you. Be comfortable when you masturbate. Stay away from cold places. Sex seems to thrive in warmer, damper climates. If you like the dark, pull down the shades during the day or turn off the lights at night. Certainly, don't watch TV or listen to the radio when you have sex. Don't program yourself into a regular schedule: self-stimulation every Monday, Wednesday and Friday at 4 P.M. Get as much practice in being proficient about sex as you can, but do it more when the mood strikes you. You can't hurt yourself by too much simple masturbation, but your genitals may become sore for a day or two if you are excessive.

5. Don't just masturbate with your genitals. Use your whole body as a source of stimulation. Take some time to orient to sensations you feel when you touch other parts of your anatomy. You like the feel of a vibrator on your belly? Great. Vibrate your belly as you masturbate. Does it feel better when you move your legs and buttocks? Good. Do that as you masturbate also. Do you sweat a lot in masturbation? If so, run your hands over your sweaty body. Notice how this is more sensual than when your skin is dry. Check on your breathing. Does it get faster and then slower when you do certain things? Faster breathing generally means more arousal. Do you give short gasps of breath sometimes? That usually means more sexual arousal too. Practice breathing rapidly and in gasps, and orient to the sounds you make as you do it. This is a good way of getting to like the sounds of sex, and it's a neat way to arouse your next sexual partner too.

6. Most importantly, remember that sex is not just an affair to be experienced, but also to be enjoyed. So the procedure is a bit different from eliminating any other phobia. You don't want to be just nonphobic about sex; you want to be philic about it—to love it. So you orient during sex *only to bodily and sexual feelings.* Don't contemplate the *Rights of Man, War and Peace,* the

Dow Jones Index or your latest calculus assignment. Pay no attention to anything that has no sexual relevance. Instead—but without making a chore out of it—concentrate your attention on the sensation that masturbation and your sexual fantasy give you.

If you have a habit of orienting to other things during sex, this may relieve your anxious or guilty feelings and you may therefore feel more comfortable, but it isn't likely that you will become aroused enough for orgasm. Attend only to your bodily sensations—the sexy feelings, the goosebumps on your arms and legs, the sexual flush on your face and neck, your erect nipples (both men and women), the tautness of your legs and hips, feel of the bed, couch or bearskin rug as it presses into your back and buttocks—and nothing else.

Set up a program for yourself using these general instructions. Doing all these things will take some time. Start off slow and try not to be impatient. Give yourself lots of leeway and don't demand instant results from yourself. Your success will come a lot faster if you don't set up the frustrating goals of, "I have to do it now!" Remember, behavior therapy and orienting don't require heroes and heroines. All it needs is good percentages and odds. In changing your emotions and behavior, remember the behavioral motto: ALL I WANT IS AN UNFAIR ADVANTAGE.

Preintercourse anxiety and orgasmic program

This program is primarily for women who have reliable orgasm during masturbation but who think themselves "frigid" with a sexual partner. It, like the *preorgasmic program*, is basically a masturbatory one, but here a potential sexual partner is gradually brought into the act. Aimed at women's problems, it is designed as a first step prior to having orgasmic intercourse with a spouse or lover, since sexual anxiety brought about by the presence of another person is most likely the prime cause for 70 percent of all masturbatory–orgasmic women reporting lack of orgasm with sexual partners.

This sexual retraining program is in two parts: first, the *vaginismus retraining program* and second, the *conjoint orgasmic program.* If you are vaginismic and/or conjointly nonorgasmic, use both programs to reduce your sexual anxieties, preferably the one dealing with vaginismus first and the conjoint nonorgasmicity second.

Eliminating Vaginal Constrictions that Make Intercourse Impossible

Vaginismus is the professional term used to label the involuntary constriction of the circular muscle at the entrance to the vagina (the vaginal sphincter muscle) when any object tries to enter. If you find that this happens when you try to insert anything into your vagina, you have a "local conditioned muscular reflex." Now, that label isn't something to get more anxious about. The behavioral treatment of vaginismus is quite short and quite successful. I myself have never heard of a failure except for deliberate foot-dragging where the private wish of the patient is not to have sex with a spouse.

Vaginismus is often caused by painful intercourse, where infection, muscle separations, virginity or a tight vaginal opening are the causes of the pain, and the involuntary response is a severe constriction of the vaginal sphincter muscle. If painful intercourse is repeated a number of times, learned vaginismus may result. Some women with this problem report that their vaginal sphincter is not very discriminative. It can't "tell" the difference between an erect penis seeking entrance and the woman's own index finger. It rejects the attempts of both.

Clearly, this condition is not sexual inhibition as

a result of naivete, modesty, negativity or any other mental disposition to sex. It is a conditioned reflex that is not subject to control by thought, and it is identical to eye tics conditioned in the psychological laboratory with a puff of air or finger withdrawals to mild electric shocks. With a conditioned muscular reflex of this type, sexual intercourse between man and woman is impossible.

To eliminate vaginismus, you will want first to gain some control over the flexing and relaxing of your pubococcygeal (PCG) muscle. This muscle runs from your pubis (the hairy mound in front) to your coccyx (the tail bone in the back). Parts of it are the sphincter muscles, which open and close the three body orifices in this area: the urethral duct through which you urinate, the vagina and the anus.

The PCG exercise is simple. Orient to the sensations coming from the PCG muscle when you urinate. Pay attention to what you do to relax the urethral sphincter when you want to urinate. As you sit on the john, practice stopping the urine flow until you are able to do so whenever you wish. Then, at odd times during the day for several weeks, practice the same muscular tightening and relaxing when you don't have to urinate.

This exercise does two things for you. It gives some voluntary control over your vaginal sphincter so that when it closes without your wishing it, you will have some way of jogging it back into a less constricted state. Also, if you have a *partially relaxed PCG muscle* your difficulty in reaching orgasm during intercourse may be caused in part by this condition. The PCG muscle operates like the heart muscle. It is constricted (except when you voluntarily relax it) keeping the vaginal, urethral and anal openings closed twenty-four hours a day for all your life. A partially relaxed PCG muscle may be caused by poor toilet training in childhood or by physical injury during labor where the interior vaginal muscles are torn, stretched or separated. With the relaxed condition of the interior vaginal muscles, the sensory nerve endings in the vagina make very little contact with the penis and do little to arouse or stimulate the woman. Some nonorgasmic women with a relaxed PCG muscle have reported satisfactory orgasm after having increased the PCG muscle tonus using the urinary stopping exercise.

When you feel that you have good control over tightening and relaxing your pubococcygeal muscle, then go on to the next step for vaginismus retraining.

For this part of the program, secure a series of candles, chopsticks, dowels, etc., that range in size from a birthday cake candle up to the diameter of a penis. A phallic vibrator is excellent for the largest size. Starting with the birthday cake candle, lie relaxed on your bed and insert it through the vaginal opening. If you find you cannot penetrate with this small a stimulus, lie back and go through your PCG muscle exercise. Try, if possible, to increase the tightness of the vaginal sphincter, more than it constricts on its own when you try to insert something. Do this several times while concentrating on the sensations coming from the vaginal muscle. Tighten greatly, then relax. After a few exercises, the vaginal muscle is likely to relax when you relax. Then go back to the insertion of the birthday candle. Repeat this procedure as many times as necessary until the PCG does not automatically constrict when you insert the birthday candle. Then select the next larger aid, roughly about the size of a chopstick. Repeat the whole procedure you used for the birthday candle until the PCG muscle does not automatically constrict when you insert the chopstick. Then use your finger as the next implement and go through it all again. Keep increasing the size of the object inserted after each step until you can successfully insert the phallic vibrator.

This portion of the program may require as much

as three weeks of practice for about fifteen minutes per day, depending on how severe the vaginismus constriction is. When you have completed it, then go on to the next program for conjoint orgasmic anxiety.

Making Yourself Less Anxious in the Presence of a Sexual Partner

Many of us fail to reach orgasm with a sexual partner because of learned anxiety about shared sex and one's attitude about revealing private things to another person. Old-fashioned modesty, it seems, still plays an inhibiting role for many of us.

While it's okay to be sweaty, breathing hard with glassy eyes, thrashing around in an uncontrolled manner by yourself, it's a no-no to behave like that in front of, underneath, or on top of someone else. So the point of this program is to gradually bring a sexual partner into a situation where you are already successfully orgasmic: masturbation. And while this gradual introduction of a sexual partner is going on, you continue to orient to the sensations of sexual arousal caused by your self-stimulation, and you do not pay attention to what your possible sexual partner may be thinking, feeling or imagining.

This program is simple, basic and short. All you need do is:

1. Masturbate to orgasm a number of times while gradually bringing a potential sex partner into the room where you are.
2. During masturbation, orient exclusively to your own sexual stimulation and sensations, ignoring your potential sexual partner as much as is possible and not dwelling upon what he or she may be thinking and feeling.
3. Use all the masturbatory techniques you know you like, or use ones that you have learned from your pre-orgasmic program.

The key to introducing the anxiety agent, your potential sexual partner, is to do it gradually. Try the following sequence of sessions:

1. Masturbate lying on your bed nude with the fully clothed sex partner outside the room with the door closed.
2. With door half open and partner not looking.
3. With door fully open and partner not looking.
4. With partner in doorway and not looking.
5. With partner at foot of bed and not looking.
6. With you clothed and partner looking.
7. With you nude.
8. With partner at side of bed.
9. With partner sitting on bed holding your hand and gently rubbing your shoulder.
10. With partner lying on bed with you.

If you find you have some difficulty at any step, say, for instance, step six where your partner is at the foot of the bed and looking at you, retreat to where you were previously orgasmic at step five when your partner was not looking at you. Repeat the previous step twice, and then go on to try the next one again. You may find that you will need to go two steps forward, one step back, throughout the entire program. This is perfectly okay. Most people go through behavioral programs in exactly this fashion. Try having two sessions a day: one in the morning and one in the evening, giving your nervous system some time to recover between orgasms.

After you have completed the program through step ten, repeat the whole procedure once more but this time with both of you nude during all the steps. One precaution—explain to your possible sex partner that you will not have sex with him or her during the entire retraining and the only sexual contact will be what is described in each program. Your partner has to be cooperative or the program is likely to be of little help in making you conjointly orgasmic.

When you have finished both parts of this program, go on to the remaining sections that concern you.

A sexual program with your partner

When you read the German Army Field Cooking Manual, the opening line of the initial recipe says, "First capture a field kitchen . . ." The opening statement for this program is similar: First you get the services of a cooperative partner. This partner certainly must be sexually attractive to you. Without that quality, you will get nowhere. He or she must also be your friend. That may be hard to find in some lovers but is necessary for this program to be of any use to you. If your partner is primarily concerned with his or her own gratification, find another partner. If you find yourself always nervous around your partner, find another partner. At least during this program, your sexual needs are to be met. Your partner's desires during this program are of no importance. If you are his or her only sexual resource, your partner can get relief through solitary masturbation. While a few strokes, a tickle and a giggle thrown in will cost you nothing, impress upon your partner that too many German Field Army cooks spoil the soup. While this is a conjoint effort, you are the boss and are primarily going to decide what will happen, based upon your own needs of the moment. After you have achieved your common goal of making *you* fully functional, both of you can then negotiate who does what to whom and in which way.

Orienting to Bodily Touch

Step one for men or women: To practice orienting to sexual things with a partner, follow the procedures outlined by Masters and Johnson (*Human Sexual Inadequacy*, New York: Little, Brown, 1970) called *sensate focusing*. With you and your partner nude, move the bed up against a wall where you have some support. Then get in a bobsled position with you sitting in front, between your partner's legs. Rest your back on your partner's chest and bring your partner's arms around you. Take his (or her) hand and guide it over different parts of your body. Orient to the feelings in your skin that this touch gives you. Experiment by touching and instructing your partner where to touch, how much, in what way and how long. Do this to different parts of the body for fifteen minutes. Then concentrate attending on sexual stimulation of the genitals, breasts and buttocks, using the same hand-guiding method. Orient to these sexual sensations and vary the way you guide your partner. Do this to try to achieve the same control over your arousal as you have in self-stimulation. Most importantly, pay attenton to your own sensations rather than what your partner is thinking or feeling.

Controlling Sexual Sensations and Arousal (Women)

Step two for women: Have your partner lie flat on his back. Mount him in a kneeling position so his erection lies up against the pubic hair on your abdomen. Lean forward and have him caress the parts of your body that you want him to caress in the way you showed him before. Raising your hips up, stroke his erection through the lips of your vagina and into the area of your clitoris until you can feel your lubrication flow. When you are wet, the arousal state has been well started. Pay attention to the sensations arising from this stimulation. Relax your breathing. If it catches, don't try to regulate it.

Very slowly insert the tip of his erection into the opening of the vagina. Sit back allowing the penis to penetrate you slightly, then rock forward again until it is just at the vaginal opening. Sit back again and allow the penis to penetrate further, then rock forward until it is almost out again. Repeat this motion slowly, over and over again, each time allowing further penetration. During this rocking period, attend to the sensations arising from the strokes back and forth. If you find the sensations from your clitoris are only minimal, you can adjust your position backward, forward or from side-to-side to insure its stimmulation. You may find that maximal stimulation comes from holding onto your partner's upper arms and forcing your hips down to achieve maximum penetration and then gently rocking back and forth —more back than forth—to get the best mechanical contact between the penis, the pubic mound and the upper area of the vaginal lips.

The purpose of this step is not to have intercourse, but to train you to orient to the different sensations that arise from the various hip movements you can use to change the contact between your vaginal area and your partner's erect penis. Go through this procedure a number of times until you become adept at using the male member in arousing the same sensations you already know how to achieve through masturbation. As you practice this, you will be doing two things simultaneously: By orienting to different sexual stimuli, you will reduce any anxiety you have and also learn how to stimulate yourself maximally during intercourse. When you achieve the same skill in stimulating yourself during intercourse as you have in masturbation, orgasm rate will be more under your voluntary control. Then you and your partner can evolve your own system of meeting each other's sexual gratification needs.

After you have achieved competence in bringing on orgasms in the straddled position, you may wish to experiment with other positions and practice attending to their particular sensations to achieve maximum control over them. For detailed instructions on these alternate ways of intercourse you might refer to Masters and Johnson, *Human Sexual Inadequacy*

(Boston: Little, Brown, 1970), Alex Comfort, *The Joy of Sex* and *More Joy* (New York: Crown, 1972, 1974) or Patricia Raley, *Making Love* (New York: The Dial Press, 1976).

Making Yourself Less Anxious About Your Erection — Or Lack of It

Step two for men: The purpose of this practice is to reduce learned anxiety, which causes you to lose your erection and to ejaculate prematurely. As I pointed out before, both loss of erection and premature ejaculation are due to anxiety operating on your primitive nervous system, not any hidden psychological deficit or personality quirk. Its cause is usually not mysterious; it may, from time to time even be a direct result of your own dumb decision in trying to make it with somebody's wife just before he is due home for dinner. The anxiety may have been introduced into your sex life a long time ago or just recently. If your sexual problem persists, it is likely that you have been incubating it through expectation of failure and making yourself anxious this way. At the first sign of detumescence, your anxiety goes up and your erection goes down. What would have prevented this conditioning of your anxiety? Any experiences that would have shown you that you could lose your erection and then regain it within minutes. Such experiences would have taught you that erections are a dime a dozen. If you don't have this perceptual experience, the simplest way to erase your fear of losing your erection is practice getting an erection, losing it and then becoming erect again —over and over and over.

With both of you nude and comfortable, have her stroke and tease your penis—with hand and/or mouth —until you are erect. As she is doing this, *orient to the sensations she causes, not to the state of your erection.* When you become erect, what do you do then? Stand up and cheer? No! Instead, as soon as you are fully erect, your partner stops stimulating you. You both lie back and talk about basketball scores, stock prices, the weather, politics, whatever. When you have lost your erection by orienting to other nonsexual things, have your partner begin the same teasing procedure again. Repeat this cycle at least three times. Practice this once a day for about a week or until you find you consistently orient to how teasing feels and are no longer wondering if you are erect, will be erect, or how fast you are losing your erection.

If you have a problem with premature ejaculation during intercourse or foreplay use the simple squeeze –pinch technique to stop your ejaculation. To do this you need to orient to the sensations arising just before you ejaculate: the tightening of the pelvic muscles, the sensations in the testicles and internal gut, etc. Pay attention to these feelings and when you can reliably tell you are close to ejaculation, grab your penis between thumb, pressed on the top of the corona (the head), and the forefinger, pressed on the soft underside. Firmly squeeze your penis. This is a reflex action that shuts off the ejaculatory process if it has not already begun to pump out semen. If it has, take the pressure off and let the semen flow. It's similar to pressing into your upper lip to shut off a sneeze. Show this technique to your partner and let her practice it. Then she can use it during this and other practices when you tell her that you are about to ejaculate.

When you have achieved your goals in this part, go on to the next step in the program.

Controlling Sexual Sensations and Arousal (Men)

Step three for men: In this step the purpose is not to have intercourse but to orient to sexual stimulation as a means of reducing learned anxiety, maintaining the primitive nervous system in the arousal or plateau states, and consequently maintaining an erection.

There are two positions that work well for this practice: with yourself flat on your back and your partner straddling you on her knees or with your partner kneeling on the bed and you standing and entering from the rear. The least desirable position, as it turns out from therapy experience, is the missionary one with the man atop the woman. Try both positions alternately and see which is best for you.

Run through the last step once more. On the third time you become erect, get into the position you have chosen and have your partner stroke your penis between the lips of her vagina until it becomes well lubricated. Then have her insert it only partially. With your hips, slowly move it in and out of the vagina with a shallow penetration. Attend to the sensations you feel from this action. Do this for ten strokes, withdraw and then both of you lie back and relax until your erection is gone. Then have your partner tease you up, and repeat the procedure once more, this time thrusting slightly deeper. Withdraw, and keep going through this procedure gradually until you are making full strokes each time. With each cycle, concentrate on the sensations arising from your penis as you stroke in and out, not on what your partner may be feeling. If at any time you lose your erection, stop, both of you lie on the bed and, after your erection is completely gone, have her tease it up again. Then make your insertion only as far as you went before without becoming limp. If you tend to ejaculate prematurely, let your partner know if it is about to happen and have her give you the squeeze –pinch to suppress it. Repeat this step adding ten strokes each time until you find yourself making sixty or more strokes with no loss of erection and you have formed a habit of orienting to your own sexual sensations and arousal. After that, stroke to orgasm. Repeat this sex act for about a week. Then you and your partner can begin negotiating on what satisfies your individual needs.

These OR sexual retraining programs are all based on the notion that your learned anxiety about sex has something to do with the *sexual act, foreplay, the partner you choose, how you respond sexually*, etc. The program assumes that the stimuli that make you phobic about sex are included in this complex of sexual things you do and that are done to you. If you find you have little luck in correcting your anxiety problem using the OR methods, then you might consider some consultation with a professional who may be able to determine the actual source of your anxiety. It may, for instance, be prompted by an attitude that having orgasms and a matter-of-fact sexual relationship with your partner requires you to give or receive a personal commitment of some sort. This, or some other similar private feeling, may cause anxiety that is not directly related to what's going on during sex, but that may still cause you problems. These kinds of feelings are not directly treatable with the behavioral methods used here because the anxiety source—being trapped into some commitment —is an abstract one. We can't really point our finger at an abstract cause of anxiety during sex and say that these *stimuli* are the ones you respond anxiously to, so let's do *this, this and this to recondition them.* If you find such is the case with you, it's very likely that you are a bit nonassertive sexually and will feel much better with some assertive skills to deal with social fears such as, "I'm afraid I will have to make a commitment or hurt someone's feelings." I recommend then that you enroll in a systematic assertiveness class at your local university, college or high school to learn how to reduce such social guilt and anxiety. These programs are very popular now and generally given in the evening extension program. It's simple to find out where they are offered: just dial your local adult education system and ask.

The purpose of this entire book is to point out one simple idea. Fears and phobias are not unnatural or signs of psychological sickness, and you yourself can deal with them effectively, if you wish. There is nothing mystical that we professional therapists do in treating them. I think that the greatest help we give sometimes to patients is our expert reassurance that the problem is not as exotic and difficult as they often believe it to be. And this reassurance we give is not too much different from the support you can get from a sympathetic and trusted friend.

The technical advice we give is amazingly simple: If you have a phobia, do anything in the phobic situation which makes your anxiety go down. As it turns out, this practical, experience-based advice boils down to anything which keeps you physically and/or mentally active in the face of whatever you fear. Now this advice seems to contradict common sense at times, but only superficially. In the pressure cooker of our overpopulated modern civilization, we anticipate with relish and start leaning obliquely on Thursday toward the relaxed suburban weekend with its peace and quiet, seeing this escape as the ideal antidote for our tiring weekday life. Unfortunately, many of us, it seems, have come to look at peace, quiet and relaxation as the be-all and end-all—the nirvana to be sought, the payoff, the good island in an unpredictable sea of troubles. The only fly in this idyllic ointment is that peace, quiet and relaxation are not the environmental ambiance Mother Nature had in mind for our routine living when she designed our amazingly adaptable, efficient nervous system and constitution.

If you doubt this viewpoint on our makeup, think back to your last vacation lying on the beach at some beautiful resort and remember how long it took before you became totally fed up with being completely relaxed and isolated.

Because of the often intense pressures of our modern life-style, you, like many of us, may assume that quiet and relaxation is the only antidote to feeling bad or even fearful. In reality, these tranquil states are nonstates or psychological resting points where your physiological engine is on idle, only waiting for the chance to become involved with the business of life again. Relaxation and psychological isolation are excellent remedies for an abused, overworked body and nervous system that is running at full speed. We have even worked out a clever system using the orienting reflex called transcendental meditation to achieve short, restful periods of twenty minutes during the workday. We concentrate on our personal mantra, directing and redirecting our attention until the magnitude of this self-instructed orienting reflex blocks out our perception of all the other busy stimuli surrounding us.

But just as our physical frame is designed to demand exercise in order to work well and remain in good health, our neurological and psychological makeup demands activation, not relaxation and isolation, for us to feel good. We are active animals, members of the species which has conquered this planet. And everything I have learned in the laboratory, in the clinic, from colleagues and from everyday living tells me that we are still active animals built to apply ourselves *to any purpose we choose*. Mother Nature commanded us to innately orient to the basic things needed for survival of the species through our individual survival. But Mother Nature also threw in a bonus beyond survival: She gave us an evolutional legacy that is open-ended. From whatever each of us chooses to orient to, whether its purpose be grand or mean, we automatically get psychoneurological motivation, sustenance and reward. You and I can orient to anything we choose without evolutional, physiological or philosophical restriction; even to our fears and phobias if we like. And having that choice, we can eliminate them.

Orienting Reflex Checklist

Scan the list of topics below. As you can see, it is just a list of things you may be interested in. The purpose of going through this OR checklist is to look purposefully at some of the things in your life that interest you, that you pay attention to without much effort, and those things that are rewarding to you. With these areas in your life identified, you can use them to help overcome your learned fears and anxieties.

If you find you have other interests that are not listed here, write them in the blank spaces provided at the end of the checklist.

ACTING
ANIMAL HUSBAND-
    RY
ANIMALS
ANTHROPOLOGY
ANTIQUES
ARCHITECTURE
ART
ASTRONOMY
ASTROLOGY
AUTOMOBILES
BACKPACKING
BACKGAMMON
BASEBALL
BEEKEEPING
BIOLOGY
BOATING
BOTANY

BRIDGE
BUSINESS
CALLIGRAPHY
CATS
C.B. RADIO
CERAMICS
CHEMISTRY
CHESS
CHILDREN
CITIES
CIVIL WAR HISTORY
CLUBS
COINS
CONSERVATION
CONSUMERISM
COOKING
CREWEL
CRYPTOGRAPHY

CULTURE
DANCING
DECORATING
DIVING
DOGS
ECOLOGY
ECONOMICS
ELECTRONICS
ENGINES
ENTERTAINING
FADS
FASHION
FISHING
FOOTBALL
FORESTRY
FRONTIER HISTORY
GAMES
GARDENING
GEM STONES
GEOGRAPHY
GEOLOGY
GOLF
GOURMET FOOD
GOVERNMENT
GUNS
GYMNASTICS
HAM RADIO
HANDICRAFTS
HARDWARE
HAUTE COUTURE
HISTORY
HOBBIES
HORSES
HOUSES
HUNTING
INTERIOR DESIGN
JAMS AND JELLIES
JEWELRY
KNITTING
KNIVES

LANGUAGES
LAW
LITERATURE
MATHEMATICS
MECHANICS
MILITARY AFFAIRS
MILITARY HISTORY
MONARCHIES
MONIES
MOTORCYCLES
MOTORS
MOUNTAIN CLIMB-
   ING
MOVIES
MUSIC
MYTHOLOGY
NEEDLEPOINT
NEEDLEWORK
ODDITIES
OIL PAINTING
PETS
PHOTOGRAPHY
PHYSICS
PLANTS
POETRY
POLITICS
PSYCHOLOGY
RACING
RADIO BROADCAST-
   ING
REAL ESTATE
ROWING
SAILING
SCIENCE
SCUBA DIVING
SCULPTURE
SEWING
SHOP WORK
SKIING
SOCCER

SOCIAL CONTACT   TRAVEL
SPORTS   VOLCANOS
STAINED GLASS   WEAPONS
STAMPS   WINES
STOCK MARKET   WOODWORK
SWIMMING   WRITING
TENNIS   YOUTH CLUBS
THEATRE   ZOOLOGY
THEOLOGY   OTHER INTERESTS
TOY SOLDIERS   NOT LISTED
TRACK AND FIELD

Now go back over each of these topics you have checked off and rate them from most interesting to less interesting. Rate your most interesting topic as 1. The next is 2, the next 3, and so on with the least interesting topic you checked having the highest number. Make sure you have checked off and rated at least a half-dozen topics.

IDEALIZED SEXUAL AROUSAL CURVE

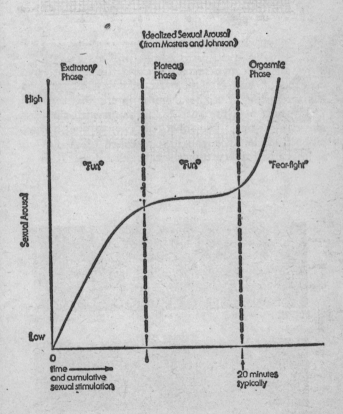

Idealized Sexual Arousal
(from Masters and Johnson)

POLYGRAPH RECORDINGS

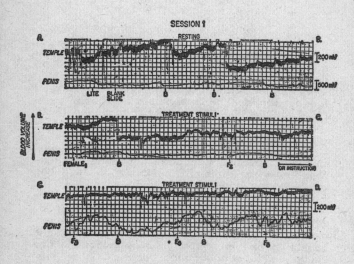

SESSION 1

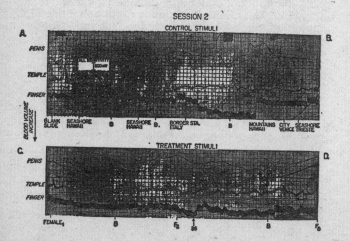

SESSION 2

Suggested technical reading

Bandura, A., Ross D. and Ross, S. A. "Vicarious reinforcement and imitative learning." *Journal of Abnormal and Social Psychology*, Vol. 67 (1963), pp. 601–607.

Boulougouris, J. C., Marks, I. M. and Marset, P. "Superiority of flooding (implosion) to desensitization for reducing pathological fear." *Behavioral Research and Therapy*, Vol. 9 (1971), pp. 7–16.

Cole, M., and Maltzman, I. M., eds. (1969) *A Handbook of Contemporary Soviet Psychology*. New York: Basic Books.

Frankl, V. E. "Paradoxical intention: a logotherapeutic technique." *American Journal of Psychotherapy*, Vol. 14, (1960), pp. 520–535.

Jones, M. C. (1924) "A laboratory study of fear: The case of Peter." *Pedagogical Seminary and Journal of Genetic Psychology*, Vol. 31 (1924), pp. 308–315.

Lazarus, A. A. and Abramovitz, A., eds. "The use of 'emotive imagery' in the treatment of children's phobias." In *Case Studies in Behavior Modification*. Ullmann, L. P. and Krasner, L. New York: Holt, Rinehart and Winston, (1965).

Lisina, M. I. "The role of orientation in the transformation of involuntary reactions into voluntary ones." *Orienting Reflex and Exploratory Behavior*. eds. Voronin, L. G., et al., American Institute of Biological Sciences, Washington, D.C., (1965).

Maltzman, I. M., Smith, M. J., Kantor, W. and Mandell, M. "Effects of stress on habituation of the orienting reflex." *Journal of Experimental Psychology*, Vol. 87 (1971), pp. 207–214.

Marushevsky, M. "On the interaction of the two signal systems in orientation reactions." *Problems of Psychology*, Vol. 3 (1957).

Meyer, V. "The treatment of two phobic patients on the basis of learning principles." *Journal of Abnormal and Social Psychology*. Vol. 58 (1957), pp. 261–266.

Ritter, B. "The group desensitization of children's snake phobias using vicarious and contact desensitization procedures." *Behavioral Research and Therapy*, Vol. 6 (1968), pp. 1–6.

Sokolov, E. N. *Perception and the Conditioned Reflex*. New York: Macmillan, (1963).

Watson, J. B. and Rayner, Rosalie (1920) "Conditioned emotional reactions." *Journal of Experimental Psychology*, Vol. 3, (1920), pp. 1–14.

Wolpe, J. *The Practice of Behavior Therapy*. Oxford: Pergamon, (1969).

ABOUT THE AUTHOR

Clinical-experimental psychologist MANUEL J. SMITH is the author of *When I Say No, I Feel Guilty*, which has sold over 2 million copies. A therapist in private practice and assistant clinical professor of psychology at UCLA, Dr. Smith has done research in social psychology, learning, phobic states, psychophysiology and sexual functioning. His work has appeared in various professional publications including *The Journal of Experimental Psychology, Psychology Report, Current Research in Human Sexuality*, and *Experimental Methods and Instrumentation in Psychology*. He is a member of the American Psychological Association, the Society of Psychophysiological Research, the Western Psychological Association and the California State Psychology Association, and has lectured widely in his field. Born in Brooklyn, New York, in 1934, Dr. Smith received both his B.A. (1950) and M.S. (1960) degrees from San Diego State College, and his Ph.D. from the University of California at Los Angeles (1966). He and his wife live in Los Angeles.